The
Strained
Alliance

The
Strained
Alliance

Peking, P'yŏngyang, Moscow
and the Politics
of the Korean Civil War

Robert R. Simmons

THE FREE PRESS
A Division of Macmillan Publishing Co., Inc.
NEW YORK

Collier Macmillan Publishers
LONDON

60-877-392

The Free Press
A Division of Macmillan Publishing Co., Inc.
866 Third Avenue, New York, N.Y. 10022

Collier–Macmillan Canada Ltd.

Library of Congress Catalog Card Number: 74–4891

Printed in the United States of America

printing number
1 2 3 4 5 6 7 8 9 10

Library of Congress Cataloging in Publication Data

Simmons, Robert R
      The strained alliance; Peking, P'yŏngyang, Moscow
and the politics of the Korean War.

      Includes bibliographical references.
      1. Korean War, 1950–1953—Diplomatic history.
2. Korean War, 1950–1953—Causes. I. Title.
DS918.S55   951.9'042   74-4891
ISBN 0-02-928880-0

To my parents,
with all of the love and admiration
that a printed page can convey

Contents

Preface

Hindsight tends to be 20–20. Because of the urgency of a given political crisis and the complexity of the issues involved, historians and political scientists tend to be myopic, seeing each such emergency as an isolated occurrence. In fact, however, such events are connected to other, earlier ones. It is clearer now than it was in 1965, for example, that the Indochina War was not an event peculiar to the early 1960s, but rather was intertwined with the history of at least the previous three decades.

Similarly, the so-called "Korean War" has popularly been viewed as a battle of the Cold War, to be understood solely within the context of post-1945 Great Power politics. This may have been because most of us have a propensity to simplify history, to see it within some form of a relatively simplistic devil theory. Now that the war has receded into our collective memories, however, perspective on its development has become more lucid. The general anticommunist hysteria of the 1950s has faded, making us less compulsive and rigid in our beliefs about Communists and communism.

This book began in the late 1960s as a typical product of the monolithic conception of international communism. I was fortunate enough, however, to read Donald Zagoria's study of the intricate relationships, primarily of the 1960s, between Moscow, Peking, and Hanoi.* Prof. Zagoria, however, while taking note

*Vietnam Triangle: Moscow, Peking, Hanoi (New York: Pegasus, 1967), pp. 18–20.

xi

of China's reluctance at being considered a junior partner of the Soviet Union in the early 1950s, nonetheless saw the Sino–Soviet bloc in that period as being "monolithic."

Encouraged by the insightful analysis which Prof. Zagoria brought to the Moscow–Peking–Hanoi alliance, I sought to learn if any analogous features characterized the earlier Peking–P'yŏngyang–Moscow alliance. As these pages demonstrate, the intrarelationships of the earlier coalition were more subtle than those of the 1960s—because the earlier alliance was ostensibly united, whereas the Vietnam alliance of the 1960s was carried out against the backdrop of an open Sino–Soviet split.

An observer sensitive to the strains between the three partners during the 1950–53 war will be alert to various, otherwise obscured, aspects of the conflict. Studies on the war which assume unified foreign policies on the part of Peking, P'yŏngyang, and Moscow largely neglect, for example, the importance of nationalism to each of the three partners. This factor propelled each partner to devalue the needs of the others during the war.

In mentioning the benefit of Prof. Zagoria's book, I should like to discredit the canard of the unhelpfulness of scholars. The myth is that academics do not help each other in research because of the fear that their ideas may be "stolen." On the contrary, while it is required to affirm that I bear the responsibility of all of the mistakes found in this volume, it is also necessary to declare that all of the writers who are cited in this book were of great assistance to me in fully and freely sharing their ideas. Through our conversations and correspondence, they became partners. I am grateful that what began as an historical quest has resulted in the formation of many friendships.

At the same time, it should be said that these scholars have often disagreed with my conclusions—just as I have questioned theirs. In the same spirit, I hope that many of the readers of these pages will challenge some of my findings and pursue further research on some of the topics briefly touched upon here.

Finally, I should like to take this opportunity to thank a few
of the many people who have kindly helped this research. Steven
Spiegel's encouragement and advice were more helpful than he
probably knew. Richard Baum gave the first draft a thorough
reading. Alynn Nathanson, Harold C. Hinton, Roy U. T. Kim,
Donald W. Klein, Chong-Sik Lee, John Melby, Glenn D. Paige,
Robert Scalapino, and Allen Whiting have each set standards
which I have tried to meet. Masao Okonogi and Tatsuo Yamada
introduced me to Japanese resources in Tokyo.

Most of all, I thank Barbara, who during the past four
peripatetic years has made our many nomadic tents into homes.

A Note on Methodology and Sources

A brief explanation of the more seldom-used prim-
ary materials upon which this study is based is in order. The files
of the United States Army's Intelligence Section (G-2) [†] from
1945 to 1952 proved to be very useful. Because the sources of
G-2's information varied, each intelligence report usually led
off with an evaluation of its reliability and accuracy. I have
used only those reports which G-2 at the time labeled as the
most credible. These files, classified during the war as "secret,"
are now held in the United States Federal Records Center in Suit-
land, Maryland. After later 1952, these records become meager
for unknown reasons either because of their present security status or simply because G-2 diminished its reports after this date.

The second major, but little-used, basis for research was
the daily translations of Chinese, North Korean, and Russian
radio broadcasts. These were published in the United States as
the *Foreign Broadcast Information Service Daily Reports* and in the
United Kingdom as the British Broadcasting Company's
Summary of World Broadcasts, Far East. Most large libraries have

†This source appears in the chapters as *United Nations and United States
Far East Command, Intelligence Summaries.*

holdings of either one or the other translation series. Therefore, the footnotes relate only the date of the radio transmissions. From close textual readings of the transcripts from the 1950–53 period, it is frequently possible to determine shifts in attitudes between the three communist states. This is particularly true when a radio broadcast is being beamed to one specific country in that state's language. This often allows for a highly illuminating comparison of disparate goals and positions, and serves as an indicator of the differences between the three states. Because each often guised its intraalliance communications in esoteric language, a careful analysis of these radio transmissions from their originator's context is necessary in order to understand what each was saying to the other.

Robert R. Simmons
Guelph, Ontario
June, 1974

Introduction

The proper study of the Korean war should, while recognizing that both Moscow and Peking were intimately involved, emphasize its civil nature. The causes of the war must be sought on the Korean peninsula itself, an intensely nationalistic land whose people had been arbitrarily divided at the end of World War II. The opposing nature of the ideologies resident in the two halves of the nation served only to reinforce the passionate desire for reunification. In short, the proper appellation for the conflict is the Korean Civil War.

Conventional wisdom regarding the Korean Civil War has hitherto suggested that Korea between 1945 and 1953 should be seen primarily as an integral part of the Cold War, and that the origins of the war should thus be sought outside the peninsula. Behind this assumption is the belief that the genesis of the conflict is to be found in the largely unified wishes of the Soviet Union, China, and North Korea, with most of the control emanating from Moscow.

On the contrary, however, it is our contention that we can better gauge the fount of the beginnings of the war, the relationship between the three communist states during the war, and the war's termination by rejecting these shibboleths. An investigation of the war which neglects the internal situation on the peninsula, the patterns formed by Asian history relevant to Korea's relations with its two giant neighbors, and the nature of the ties between these three countries is incomplete and inconclusive.

Because the stress previously has been upon American strategic actions and reactions, most studies have largely ignored the communist side during the war.* The political context which actually formed and framed the Korean Civil War is usually pictured as mere background when, in reality, politics was almost always in the foreground.

Related to this is the common impression that the United States was merely *reacting* in the course of the war, and to a united, monolithic enemy. Actually, in goals and purposes the three allied communist states were frequently at odds with each other—a fact which has been largely neglected in the belief that the war and the armistice negotiations that ended it were directed by a monolithic foe. Conceivably, a realization of these allies' differing motivations might have led to other negotiating or military postures on the part of the United States. Washington, it should be further noted, was not simply "reacting" to the war, but rather took positive stances of its own to which the communist states felt impelled to reply.

Because social scientists are permitted partial access to the antechambers of power only to take notes, their summations are usually incomplete, and often distorted. This problem is compounded when dealing not merely with one state, but, as here, with three diverse, authoritarian regimes. A thorough study of the Korean Civil War is made even more difficult because not only have the archives of Moscow, Peking, and P'yŏngyang remained closed, but so also have the more sensitive files of the United States Government. We are, for example, as yet incom-

---

*Two major exceptions are Allen S. Whiting's *China Crosses the Yalu: The Decision To Enter the Korean War* (New York: Macmillan Co., 1960) and *Communism in Korea: The Movement* by Robert A. Scalapino and Chong-sik Lee (Berkeley and Los Angeles: University of California Press, 1972). Prof. Whiting's pioneering book remains a model for observers who wish to read Chinese publications of this period in an attempt to explain Peking's entrance into the Korean Civil War (although the reader will note that parts of this volume explicitly differ with *China Crosses the Yalu*). Scalapino and Lee's comprehensive study utilizes interviews with North Korean defectors that are highly valuable to any study of the war.

pletely informed on American activities on the Korean peninsula directed by General MacArthur between 1949 and 1951, and on the messages and signals exchanged by Washington and the three communist states throughout the war.

Because of this lack of facts regarding each of the four principally involved countries, this is not a definitive work. Rather, it attempts to present data and raise hypotheses not usually considered. This is done with the belief that it is as worthwhile to ask questions and to suggest new viewpoints as to merely repeat what appear to have been the unsatisfactory answers previously advanced about the war. Therefore, not much space is devoted either to arguments which are now generally accepted, and to which we agree, or to earlier hypotheses which seem inadequate explanations to important questions. Instead, notice is given in the footnotes that a body of literature already exists giving differing points of view from those which are suggested in these pages.

Material in one chapter may be more familiar than topics covered in another section; consequently, one reader may feel that too much space is devoted to one subject, while another reader may think that not enough attention is being given to another. This is perhaps inevitable in a book which covers disparate developments in Korea, China, the Soviet Union, and, to a lesser extent, the United States. In this exploratory book I have attempted to walk a middle line between widely known and less familiar data, hoping that others will be prompted to research further some of the hypotheses pursued here. At points in the narrative where the facts of a situation are well known and widely accepted, the story is touched upon only to provide context.

The major primary and secondary sources used for this study contained, of course, mixtures of fact and opinion, hard data and propaganda. These materials included interviews with communist defectors, particularly from China and North Korea, a careful reading of the Chinese, Russian, and North Korean radio broadcasts, the intelligence reports of the United States Army during the war, and, finally, an examination and comparison of the various publications meant for internal distribution to the cadres of the Chinese, Russian, and North Korean regimes. I have tried to sift carefully through this mixture, and select only that information which appears to be accurate on the basis of internal and comparative consistency.

Outline

Because international crises are seldom divorced from past geopolitics, our first chapter briefly sketches the background of the Korean peninsula in Northeast Asian history. Several important conclusions emerge from this short survey, all relevant to an understanding of the twentieth-century war. One is that Korea has traditionally been a battleground between China, Russia, and Japan, each of which considered Korea vital to its security. Consequently, each has sought to control events on the peninsula. This was accomplished either by military occupation or by exerting influence on Korea's politically fragmented domestic factions.

Interestingly, the United States had become involved in Korean politics in the late 1800s, by promising to protect Korea's fragile neutrality between her neighbors. The United States–Korean agreement, however, turned out to be impotent; that memory might well have prompted Koreans in 1950 to expect that America would not intervene in their civil war.

The overriding fact of Korean history has been the keen nationalism felt throughout the peninsula. Factions aligned with foreign powers for the purpose of perserving both their own authority and Korea's independence. Within this context, Kim Il-sŏng's (and Syngman Rhee's) association with an external power should be seen as an extension of a pattern well understood on the peninsula.

Building upon this history, the second chapter then examines the political system of North Korea between 1945 and 1950. This system was in many ways an extension of the earlier pattern. Politics were both factionalized and highly nationalistic. The background of the war must be considered in the light of these factional struggles. This explanation underscores the domestic causes of the war, while stressing the fact that Kim Il-sŏng's authority was in large measure born of his nationalist credentials combined with the support of the Soviet occupation army.

Also vital to an understanding of events after June, 1950, is an appreciation of the general strains between China and the Soviet Union, including their struggle for influence on the peninsula. Chapters 3 and 4 shift focus away from the peninsula in an effort to explain several of the differences between its two giant neighbors. Chapter 3 presents some of the available evidence indicating that the ultimate alliance between China and the Soviet Union, sealed by the Korean Civil War, was not inevitable. The Chinese Communist Party had suggested its interest in maintaining communication and compromise with the United States before the war began. This was in part because of the strains that had existed historically both between Russia and China and between the Communist parties of the two states.

The following chapter presents an example of the causes of stress between the two states. This section contends that the Soviet Union deliberately froze China out of the United Nations in January of 1950 in a calculated effort to cut off all of China's potential contacts with the West. These two chapters, together, suggest that there was a strong possibility that if not for the Korean Civil War and the subsequent conflict which it brought about between China and the United States, these two states might well have reached a rapprochement, similar in some respects to the one which they have achieved in the 1970s.

Chapter 5 returns the center of attention to events on the Korean peninsula. In examining the fierce factional fighting between North Korean leaders in the post–World War II period, this chapter argues that the timing of the beginning of the war was chosen by Kim Il-sŏng as a result of these internal divisions combined with fears of a South Korean invasion. This chapter is the most speculative of the book; there is little hard primary data on exactly why the war began on June 25, 1950. On the other hand, the customary interpretations of the causes of the war have so far unsatisfactorily answered such questions as why the Soviet Union was absent from the United Nations at the time, why China did not take Taiwan before the beginning of the war, or why P'yŏngyang did not receive more aid from its allies. The hypothesis presented here has the value of focusing attention upon the *Korean* bases of the war, a most important aspect of a conflict which is usually viewed as being largely a Cold War battle. Although the hypothesis is founded largely upon circumstantial evidence, it has the advantage of being the most parsimonious explanation available to answer several hitherto puzzling factors associated with the war. Moreover, it encourages the introduction of data which are often not taken into account when considering the beginning of the war.

Chapter 6 discusses the hesitation with which China entered the war. Crucial to an understanding of Peking's attitude is the fact that the celebrated American naval "interdiction" of the Taiwan Straits in the summer of 1950 was almost entirely a merely *verbal* one. China was therefore hopeful that President Truman would reverse his formal statement—meant largely for domestic American consumption—once Washington realized that China was not involved in the war. Instead, of course, the United States acted in a reverse manner and appeared to be threatening an invasion of China as the war entered the fall of 1950.

Both China and North Korea hoped that the Soviet Union would assist P'yŏngyang as the tide of battle turned. The usual interpretation of China's entrance into the war has been that it was done cautiously, in an effort to protect her territorial security. While this idea is accurate insofar as it goes, it is an insufficient explanation of the circumstances surrounding China's crossing the Yalu. These can be fully understood only in the context of the interrelationship between the three communist states.

The Soviet Union was as concerned as was China about the possibility of an American invasion of its territory as General MacArthur advanced north along the Korean peninsula in the fall of 1950. Although most studies of the war recognize that U.S. troops were threatening China, they neglect the significant fact that these forces were also approaching the *Soviet* border. Moscow therefore encouraged China's intervention, but Peking entered the war only when it became obvious that Russia steadfastly refused the use of its own troops on the peninsula. Consequently, the Sino–Soviet Treaty of Mutual Assistance, conceived in Moscow in February of 1950, was aborted on the Korean peninsula in October of the same year.

Koreans, moreover, learned not to expect altruistic aid from either neighbor when their national survival was at stake. This last goes a long way toward explaining North Korea's "sudden" display of independence from both China and the Soviet Union after the mid-1950s. And it applies equally forcefully to the lesson which China learned about the nature of Russian assistance during a crisis. In fact, the serious split between the two communist allies may be dated from China's unsatisfactory experience with Soviet aid during the Korean Civil War.

The next two chapters examine the causes of the strains between the three communist allies during the war. In particular, these pages point up the fact that Moscow consistently supplied its two neighbors with second-line military equipment that was inadequate to overcome American technology. Similarly, Soviet economic aid was not considered sufficient by either China or North Korea. Meanwhile, the Soviet Union dictated most of the political decisions affecting the war. For exam-

ple, the initiatives for the beginning of the P'anmunjŏm armistice negotiations apparently came as a surprise to both Peking
and P'yŏngyang when they were first proposed by Moscow.
P'yŏngyang's influence upon the tactics of these talks, in particular, was nil.

The last substantive chapter argues that, beginning in the
late spring of 1952, China and North Korea brought pressure to
bear upon the Soviet Union to accede to their desire to leave the
war. By the fall of that year, as a result of the combination of her
allies' entreaties and its own domestic politics, the Soviet Union
began to signal its own decision to reach a compromise solution
at P'anmunjŏm.

The wartime coalition, in short, was a strained alliance. But
just what is an "alliance?" How and why does one come into
existence? Does an alliance evolve? Why does it end? Can we
examine one particular alliance and draw some conclusions that
will apply generally to this type of international relationship?
The ubiquitous and ambiguous term "alliance" presents a problem, because its nearly univeral use masks the fact that interstate
relationships are dynamic events.

States enter into alliances for reasons of military security in
the face of a present or imminently expected crisis. Because each
state enters the alliance for different purposes and propelled by
differing histories, and each is willing to expend a different
proportion of its national resources for the common effort, there
is an inevitable tension within the alliance. Each state is anxious
that it receive the maximum possible aid from its allies, and is
affronted when expected aid is not forthcoming.

The final chapter examines various types of alliances and
advances the idea that different states within an alliance may
well perceive the alliance differently. This asymmetry of goals
and expectations leads to strains between the alliance partners.
This is, in fact, what occurred to North Korea, China, and the
Soviet Union. Each was involved in the war for different pur-

poses, and each had conflicting expectations of support from the other two. It was a strained alliance; the strains made manifest during the war (and present in the relationship before the war) were to become clearer to us in later years.

The
Strained
Alliance

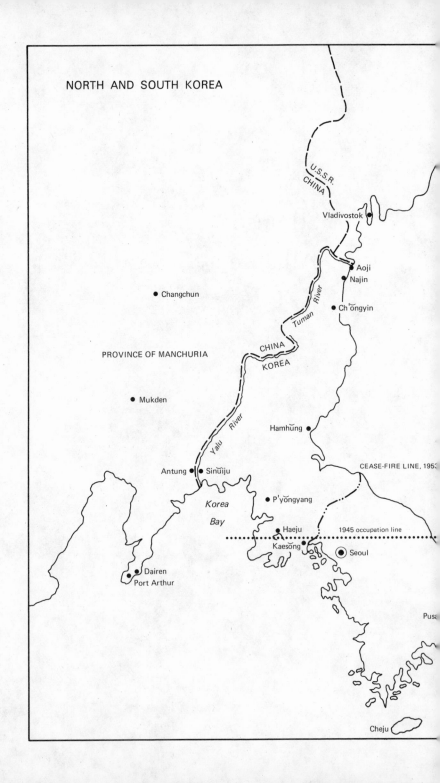

NORTH AND SOUTH KOREA

U.S.S.R.
CHINA

Vladivostok

Aoji

Najin

Changchun

Turman River

Ch'ŏngyin

PROVINCE OF MANCHURIA

CHINA

KOREA

Mukden

Yalu River

Hamhŭng

CEASE-FIRE LINE, 195:

Antung Sinŭiju

Korea
Bay

P'yŏngyang

1945 occupation line

Haeju

Kaesŏng

Seoul

Dairen
Port Arthur

Pusa

Cheju

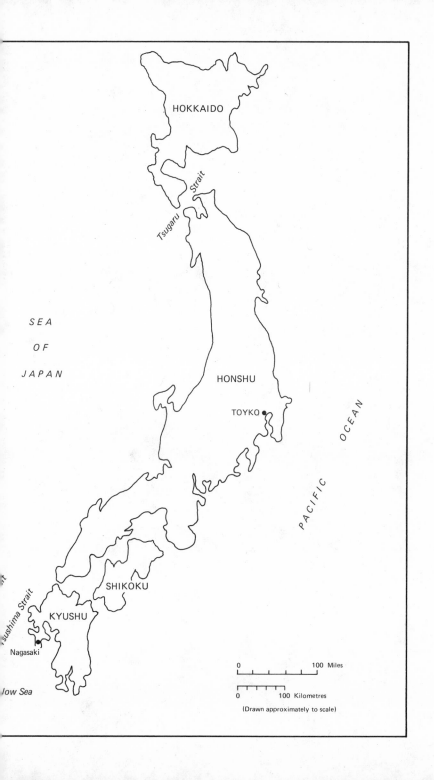

HOKKAIDO

Tsugaru Strait

S E A

O F

J A P A N

HONSHU

TOYKO●

P A C I F I C

O C E A N

SHIKOKU

Tsushima Strait

KYUSHU

●
Nagasaki

low Sea

0   100 Miles

0   100 Kilometres

(Drawn approximately to scale)

1

A Partial Korean Genealogy of the Korean Civil War

States are not born *ex nihilo*. Every state possesses a collective historical memory, informed perhaps by one or more traumatic experiences endured *ante*-state and transmitted through socialization, which shapes the way in which the world is perceived and interpreted. Any study of the inputs to foreign-policy formulation must take account of these primitive psychic forces, which, in important measure, predispose a state's perception of its self-interest.[1]

To understand the attitude of the People's Republic of China (PRC) toward Taiwan over time, for example, it must be noted that Mao Tse-tung's generation grew to revolutionary maturity nurtured not on an irredentist urge toward Taiwan—a Japanese colony too far away—but rather on hostility toward the West, including Russia and Japan, for their economic exploitation, and often territorial detachment, of sections of China closer at hand. Taiwan became a Chinese Communist rallying cry only after Chiang K'ai-shek had made it his island fortress. Furthermore, it can be persuasively argued that Taiwan did not become a vital issue between the United States and China until after the United States had intervened in the Chinese Civil War by verbally interdicting the Taiwan Straits with its Seventh Fleet on June 27, 1950.[2]

1

Similarly, the Chinese leadership's hostility toward the Soviet Union can best be understood not simply as a reflection of the ideological conflict between the two states but as a reaction to Russia's repeated historical intrusions on Chinese territory, a memory still fresh in Peking. And China's present fears of Japan likewise reflect the trauma of past Japanese invasions. Finally, Chinese and Soviet attitudes toward the Korean peninsula are born of parallel past experiences.

The leaders of the Democratic People's Republic of Korea (DPRK) likewise act from a historical consciousness. They recall vividly who their country's friends and enemies were in the past and who could be relied upon under what circumstances, and then draw conclusions as to the lessons that should be learned from their national heritage, and from past mistakes. It is not giving the story away to say that the most obvious lesson to be gleaned from a brief look at the political history of Korea over the past several centuries is that no external power could be relied upon to come to the aid of Korea for motives other than those of largely self-interest.

This notion of an historical "mythology" (as Mannheim calls it) is an instructive one with regard to the study of alliances. If nations, and national leaderships, have primitive collective memories which are instrumental in determining which options of policy are likely to be considered (i.e., seen as possible), then some alliances are more likely to form than others, and some are more likely than others to survive, to remain credible to both itself and to others, and to evolve into more than "mere" alliances. [3] This is examined in greater detail in the final chapter.

If indeed the past, as it is remembered within the collective consciousness of nations, significantly affects how nation-states see, and act on, the present, then we need to know more about Korean history prior to 1950 to understand the Korean Civil War and the alliances that developed during it. (In this context, it is not irrelevant that John Kennedy and Lyndon Johnson, two American presidents of quite dissimilar background, were both men who had spent their boyhood idolizing the Western heroes in cowboy movies. Kennedy formed his own cavalry, the Green Berets, under the transparent symbolism of the "New Frontier"; Johnson told his men to "bring back the coonskin" with the twentieth-century equivalent of the Winchester repeating rifle, the B-52 bomber. Henry Kissinger, in a late-1972 interview, expounded further on the frontier theme: "The main point comes from the fact that I have acted alone. The Americans love this immensely. The Americans love the cowboy who leads the convoy, alone on his horse . . . He acts, and that is enough, being in the right place at the right time. In sum, a western.")[4]

Korea Before 1895

The sporadic encounters of China, Japan, and Russia on the Korean peninsula prior to 1945 provide a classic case of how collective national memories—of spent blood, treasure, and dreams—can affect events decades later.

The peninsula of Korea has attracted, and endured, the attentions of her neighbors for much longer than the single past century upon which this chapter will concentrate. Shaped something like the state of Florida, and twice as large, Korea is a land of mountains in its northern and central sections, tacked onto Manchuria and Siberia, tilted toward the East and sloping toward the West.

This nexus of Northeast Asia—Seoul, the traditional capital is (in air mileage) 587 miles from Peking, 462 miles from Vladivostok, and 715 miles from Tokyo—has been seen by each of its neighbors as either a dagger pointed at its heart, a land bridge that could provide an advantageous invasion route, a buffer state, or a rich prize in itself. In a loose geographical analogy, Korea could be thought of as the Palestine of East Asia.

Internally, Korean society had two characteristics which directly affected Korea's relationships with other countries. First, Korea is, and has been for well over a millenium, what today would be termed an almost pure nation-state: the people living within its borders share a common history and sense of destiny and a perception of themselves as a unique people, bound together by a common language, culture, and religion. Boundaries of water on three sides of the peninsula, and the presence of jagged mountains along with two major rivers serving as the northern boundaries, enhanced the feeling of distinctiveness and encouraged a strident sense of nationalism and a loathing of foreign domination.

The traditionally high degree of both factionalism and corruption (within a strongly centralized government) in the Korean political system is a second factor that has strongly influenced her foreign relations. In particular, it has led to the weakening of Korea's ability to withstand Great Power incursions. By the same token, internal political fragmentation made Korea more of an alluring target and treasure for her neighbors, as each sought to ally itself with a domestic faction. The various factions, centered in Seoul, sought both to enhance their own particular strength and to maintain overall Korean autonomy by playing off the Great Powers and selectively aligning with them; in the end, they demonstrated only that factional politics and national autonomy were incompatible.[5] The pattern continued, however, in North Korea after 1945, as we shall see later.

Until the late 1500s, Korea's political and military dealings had been almost solely with China. Relations with this vast neighbor to the northwest were governed by an extrapolation from the Confucian familial system, rather than by formal treaties. Confucianism, with its hierarchical relationships and rigid sense of commitments, became the dominant ethos of Korea, both domestically and in external dealings. Relations between China and Korea were described by both countries as that of "sadae": the younger brother serving the older brother, with the older brother recognizing a duty to his younger brother.

Traditionally, Korea was a buffer state for China. The Chinese first occupied Korea and made it part of their empire in the Han period (ca. 200 B.C.–200 A.D.). The invasions which Korea suffered during the next thousand years were all from the direction of China. For example, in the thirteenth century Genghis Khan made Korea his vassal (1219). There were two Mongol incursions in the first half of the century (1231 and 1232); Khublai Khan invaded Korea twice in 1274 and 1281. These invasions did not penetrate deeply into the Korean political fabric, however, since each aggressor withdrew either under pressure of Korean arms or by virtue of the skill of Korean diplomacy.

A turning point came late in the sixteenth century. Toyotomi Hideyoshi, the Regent of Japan, invaded Korea in 1592 and 1598 in vain attempts to subjugate China. The Hideyoshi invasions not only introduced to Korea the threat of armed aggression from a country other than China, but also devastated Korea on a scale not previously known. Soon thereafter came another great invasion: the Manchus attacked and occupied parts of Korea several times between 1625 and 1636 as part of the Chinese dynastic war then raging between the emerging Ch'ing (Manchu) and the reigning Ming. In 1636, King Injo of the Yi Dynasty signed a treaty acknowledging Manchu suzerainty over Korea. On the basis of this treaty, Korea sent tribute missions to Peking as late as 1893. [6]

The misery and general xenophobia engendered by these successive invasions led King Injo to declare a policy of drastically minimizing relations with both China and Japan. Korean diplomacy was now exemplified by the longer, and isolationist phrase "sadae kyorin," where "kyorin" referred to friendly relations with the Japanese neighbors who had proved to be so close. [7] After 1636, for example, Korea suspended even the mining of gold and silver, lest such industry should attract further foreign interest. [8] This attempt at the suspension of all but pro forma relations led to "hermit kingdom" status for Korea in the mid-1800s.

Meanwhile, during this period when Korea was maintaining "correct" relations with both China and Japan, the balance of power between the latter two countries was undergoing change. China had grown weaker, her rebellions of the mid-nineteenth century having been accompanied by an increase both in regionalism and in western influence. Japan, on the other hand, had waxed strong under an essentially orderly assimilation of western technology, during which time the restoration of the Emperor's rule in 1867 led to the abolishment of the Shogunate and of feudalism. A mood of expansive Japanese nationalism prevailed in Tokyo.

On September 19, 1875, a Japanese man-of-war, the *Unyō*, provoked the fire of Korean soldiers by intentionally violating Korean territorial waters off the island of Kanghwa, near Inch'on.[9] Thereupon "in retaliation," the *Unyō* completely destroyed the town of Yongjong. By this action, Japan sought to accomplish the dual purposes of ending Korea's attempt at "hermit" status and modifying China's continuing influence on the Peninsula. In pursuance of the latter end, the Japanese government sent an envoy to Peking in order to determine the exact relationship between Korea and China. The Chinese, fearing involvement with Japan in a war over Korea, virtually acknowledged the independence of Korea.[10] Twin lessons were thus imprinted upon Korean consciousness, to be repeated several times over the succeeding decades: military incidents are provoked by a stronger power in order to gain political ends, and true independence cannot be granted by a foreign power, but must be struggled for.

The conclusion of this train of events was "The Treaty of Peace and Friendship Between the Kingdom of Chosŏn and the Empire of Japan" signed on February 26, 1876, an agreement which underscored Japan's new economic influence in Korea. In this treaty, Japan essentially imposed the same sort of unequal terms on Korea as those which the Western Powers had extracted shortly before from both Japan and China. Three seaports were opened to Japanese traders, extraterritorial rights were granted Japanese citizens in Korea, and, in an August, 1876, supplement to the treaty, the use of Japanese currency in Korea was given legal status.

Japan's success in concluding this treaty was due in part to the emergence of a newly powerful faction within the Korean court, that of Queen Min, that was amenable to increased Japanese influence as a means of countering their domestic rivals, who followed a strongly xenophobic foreign policy. Within the Korean court at this time, there were four, often cross-cutting, factions: two of these were based on personal loyalties, either to Queen Min or to the Taewŏn'gun, the regent for the king, while the other two factions divided along progressive or conservative lines with respect to their attitude toward maintaining Korea on the "hermit kingdom" path. When the king came of age in 1874, Queen Min used her influence to cause the semiretirement of the Taewŏn'gun, and to encourage an opening to Japan. She filled government posts with her supporters, and allied with the progressive faction in its desire to open up the country to outside influences. But innovations were slow, for the temperament and institutions of Korea hindered any rapid shift in attitudes.

A "radical" faction soon arose, however, composed largely of leaders who had resided in Japan. These Japanophiles introduced and pushed for changes (e.g., more contact with the outside world) beyond those which the Min faction was willing to sponsor. As these reforms gathered force and gained in popularity, a split developed between the "radicals" and the Min faction (and between these two and the conservative and anti-Min factions); not really over the reforms, which each of these factions largely supported, but rather over the power which success would bring.

In reaction to the growing Japanese influence upon the radical faction, the Mins turned to China for support. The Min faction thereupon became allied with the conservative faction, who had themselves allied with China in an effort to stem Japan's growing influence in Korea.[11]

The senior grand secretary of China at this time who conducted China's relations with Korea, Li Hung-chang, proposed that Korea should both increase its own military strength and conclude treaties with Western powers "in order to check the poison with an antidote."[12] Li strongly suggested the United States as the best partner for Korea's first treaty with a non-Asian state. This resulted in the Chemulp'o (Inch'ŏn) Treaty of May 22, 1882. To counter possible objections on the part of the "'radical' pro-Japanese" faction with regard to the need for such a treaty, the Min party relied upon the arguments of Li Hung-chang. Two scholars note that "by letting China take the lead and carry the main burden of negotiation, the Korean leaders paid the least possible price of political commitment and maximized their defense against attacks from the powerful isolationist groups at home."[13] This was not the first, nor the last, time that foreign encouragement was used by a Korean faction in order to further both its domestic and foreign goals.

The first article of the United States–Korean treaty of 1882 declared that "should either party become subject to unjust or oppressive treatment by a third nation, the other party to this treaty will exert its good offices for an amiable arrangement, thus showing their friendly feelings."[14] The significance of this clause shall be noted shortly.

Shortly after the conclusion of this treaty, the Min faction was faced with domestic rebellion. A military reform had led to the dismissal of over 1,000 old or disabled soldiers. This triggered a revolt on July 23, 1882, against both the Mins and, in a rage of antiforeign feelings, the Japanese. The Taewŏn'gun was reinstated in power by the rioting soldiers. Queen Min, in turn, sent a strong protest to Peking demanding Chinese protection and pointing to the Taewŏn'gun as the guilty party.[15] Li Hung-chang sent a force of 3,000 Chinese troops plus 2,000 Korean soldiers under Generals Wu Ch'ang-ch'ing and Yuan Shih-k'ai to put down the rioting. The Chinese abducted the Taewŏn'gun to China and brought Queen Min back to power.

Although Chinese influence was again predominant, 200 Japanese soldiers were stationed in Seoul, and served as a means of maintaining a Japanese presence in Korea. In order to stabilize Chinese influence, P.G. von Möllendorff, first German Consul at Tientsin and then an official of the Chinese Imperial Maritime Customs, established a customs service in Korea and acted as an advisor to the Korean Foreign Office (which had been established only in 1882). The Court, now conservative and backed by a Chinese garrison, blocked the radicals from exercising power. The radicals staged an attempted coup d'etat on December 4, 1884, with the help of the Japanese legation guards. The Chinese garrison force, outnumbering the Japanese seven to one, defeated the radicals and forced the Japanese to withdraw from Korea for a short time. [16] Chinese influence in Korea was dominant until the Sino–Japanese War of 1894–95. Meanwhile, Koreans had learned that foreigners would use their troops directly on the Peninsula in order to support the faction of their choice.

China, as the weaker power, still did not want to provoke a war with Japan, however. The subsequent Treaty of Tientsin (April 18, 1885) sought to prevent a spark from igniting the powder that was Korea into a general war between Japan and China. [17] The treaty forbade either country from sending military advisors or troops into Korea without the consent of the other. This opened the way for Korea to seek military help from a third country, and Seoul proceeded to seek this help from its third neighbor, Russia.

Von Möllendorff, with the king's permission, conducted secret meetings with Russia to get military advisors. On his own initiative, the king sent a secret mission to Vladivostok with a similar request. These intrigues failed, however, because of objections from other high Korean officials, who were fearful of Chinese or Japanese remonstrances. As a result, von Möllendorff was expelled from Korea, to the accompaniment of the king's protestations of his own innocence. [18] China, in an expression of her irritation with the Min court and as a warning, subsequently returned the Taewŏn'gun to Korea—over Min objections—and appointed the arrogant 26-year-old Yuan Shih-k'ai as Chinese "Resident" in Korea, a title that brought with it the power and influence of a pro-consul. China consequently retained most of her influence in Korea, but at the price of unpopularity.

This incident in Korean history was to engrave upon the memories of later decades the lessons that foreign treaties made over Korean heads were not to be trusted, and that it is common for all leaders, including the Korean king, to deal covertly in matters of state, both foreign and domestic.

Corruption, an ever-present side effect of the nepotism and factionalism in the Korean court, increased while the government sought to cope with the various economic and political foreign penetrations. Excessive taxation and the selling of offices were now the norm. This situation led to several fierce rebellions in the provinces. The most serious of these was that of an antiforeign religious sect, the Tonghak.[19] On June 1, 1894, the Korean government appealed to Yuan Shih-k'ai for military assistance. Yuan acted promptly: 1,500 soldiers and two warships were dispatched to Seoul, landing south of the city on June 8.

Japan, feeling that the Treaty of Tientsin had been abrogated, landed 400 marines at Seoul on June 10; soon, there were 4,000 Japanese soldiers in the Seoul vicinity. Fearful of the threat to its tenuous independence that the reintroduction of foreign troops represented, the Korean government announced the capture of the Tonghak capital and demanded the withdrawal of both the Chinese and Japanese forces. Li Hung-chang, negotiating from a position of weakness, offered to call his troops back to China. The Japanese replied by sending an additional infantry regiment to Korea.

On July 4, 1894, the militarily superior Japanese occupied the Palace in Seoul and formed a new, pro-Japanese cabinet, most of whose members either were returned Japanese students or had taken part in an abortive pro-Japanese coup in 1884, or both. On July 25, 1894, at Japan's insistence, Korea renounced all past treaties which interfered with Korea's independence. The April 17, 1895, Treaty of Shimonoseki marked China's formal acknowledgment of the end of her significant influence in Korea, a condition which had in fact existed since the summer of 1894. On the other hand, the Triple Intervention of Russia, Germany, and France, which immediately followed the Treaty of Shimonoseki, forced Japan to retrocede the Liaotung Peninsula to China (actually, of course, for the Western states' use), and also bound Japan to honor her proclamations of aiding Korea's independence.[20] Financially drained by the Sino–Japanese War, and uncertain of the new international realities created by the Triple Intervention, Japan decided to relax somewhat its control over the Korean government.

As a result of the above events, knowledgeable Koreans became more aware of the existing Great Power machinations and conflicts on the peninsula. The importance of returned students in the political system was brought home, and distrust of them heightened. Finally, Russia, China, and Japan became more convinced than ever of the importance of the Korean peninsula to their own international rivalry.

On October 8, 1895, Japanese officials in Seoul, in defiance of Tokyo, launched a coup against the Min court, in which Queen Min was murdered. The coup arose out of the fact that a coalition cabinet, composed of the Mins and an emerging pro-Russian faction, had been organized two months earlier. In response to the formation of this cabinet, with its anti-Japanese coloration, the Japanese officials conspired with the Tae-wŏn'gun for its overthrow. They agreed to support the Tae-wŏn'gun only in exchange for his pledge to grant large-scale commercial and political privileges to Japan and to renounce any active role in the administration of his country.[21]

The Russian–Japanese Rivalry over Korea

The Treaty of Shimonoseki and the Triple Interven-
tion signaled the replacement of China as Japan's major rival in
East Asia by Russia, which, under Nikolai Muraviev, was ex-
tending her influence to the borders of Korea and on to Sakhalin
Island. As early as 1864, Russia had crossed the Korean border at
Kyonghung demanding trade. Then, in 1866, she sent a fleet to
Wŏnsan demanding that Korea open her ports for trading with
Russia.[22] During the next three decades, as exemplified by von
Möellendorff's negotiations of 1885, Russia consistently sought
to penetrate the Korean political system, but was constantly
hindered by Chinese or Japanese actions.

In 1880, for example, the Chinese legation in Tokyo wrote a
memorial to a visiting Korean goodwill delegation stating that
the greatest danger to Korea was from Russia and that an alignment should therefore be made with the United States. Upon
returning to Peking from Shimonoseki, Li Hung-chang in 1895
said: "Russia is today our greatest friend and our most-to-be-
feared enemy. She is our friend because . . . . she wants to be a
greater friend than they [France and England]. She is our greatest
enemy because what the Russians call the trend of their destiny
makes her so. . . . She will help us to keep Japan out because she
herself wants to get in."[23] Li was accurately voicing what were to
be China's emotions in 1950.

Japanese feelings were expressed by Marshall Yamagata
Aritomo, a high Japanese statesman, in 1903, just before the
outbreak of the Russo–Japanese War, when he commented that
"if you will look at the geographical position of Korea, you will
see that it is like a poinard pointing at the heart of Japan . . . . If
Korea is occupied by a foreign power, the Japanese Sea ceases to
be Japanese, and the Korean Straits are no longer in our control."

Russia sought influence in Korea for several reasons: for
Korea's rich forests and mineral resources, as a buffer state
against potential Japanese territorial incursions, as the site of a

warm-water port,[24] and, especially after the Triple Intervention resulted in Russian control of Port Arthur, as part of a coastline which connected that facility with her major Far Eastern naval port, Vladivostok. Indeed, Lamsdorff, the Russian Foreign Minister from 1900 to 1905, frankly told Japanese Prime Minister Ito during a conversation on December 2, 1901: "If Japan should build fortresses along the Korean coast, it would cut off communications between Vladivostok and Port Arthur, a thing which Russia, for her own protection, cannot overlook." In response, Ito told Lamsdorff that "it goes without saying that the problem of Korea is almost a matter of life and death to Japan. The Japanese, moreover, are constantly entertaining the fear that Korea might some day be absorbed by Russia. . . ." [25]

The Russian "party's" influence was strengthened after the murder of Queen Min due to Korea's rapidly growing anti-Japanese feeling; widespread anti-Japanese rioting broke out in the provinces. Japan recognized the fact that Russia had now replaced China as the natural counter on the peninsula to her own intrusion by relaying to Russia her protestations of innocence for the grisly murder of the Queen.

On February 9, 1896, 100 Russian marines landed at Inch'ŏn in order to increase the guard at the Seoul legation to 160 men. The leader of the Russian party, Yi Pom-jin, then prevailed upon the king to seek asylum at the Russian legation; he did so on February 11, 1896. The Seoul populace, in a surge of loyalty to the king combined with anti-Japanese feelings, murdered many of the pro-Japanese government figures. King Kojong remained in the Russian legation for the following year, running his government with a natural favoritism toward those ministers who were pro-Russian.

Russian influence grew to such an extent that King Kojong sent the brother of the deceased Queen Min to the coronation of Czar Nicholas II in the summer of 1896 in order to seek a Russian protectorate over Korea. Also attending the coronation, and thus turning it partly into a Great Power conference on Korea, was

Japanese Marshall Yamagata Aritomo. Yamagata proposed a division of Russian–Japanese influence at the Korean 38th parallel.[26] Russia formally rejected this specific notion, but signed instead the more comprehensive Lobanoff–Yamagata Protocol in Moscow on June 9, 1896. This agreement promised that each state might afford assistance to Korea and grant it foreign loans to allow the peninsula to form a national army and police sufficient for internal needs. The protocol decided that Japan should continue to manage its telegraph line in the south, while Russia reserved the right to build its own line from Seoul to the Russian border.

Prince Lobanoff suggested that the agreement include a secret article providing that, should Russia and Japan ever again decide to send their troops into Korea, "each would define the area to be occupied so that a buffer zone would be created to prevent conflict between them."[27] It was in such an event that the 38th parallel would become important as a de facto division between Russian and Japanese influence.

In sum, the Lobanoff–Yamagata Protocol was a joint protectorate over Korea which expanded Russian influence at Japan's expense, particularly in the north. For example, it was now Russian officers who were to instruct the Korean army. Russia apparently expected her influence over Korea to eventually freeze Japan out of the peninsula. As Lamsdorff later stated Moscow's belief: "The fate of Korea, which was bound to become a component part of the Russian empire because of political and geographical conditions, was determined by us in advance."[28]

The Korean army obtained Russian advisors and arms to replace Japan's; a Russian-language school was established at the Russian legation. Russian economic penetration grew with financial arrangements by Russian banks, as well as a timber concession along the Yalu River. The decline of Japanese authority made the rise of Russian influence only more obvious.

Consistent with the Korean pattern of factional jockeying, opposition to the Russian "party" began to develop. This group of older conservatives and younger, more nationalist, officials urged the king to leave his residence in the Russian legation. He did so in February, 1897. In March, 1897, the Japanese published the articles of the Lobanoff–Yamagata Protocol which indicated the de facto division of Korea into spheres of influence, engendering Korean protests against both countries of Japan and Russia.[29]

Russia, meanwhile, was becoming increasingly fearful of Japan's aggressive intent both toward Korea and toward Russia herself. In September, 1897, the Russian minister in Tokyo warned his government that "it cannot be doubted . . . that the immense armament of the Japanese is directed against us and that Japan is eagerly preparing for an armed conflict with us. It is equally unquestionable that this conflict will break out over the Korean Question."[30]

A further cause for the growing Korean dissatisfaction with Russia was the appointment of Alexis de Speyer as the new Russian ambassador in Seoul in late 1897. As had happened before with both the Chinese and Japanese "Residents" in Korea, Speyer was more oppressive toward the Koreans and more zealous in his advancement of what he considered to be Russia's interests than his superiors themselves might have wished. Impatient with Korean protests at his overbearing methods, Speyer threatened in March, 1898, to withdraw all Russian advisors unless all anti-Russian officers were expelled from the Korean army. Seoul refused, and Speyer fell into his own trap. Forced by his own rhetoric to pull all Russian officers out of Korea, Speyer thus destroyed overnight the main basis of Russian influence in Korea. Moreover, Speyer had sought to replace the efficient British head of the Korean customs and treasury with a Russian; the British then sent warships to Inch'ŏn to demonstrate their support for the incumbent, and Speyer, outbluffed, had to back down.[31]

Russia continued to maneuver for leverage in Korea, but from a now much-weakened position, while at the same time she sought a dominant position in Manchuria,[32] refusing to withdraw from Manchuria after the Boxer Rebellion. Tensions increased between Japan and Russia, with each regarding Korea as essential to its own security.[33]

The Korean government, exhausted after forty years of factional infighting and attempted manipulations on the part of the intruding Great Powers, and fearful of becoming a battleground, tried to unite. In August, 1903, Korea formally requested Japan and Russia to consider Korea as a neutral country in case of war. Direct negotiations, meanwhile, were taking place between the two protagonists; Russia demanded a neutral zone slightly north of the original division line, at the 39th parallel.[34]

At this moment, the Korean government turned to the West, principally the United States, to counter growing Japanese hegemony. But when the Korean king directly asked Washington's help in guaranteeing Korean neutrality on the basis of the 1882 treaty, he was told that the American interest in Korea was economic rather than political.[35]

Korean history thereupon held out two additional lessons for the next generation. First, that the division of the peninsula at approximately the 38th parallel was a not unexpected act on the part of external powers anxious to introduce their influence into Korea; secondly, that the United States, regardless of the fine sentiments which it offered, could not be counted on to interfere in events on the peninsula with military force. Washington, in fact, had not wished to intervene in Korea—as it had the legal right, if not obligation, to do—because the *quid pro quo* of noninterference was Japanese noninterference in the American takeover of the Philippines. Consequently, North Korea's assumption that the United States would not fight on the peninsula in 1950 was a reasonable one to make.

The long-expected Russian–Japanese War finally began on February 8, 1904, with a Japanese surprise attack on both Inch'ŏn and Port Arthur. Consequently, later Asians would not be surprised by abrupt attacks on Inch'ŏn, nor by Chinese and Russian fears of a sudden attack on Manchuria. Japan's juggernaut easily consolidated its military control of Korea. By the end of March, 1904, more than 10,000 Japanese troops occupied Korea. On March 1, General Kuroki's army had crossed the Yalu River into Manchuria, and a week later that army landed on the Liaotung Peninsula. The Japanese occupied Dalny on May 30, and Port Arthur on January 2, 1905. On March 10, 1905, Mukden fell to Japan; thereafter the war reached a stalemate north of Mukden. On May 27–28, 1905, Admiral Togo virtually annihilated the Russian fleet in the narrow straits of Tsushima. (During the Korean Civil War, the Russian Navy was to avoid the Tsushima Straits, and take a much more circuitous route between Port Arthur and Vladivostok, perhaps a measure born of this memory of four and one-half decades earlier.)

The Treaty of Portsmouth (New Hampshire) of September 5, 1905, all but granted Japan domination over Korea. This treaty, sponsored by President Theodore Roosevelt, probably reinforced the Korean view that the United States was interested less in defending Korean interests than in *appearing* as an altruistic power, without having to expend its own blood and treasure. Legal annexation of Korea by Japan, which confirmed the ultimate bankruptcy of the Korean factional infighting of the previous four decades, waited until 1910.

Notes

1. This hypothesis is explored further in *International Behavior, A Social-Psychological Analysis*, ed. Herbert C. Kelman (New York: Holt, Rinehart and Winston, 1965).
2. See Edward Friedman, "Real Interests of China and America," in *Taiwan and American Policy* (New York: Frederick A. Praeger, 1971), p. 50.
3. This view was articulated by Tolstoy in his *War and Peace*. It also received a dramatic treatment in A. J. P. Taylor, *The Origins of World War Two*, (New York: Bantam Books, 1964).

4. *Chicago Daily News,* "A Frank Interview: Cowboy Kissinger," by Peter Lisagor, November 18, 1972, p. 1.

5. Fierce factional struggles within the political elite—a small group physically centered in Seoul—even at the risk of weakening Korea or subordinating her to a foreign power, have been a constant feature of the Korean political landscape for much longer than the past century. Great national crises, such as the Japanese invasion of the 1590s or those of the Manchus in the 1620s and 1630s, did not halt the intense fragmentation within the leadership. In that epoch, "the emergence of a new faction in power invariably involved a wholesale purge and sometimes physical elimination of opposition factions. Other problems of the government and the nation appeared to have been subordinated to the requirement of this life-or-death struggle within the ruling class." Eugene Kim and Han-kyo Kim, *Korea and the Politics of Imperialism, 1876–1910* (Berkeley: University of California Press, 1967), p. 11. Also see Gregory Henderson, *Korea: The Politics of the Vortex* (Cambridge, Mass.: Harvard University Press, 1968), p. 90. For an excellent introduction to Korean history which deals with many of these themes, see William E. Henthorn, *A History of Korea* (New York: The Free Press, 1971).

6. "Sino–Korean Tributary Relations in the Ch'ing Period," by Hae-jong Chun in *The Chinese World Order,* ed. John K. Fairbank (Cambridge, Mass.: Harvard University Press, 1968), p. 90.

7. Kim and Kim, op. cit., p. 12.

8. Woonsang Choi, *The Fall of the Hermit Kingdom* (Dobbs Ferry, N.Y.: Oceana Publications, 1967), p. 12.

9. Kim and Kim, op. cit., p. 16.

10. *The Korean Review,* ed. Homer B. Hulbert (Seoul: The Methodist Publishing House, 1902), Vol. 2, p. 220.

11. Choi, op. cit., p. 17.

12. Letter from Li Hung-chang to Yi Yu-won of August 29, 1879, cited in Kim and Kim, op. cit., p. 18.

13. Kim and Kim, op. cit., p. 28.

14. Henry Chung, comp., *Treaties and Conventions Between Korea and Other Powers* (New York: H.S. Nichols, 1919), pp. 197–204.

15. F.A. McKenzie, *The Tragedy of Korea* (London: Hadder and Stoughton, 1908), p. 18.

16. For an analysis of the political cross-cutting complexities of this event, see Harold F. Cook, *Korea's 1884 Incident* (Seoul: Royal Asiatic Society in conjunction with Taewon Publishing Co.), 1972.

17. As early as 1885, Japanese Prime Minister Ito told Li Hung-chang

that Japan "needed Korea as an outlet for her surplus population and as a source of food supply." Paul Langer, *The Diplomacy of Imperalism* (New York: Alfred A. Knopf, 1935), vol. 1, p. 170.

18. Kim and Kim, op. cit., p. 62.

19. The movement was highly reminiscent of the contemporary Chinese T'ai P'ing Rebellion. Its founder, Ch'oe Ch-u, was denied advancement in the governmental bureaucracy because of his lowly birth. Following a divine revelation during a "supernatural sickness," Ch'oe initiated the Tonghak, or "Eastern Learning," in contrast with Western, or Catholic learning. Highly popular among the peasants in the populous south, the new religion combined elements of Confucianism, Taoism, and Buddhism; unlike the T'ai P'ing, it did not borrow from Christianity. It was highly nationalistic. Ch'oe was executed in 1866, but his adherents continued to grow. See Charles Allen Clark, *Religions of Old Korea* (New York: Fleming H. Revell Co.) pp. 145, 158–76. Also Benjamin B. Weems, *Reform, Rebellion, and the Heavenly Way*, Associations for Asian Studies monograph no. XV (Tucson: University of Arizona Press, 1964), chap. 2. Korea has had a tradition of successful appeals to the mass population combining a call for economic and social reform with a strident nationalism.

20. Kim and Kim, op. cit., p. 83.

21. Choi, op. cit., p. 28.

22. Chon Dong, "Korea and the Russo–Japanese War," *Korean Quarterly* (Seoul) (spring, 1960), p. 19.

23. Jae Souk Sohn, "The United States and the Opening of Korea," *Korean Quarterly* (Seoul) (spring, 1965), p. 54; Frederick Palmer, *With Kuroki in Manchuria* (New York: Charles Scribner's Sons, 1904), pp. 15–16. The next quote, ibid.

24. Czar Nicholas II, when a Prince, had travelled over the route of the Trans-Siberian Railway to Vladivostok. Realizing that Vlodivostok was not a year-round ice-free port, he expressed a wish to build a warm-water port in Southeastern Korea. David J. Dallin, *The Rise of Russia in Asia* (New Haven: Yale University Press, 1949), p. 36.

25. Dong, op. cit., pp. 41–42.

26. *Korea: Origins of the Dividing Line at the 38th Parallel* (Washington, D.C.: Library of Congress Legislative Service, June 29, 1950), p. 2.

27. Kim and Kim, op. cit., p. 91.

28. Langer, op. cit., vol. 1, pp. 125–26.

29. Andrew Malozenoff, *Russian Far Eastern Policy, 1881–1904* (Berkeley: University of California Press, 1958), p. 91.

30. Langer, op. cit., vol. 2, p. 456.

31. Choi, op. cit, p. 52.
32. In 1899 Seoul had 1,764 Japanese and only 9 Russians. Hilary Conroy, *The Japanese Seizure of Korea: 1868–1910* (Philadelphia: University of Pennsylvania Press, 1961), p. 466.
33. Thus, President Roosevelt, in early 1905, noted that Russia was the "natural enemy" of Japan "as long as Japan takes an interest" in Korea and Manchuria. Tyler Dennett, *Roosevelt and the Russo–Japanese War* (New York: Doubleday, 1925), p. 50.
34. Malozemoff, op. cit., pp. 239–40.
35. Michael Harrington, *God, Mammon, and the Japanese* (Madison: University of Wisconsin Press, 1944), pp. 325–26.

2

The Prewar
Political System
in North Korea

The Russian Occupation

After four harsh decades of Japanese rule, Korea in 1945 continued to be viewed by its new Russian ally as a buffer state. For example, General Shtykov, the Soviet representative to the Joint American–Soviet Commission on Korea, echoed the same thoughts, albeit within ideological jargon, that traditional Russia had previously held about the peninsula: "The Soviet Union has a keen interest in Korea being a true democracy and an independent country friendly to the Soviet Union, so that in the future it will not become a base for an attack on the Soviet Union."[1]

The Soviet occupation troops which liberated P'yŏngyang after forty years of Japanese rule were highly unpopular. Looting and other crude behavior was fairly typical of the liberators. Edwin W. Pauley, a member of the U.S. Reparations Commission for China and Korea, made a six-day inspection trip through North Korea in December, 1946. He reported that: "there have been so many 'incidents' between the Soviet forces and Koreans after dark that General Chistiakov was forced to issue an order that after dark a Russian must be accompanied by two others, making three in the group. Still, two or three are killed every night by Koreans who have no weapons other than a rock."[2]

In December, 1947, the Soviets suddenly withdrew all money from circulation without announcing details on a new currency. This enabled the occupational personnel, and those Koreans whom the Russians wished to favor, to rid themselves of the old money beforehand—and make a large profit on the now devalued currency. As a result, there was widespread anger toward the Russians on the part of all except those who so benefited.[3] Another factor in Korean anti-Soviet feeling was the blatant manner in which the Russians manipulated the Korean economy for their own purposes. One reliable source stated that from late 1945 through 1948 the Russians removed two billion bushels of rice, 150,000 tons of sea products, and one complete steel refinery, while providing almost no compensation.[4] As the table starting on p. 39 shows, not only was North Korea asked to export a significant proportion of its production to the Soviet Union but, even more dramatically, almost every export goal of 1949 was overfulfilled by the end of that year.

Besides the exploitative manner in which Korea was viewed by its bordering states, a second factor common to pre-1905 and post-1945 Korean politics was the pattern of factional strife and the way in which intruding powers sought to utilize this stife to impose their own influence on the peninsula.

The Russians found no single group large or cohesive enough to obstruct their influence in 1945. Unlike the American occupation authorities in South Korea, the Russians preferred to rule North Korea indirectly, through a legion of sympathetic Koreans. The Russian army operated a political control organization which was separate from the main force with its occupation-garrison duties within Korea. This group, the so-called "Romanenko Command" (named after its leader, Major General Romanenko) dominated North Korean politics through its use of bribes, the awarding of political offices, force, and control of the mass media.[5]

The political groups available to the Russians in early post–World War II North Korea for manipulation were: 1) the "Soviet–Koreans," Koreans who were either born in or resident in the Soviet Union before 1945. A leader of this group was Hŏ Ka-i, a graduate of Moscow University and former secretary of the Tashkent Republic; 2) the "Kapsan" faction, guerilla fighters against the Japanese, headed by Kim Il-sŏng; 3) the "Yenan" faction, Koreans who had fought alongside of the Chinese People's Liberation Army (PLA), led by Mu Chŏng and the venerable Kim Tu-bong. This third group had the advantage of being both politically organized and militarily trained.

In 1939, the Korean Volunteer Army (KVA) was founded in Yenan; by September, 1945, it had grown to almost 2,500, comprising mostly Korean deserters from the Japanese army and local Koreans in Manchuria. Mu Chŏng attempted to enter North Korea through Sinŭiju (on the Manchurian border) in later September, 1945, only to be halted and have his group disarmed by Russian troops. He was told that he could not bring armed troops into North Korea, but that as a compromise his arms would be returned if he would take his army back into Manchuria and continue fighting with the PLA.[6] The message appeared to be unmistakable: North Korea was to be Russian-dominated; an armed, pro-Chinese, force which could serve as a natural rival to Russian influence was not to be welcomed. Probably neither the Chinese nor the Russians, each of whom was well aware of their earlier struggles for sway on the peninsula, overlooked the significance of the Sinŭiju incident, nor did the Koreans. Beginning in the spring of 1946, small groups of the KVA were allowed into North Korea, but not in sufficient strength to pose a serious threat to Russian dominance.

A fourth group vying for power in postwar North Korea, was the "domestic" communist faction. Led by the highly respected revolutionary Pak Hŏn-yŏng, who had remained in Korea during the Japanese occupation, this faction was the first to reestablish the Korean Communist Party, on September 12, 1945, in the traditional national capital of Seoul.

The strongest and most popular political grouping in the country, however, in terms of the extent and depth grass-roots support, was that with no ties to the communists: viz., the "nationalists" under Cho Man-sik. Cho's importance was indicated by two related incidents: the Japanese governor of South P'yŏngyang Province directly transferred his authority to Cho upon the Japanese surrender, and the Russians later reinforced this decision by appointing Cho as the Chief of the Provincial Political Committee, and later of the Five Provinces' Administration.[7] Cho was so important that the Soviet occupation authorities found it expedient to have him, "for reasons still obscure,"[8] introduce Kim Il-sŏng as a Korean nationalist leader at a public meeting in P'yŏngyang in October, 1945. Kim thereupon rapidly displaced Cho, who was imprisoned in January, 1946, as a result of his uncooperative behavior toward the Russians.

One credible story has it that the Russians at first sought to form a North Korean regime with Cho Man-sik as its titular head, allowing Kim Il-sŏng to gain some seasoning. This would enable Kim's ultimate leadership in P'yŏngyang, while at the same time appealing to as many Koreans as possible. Cho, however, refused to follow Soviet directives, and subsequently vanished.[9]

There was no overwhelming protest at Cho's disappearance. This can perhaps best be explained by a reference to the Korean past, in which the political game was played out fiercely within a small group of leaders, within a limited territory (the capital), with each group assuming that it could solicit the aid of an intruding Great Power in its bid for domestic power. The major problem with applying this tradition to the North Korea of 1945–46 was that there was now only one Great Power, and thus no opportunity (except for the residual hopes of the Yenan faction) to balance off the Great Powers. Now a single Great Power held hegemony, as the Japanese had had only shortly before.

Kim Il-sŏng's Rise to Power

Did the Russians have a specific design, on their part, for North Korea, and was Kim Il-sŏng the willing marionette for Soviet machinations? Contrary to the oft-repeated assumption that Kim was a mere puppet, and analogously to the American experience with Syngman Rhee in South Korea (an experience which both Great Powers have frequently found to be repeated with their "satellites"), the Russians entered North Korea with no operational plan beyond that of establishing a "friendly regime." Kim seems to have been chosen, as was Syngman Rhee in the South, for largely negative reasons: most other potential communist leaders had been ruled out by the Russians, whereas they felt that Kim was adequately malleable and would be sufficiently pro-Russian. [10]

Kim Il-sŏng, although supported by the Soviet occupation army, needed to both lessen the influence of and compromise with the other factions in order to increase the leverage of his own "Kapsan" group. In the summer of 1948, for example, an apparently nervous Kim Tu-bong asked his Chinese friends not to visit his residence in P'yŏngyang; at the Korean Workers' Party (KWP) Congress of 1949, Mu Chŏng was censured for "heroism" and for trying to build a personal clique within the party. [11] Indeed, Mu Chŏng, potentially the most serious rival to Kim and also representing the Chinese threat to Russian influence in Korea, had been demoted in July, 1946, from a rank equivalent to that of a general to that of an artillery commander. [12]

Kim Il-sŏng himself owed sole allegience to no faction. This was probably a strong point in his favor amongst history-conscious Koreans, who had learned not to trust the "returned students" of past struggles who remained loyal to the foreign country wherein they had been educated. Kim, on the other hand, had fought with the soldiers of both the penetrating Great Powers. He joined the Chinese Communist Party (CCP) in 1931 and struggled alongside of the paramilitary forces of the PLA in Manchuria. [13] After this, it is generally thought that he spent the years 1942 to 1945 in the Soviet Union, after being chased out of Manchuria by Japanese forces—although the Koreans themselves deny this, perhaps to maintain the image of Kim staying in Korea until 1945 to fight the Japanese. In any case, this notion, let alone his specific activities during those four years,has never been fully documented. [14] In the main, however, it does appear that Kim received his early ideological training from the CCP, with later tutelage from the Russians.

A North Korean Communist Party was organized in late 1945; Kim Il-sŏng became its leader on December 17. The Yenan faction had meanwhile organized itself into a separate New People's Party on March 30, 1946. The latter attracted a wide following among the petitbourgeoisie and intellectuals; its growing popularity was viewed with alarm and jealousy by the Soviet–Korean and Kapsan-sponsored Korean Communist Party, which wished to impede Chinese influence. The two parties merged on August 28, 1946. [15] According to an eyewitness at the August convention of the new North Korean Workers' Party, the chairmanship fell not to Kim Il-sŏng but to Kim Tu-bong, leader of the Yenan faction. When Kim Il-sŏng's supporters tried to push his name through as chairman, the soviet advisor present called a recess. After a short break, Kim Il-sŏng personally placed Kim Tu-bong's name in nomination, settling himself for the first vice-chairmanship. [16] This gesture, however, was but a momentary tatic. The Soviet Union's support of Kim Il-sŏng in the north rapidly relegated the Yenan faction to a secondary position in the new party.

During this turbulent period, the year after liberation from Japanese rule, most of the "domestic" faction leadership had stayed in Seoul, the traditional national capital, now the capital of the American-administered south. This insistence upon holding onto history (and perhaps hoping to work with the Americans in the south) served the function of siphoning off the energies of the most sizeable and popular communist group; meanwhile, the maneuvering for actual power took place in the communist north. Professor Dae-sook Suh points out that this enabled the relatively unknown communists of the Kapsan, Soviet, and Yenan factions to rise to positions of prominence in the North without a direct challenge from the domestic faction. [17]

For a moment after the 1945 liberation, it may have seemed to the Russians that Pak Hŏn-yŏng's domestic faction would be triumphant in the American-administered south.

It is conceivable that the Russians during the early months of the occupation entertained the possibility that Pak Hon-yong would lead a national Communist movement if Korean unification occurred rapidly as a result of Soviet–American agreement. Certainly Pak's authority in the south was upheld by Soviet authorities at critical junctures, and he, in turn, gave his loyal support to the Russians on all matters. Did the Russians keep their options open with respect to this, at least until the spring of 1946? We cannot be certain. In any case, after the breakdown of the Joint Commission negotiations it became increasingly clear that the locus of Communist power would be in the north, not the south. [18]

Consequently, while Soviet support was the vital factor in Kim Il-sŏng's accession to power, Moscow's hedging assistance must have demonstrated to Kim that he would have to rely for his future security not totally on Soviet goodwill, but rather on his own abilities as a genuine nationalist leader.

One witness has related why the Soviet Union decided, in the end, to decisively support Kim Il-sŏng's Kapsan faction:

When the Domestic, Yenan and Soviet factions were running about in confusion in the political world of

P'yongyang, the Kapsan faction, dispersed to local districts, was doing its utmost to establish its regional organizations. . . . There was no evidence that from the outset the Soviet occupation forces had entrusted Kim Il-song with the power to control North Korea. Even if the Soviet side had such an intention, it was not an absolute one. . . . It was, therefore, after the lower organizations were completed that the Soviet Union decided to entrust to Kim Il-song and his faction the reins of government, or it may be said that such a decision was accelerated by the completion of the above organizations. . . Many people ascribe the fame of Kim Il-song to the Soviet decision. It may be one of the reasons, but the major reason was the Kapsan faction's completion of its lower organizations at this early stage. [19]

In sum, while the Russians were predisposed toward Kim Il-sŏng at the beginning of their occupation, they were also interested in seeing what other options were available to them, particularly with respect to the Soviet faction. It early on turned out to be the case that Kim Il-sŏng's faction, and not the Soviet–Koreans, had organized sufficiently at the local level so as to govern effectively; the result was, in effect, a coalition government between the Soviet–Korean and Kim Il-sŏng factions, with the Yenan and domestic factions functioning as the not-so-loyal opposition. Kim Il-sŏng, therefore, learned early in his career that much of his future success depended on his leadership qualities, rather than merely on Russian support.

Between Russia and China: Korean Nationalism

Although he knew that his rise to power was determined largely by (uncertain) Russian support, Kim Il-sŏng was well aware of the exploitation which Korea had been subjected to by its neighbors—an abuse which continued under the

Soviet occupation. An indication that Kim was sensitive to this history is a speech of November, 1946, in which he noted that some people say that power can be real

. . . only when it is framed up by someone from above or forcibly introduced from without by a foreign country. Those who make such allegations usually refer to the old society and say, "Our ancestors, too, lived that way." And what sort of power is it at all, the power framed up from above? It is a power of the rich established without the people's participation, an inequitable power of the minority against the majority. It is a fact well known to all through a long history that such a power pursued the policy of oppressing the people and defending the exploiters. And our people know better than anyone else through their own bitter experience how barbarous and predatory the power framed up forcibly by another country is.

Therefore, those who reject the power elected by the people themselves are, in fact, persons who want to return to the past when the people were subjected to oppression and maltreatment and who attempt to bring our people under the humiliating yoke of colonial slavery again.[20]

During the period when Russian occupation forces were exploiting Korean resources, Kim needed to walk a fine line between maintaining Soviet support and acknowledging to his countrymen that he was aware of the manner in which Moscow was behaving toward its newly-found small associate. For example, at a moment when P'yŏngyang was sending "out to foreign countries the raw materials which we extract from the abundant domestic sources," and while the North Korean economy was dominated by the demands of the Soviet Union, Kim Il-sŏng´ declared that

. . . we have become more firmly confident that it is quite possible for us to develop the national industry independently. Indeed, we need to receive necessary foreign aid in the future, too, but we must have a firm determination to

rehabilitate and develop the national economy and build a
rich and powerful country by our own efforts, without
seeking to rely entirely on others.

This year, the factories should be rehabilitated completely and industrial production be raised to the level of
the years of Japanese imperialist rule. And we should not
be concerned only in the quantitative growth of production; it is necessary to pay attention to gradually improving
its qualitative structure too. We should not send out to
foreign countries the raw materials which we extract from
the abundant domestic sources, as in the bygone days of
Japanese imperialist rule, but should proceed in the direction of processing all of them at home to produce finished
goods.[21]

Kim continued to reassure his nationalistic countrymen
that because of his proclaimed policy of self-reliance, coupled
with a strong political organization, external forces would not
prolong their control over North Korea:

The path our Party has traveled and the realities in North
Korea have completely belied the imperialists' slander:
"Being an inferior nation, the Korean people are incapable
of governing the state, and they cannot have a powerful
political party." We are now legitimately proud that the
Korean nation, ranking among the advanced nations of the
whole world, is creditably administering its country and
has a great political party capable of shaping the destinies
of the country and the people.[22]

North Korea and China

Although the north was dominated by the Soviet
Union, Kim Il-sŏng's absorption of several Chinese Communist
precepts is reflected in his early writings. A comparison of Mao
Tse-tung's and Kim's articles on the "mass line," for example,
indicates close ideological similarities. Mao, in his 1943 classic

"On Methods of Leadership,"[23] wrote that: "the leadership can work out correct ideas only if it sums up the views of the masses and takes the resulting ideas back to the masses so that they can gain firm mass support." In 1948 Kim echoed this notion: "We must acquire the work method of explaining matters to the masses, not commanding them, of going deep into the midst of the masses and knowing their feelings, teaching them and learning from them."[24]

Copies of Mao's works circulated widely in both North and South Korea after liberation. Probably because of this influence—and because of Kim's personal experience with the Chinese Communists during the 1930s—the KWP's analysis also coincided with the Chinese on policies of the "united front." Kim believed, as did Mao, that virtually any class which does not oppose the revolution may be part of the united front, including "the broad masses of peasants, patriotic intellectuals, and even national capitalists who had national consciousness." [25]

In sum, although Kim Il-sŏng undoubtedly owed his position in the later 1940s to the Soviet Union and was opposed to the growth of the pro-Chinese Yenan faction, it would be a misnomer to call him a Russian puppet. In fact, it is closer to the mark to say that Kim was a Soviet-supported Korean nationalist, whose power base became to a significant extent his own organization, and who reflected Chinese ideology at least as much as he articulated Russian slogans. These factors led to several ties between North Korea and the Chinese Communists,[26] and to North Korea being something other than a mere Soviet satellite.

Ties between the Yenan faction and the CCP were particularly close. The 1942 program of the Independence League (parent of the KVA) contained a provision which stated that "the CCP should play a leading role in post-war Korea."[27]

The former North Korean vice-minister of agriculture and forestry from 1945 to 1948, Chang Sang-chin, stated in his Seoul press conference, after fleeing to the South, that North Korea and the CCP had concluded a mutual assistance pact in the summer of 1946, when the Chinese Kuomintang (KMT) controlled the major city of Antung and the CCP was forced into North Korea. The Koreans supplied food and clothing to the CCP until they crossed back in 1947.[28] In March and April of 1947 there were then large-scale transfers of North Korean troops sent to Manchuria to help the Chinese Communists.[29]

A pact was concluded between the North Korean People's Committee Transportation Bureau and Communist China's Northeast Administration Transportation Committee concerning loading and unloading of Chinese cargoes passing through North Korea, dated November 6, 1947.[30]

These facts, along with the presence of large numbers of Korean soldiers fighting alongside of the Chinese in the PLA, lends credence to later Chinese expressions of brotherly affection for North Korea and a sense of responsibility toward her. Although documentary evidence is lacking, it appears that this tie between the two states blossomed into a bilateral defense treaty in March, 1949, in Moscow (under the watchful eye of Stalin).

Why would Kim Il-sŏng sign a bilateral defense pact not with his mentors, the Russians, but rather with the sponsors of his major domestic rivals, the Yenan faction? In the spring of 1949, Kim Il-sŏng allegedly told the Soviet Union's ambassador to North Korea that his forces were intent upon attacking the south. According to Japanese sources, Kim said, "If the attack failed, by the intervention of a third country, there would be a temporary retreat to Manchuria, and they would attack again at a favorable time. Therefore, he proposed a military alliance with the Chinese communists."[31]

Several other reasons suggest themselves. Kim Il-sŏng had begun his revolutionary activities with the CCP, and still felt close to them, particularly ideologically. Furthermore, history had taught the Koreans not to depend too closely upon any one foreign power. Because the post-1945 reality included only one major intruding power, it would seem to have been a wise move for Kim to try to balance off Russia's influence with at least the threat of being able to count upon another neighbor. Another suggestion as to why North Korea would sign a military agreement with Communist China is contained in a Russian shortwave broadcast to North Korea, *in Korean,* during the period when the North Korean leadership was in Moscow. Entitled "The Faithful Friend and Protector of the People's Republic of Mongolia, the Soviet Union," the commentary concluded that "twice in the past twenty-eight years the armed forces of the Soviet state gave the Mongolian people military assistance, aiding them in the struggle for independence against foreign imperialism." The message was clear: the price of Soviet military aid was to become a mere Soviet satellite. [32] Finally, there is the possible factor of race and the historically closer ties to China, because of which the Russians may have been less trusted than the Chinese.

If there were indeed a treaty, then, why should it have been secret? Perhaps primarily because to publicly announce it would have amounted to an open admission on the part of the Soviet Union of China's legitimate interest and influence in North Korea—a premise that Moscow did not wish to recognize.

Stalin's cautiousness in foreign policy, his willingness to risk adventure only when the odds appeared favorable, probably led him to approve of the alleged military alliance between China and North Korea. Most likely, he felt that he had gotten the best of both worlds: Soviet influence remained paramount in Korea, while in the event of war, it would be the Chinese Communists who would be called upon to rescue the North Koreans. On the Chinese side, the treaty afforded an opportunity to maintain an interest in her former suzerainty-state.

The South Korean army has published what it states is the text of the March 18, 1949, treaty. The operational phrase reads: "Each side has the responsibility for the common defense from any kind of invasion. If any imperialist ally attacks either North Korea or China, we two nations will carry out common acts in this common war." [33]

The Chinese Nationalists have also claimed knowledge of the formal North Korean–Chinese Communist bilateral defense treaty signed in March, 1949. It stipulated, according to them, that:

> The two sides shall take joint defensive action against aggression of whatever nature. The two sides shall take joint steps against whatever imperialist forces attack either of the two.
>
> The Chinese Communist Party shall deliver weapons and troops to North Korea between July 1 and August 31, 1949.
>
> North Korea shall retain top priority in utilizing Japanese technicians, employees and war materials in Manchuria.
>
> North Korea and the Chinese Communist Party shall exchange goods when economic need warrants it. [34]

There had been one other occasion when the Soviet Union used a second state to sign a bilateral defense treaty with one of its satellites while not directly committing itself to the latter's defense in the event of war. In 1946, Yugoslavia and Albania signed such a pact, while Albania had none with the Soviet Union. If the Chinese Communist–North Korean mutual defense treaty was, indeed, a reality, we may draw two conclusions. The first is that the new Peking government was, understandably, vitally interested in cultivating its (diminished) influence in Korea, a country in which it had a traditional interest and in which there was once again a weakening internal faction friendly to it. Secondly, the Chinese intervention in the Korean Civil War one and one-half years later takes on a new light: the Chinese, instead of merely defending what they considered to be their national integrity, were also fulfilling their part of a previously concluded bilateral defense agreement.

We shall return to the internal Korean situation in chapter 5. In the following pages, however, we shall look first at China's relationships with the external world.

Notes

1. *New York Times,* "Russian Pledges Help to Korea So It Will Not Be a Foe's Base," March 21, 1946, p. 24.
2. *New York Times,* "Pauley Discloses Korean Sidelights," December 15, 1946, p. 41. See also Robert A. Scalapino and Chong-sik Lee, *Communism in Korea* (Berkeley and Los Angeles: University of California, 1972), p. 315, which speaks of an "orgy of rape and pillage" at the time of liberation in 1945.
3. *New York Times,* "Korea Buying Panic in North Reported," by Richard J. H. Johnston, December 12, 1947, p. 16. Even those who benefited by this currency manipulation were probably not turned into complete Russophiles. The United States experience in South Vietnam, for example, has amply demonstrated that clients of intruding powers, even when they benefit financially, do not trust or necessarily love their "benefactors."
4. *New York Times,* "Korea Skeptical on Soviet Exodus," Seoul, A. P., January 1, 1949, p. 4.

    A North Korean technician at the Sup'ung Power Plant on the Yalu has stated that four of the six generators at the plant were shipped away over strenuous Korean protests. Scalapino and Lee, op. cit., pp. 1197–98.
5. Kim Ch'ang-sun, *Pukhan sip-o-nyŏn-sa* [Fifteen-Year History of North Korea] (Seoul, 1961). Translated by the Joint Publications Research Service, Washington, D.C., 1965, p. 54. Also Benjamin Min, "North Korea's Foreign Policy in the Post-War Decade, 1953–1963," unpublished Ph.D. dissertation, University of Massachusetts, 1967, p. 123. For further penetrating analysis of events briefly presented in this chapter and chapter 5, see also Koon Woo Nam, *The North Korean Communist Leadership, 1945 to 1965* (University, Ala.: The University of Alabama Press, 1974), pp. 13–83.
6. *History of the North Korean Army* (General Headquarters, United States Far East Command, Military Intelligence Section, July, 1952), p. 6.
7. Chong-sik Lee, "Politics in North Korea: Pre-War Stage," in *North Korea Today,* ed. Robert Scalapino (New York: Frederick A. Praeger, 1963), p. 8–9.
8. Gregory Henderson, *Politics of the Vortex* (Cambridge: Harvard University Press, 1968), p. 326.
9. Scalapino and Lee, op. cit., pp. 325, 338–39.

10. As Chong-sik Lee stated in "Kim Il-song of North Korea," *Asian Survey* (June, 1967), p. 378:

    > In North Korea, . . . all these ex-revolutionaries had to oper-
    > ate in the milieu of Soviet occupation, and the support or at
    > least aquiescence of the Soviet authorities was essential for
    > success. In this respect, Kim Il-song was an undisputed win-
    > ner, for he arrived in Pyongyang already annointed by the
    > Soviet command. There are grounds for doubting that the
    > Soviet forces entered Korea with a premeditated plan; it is
    > more than likely that the Soviet command possessed no more
    > detailed instruction than to establish a "friendly regime" in
    > Korea. But it is also clear that Kim was to serve as the Soviet's
    > man in this regime. In this sense, the contest for power in
    > North Korea was concluded before it ever began.

11. *North Korea: A Case Study in the Techniques of Takeover* (Washing-
    ton, D.C., United States States Department). Published with a
    "classified" status in May, 1951, released publicly in 1961, based
    upon North Korean documents taken after P'yŏngyang was cap-
    tured in the fall of 1950. Mu Chŏng's censure was an example of the
    type of factional infighting that was prevalent in North Korea. It
    was at the 1949 Congress that Pak Hŏn-yŏng was elected a KWP
    vice-chairman. It seems likely that part of the price which Kim
    Il-sŏng extracted from his rival for this post was Pak's agreement to
    oppose their common opposition, the Chinese-supported Mu
    Chŏng.

12. Kim Ch'ang-sun, op. cit., p. 84. For an insightful account of Kim's
    rise to power in North Korea, see Scalapino and Lee, op. cit., pp.
    313–81.

13. Dae-sook Suh has noted that Kim Il-sŏng "was educated and
    trained by the Chinese Communists as one of their own." *The
    Korean Communist Movement, 1918–1948* (Princeton, Princeton Uni-
    versity Press, 1968), p. 293.

14. The circumstantial evidence about Kim's wartime activities is con-
    flicting. For example, *Tokkō Geppō* (the *Monthly Report of the
    Japanese Special Political Police*), February, 1943, p. 82, and Sep-
    tember, 1943, p. 109, states that Kim Il-sŏng was operating in
    Manchuria in 1943. (Cited in Key P. Yang, "The North Korean
    Regime, 1945–1955," unpublished M.A. thesis, American Univer-
    sity, 1958, p. 54). On the other hand, *The Secret History of the Korean
    Independence Movement*, published by the Japanese Ministry of the
    Interior of the Bureau of Public Safety, n.d., p. 149 (cited in Myung

Kun Yio, "Sino–Soviet Rivalry in North Korea since 1954", unpublished Ph.D. dissertation, University of Maryland, 1969, p. 32) states that Kim Il-sŏng fought at the World War II battles of Stalingrad and Berlin with the Russians. Scalapino and Lee, op. cit., pp. 318, 326, write that Kim "spent the wartime period in the Soviet Union," although he did not participate in the battles in the West against the Germans.
15. Kim Ch'ang-sun, op. cit., pp. 97–99.
16. Ibid., pp. 99–104.
17. Dae-sook Suh, op. cit., p. 301.
18. Scalapino and Lee, op. cit., p. 327.
19. "The North Korean Labor Party's Internal Factions," originally published in the Japanese monthly *Jiyu*. Written anonymously by "The Neighboring Countries Research Institute." Translated in the *Selected Summaries of Japanese Magazines,* published by the American Embassy, Tokyo, June 26–July 3, 1967, p. 4.

    Professors Scalapino and Lee, op. cit., p. 690, note that:

    It can be argued that Kim should be given credit for the political acumen that enabled him to manipulate the Russians, moving from the position of being only one of the contenders for power to becoming *the* Soviet candidate. This assumes, of course, that the Soviets came to Korea without firm decisions regarding Korean leadership, an assumption that may be correct, but upon which differences of opinion exist.

20. "On the Eve of the Historic Democratic Election," in *Kim Il Sung, Selected Works I* (Pyongyang: Foreign Languages Publishing House, 1971), pp. 125–26.

    We are indebted for the following paragraphs to Bruce G. Cumings and Ilpyong J. Kim, "Political Organization, Nationalism, and Self-Reliance in North Korea: "An Interpretation," paper presented at the 1973 annual meeting of the American Political Science Association. A revised version of this paper has appeared as "Kim's Korean Communism," by Bruce G. Cumings, in *Problems of Communism,* March–April 1974, pp. 27–41.
21. "How to Develop State Industry and How to Manage the Enterprises?" January, 1948, in *Kim Il Sung,* pp. 188–89.
22. "Report to the Second Congress of the Workers' Party," March, 1948, in *Kim Il Sung,* p. 256.
23. Mao Tse-tung, *Selected Works* (New York: International Publishers, 1954), p. 114.

24. *Kim Il Sung*, p. 247. See similar statements in ibid, pp. 15, 150–51.
25. Baik Bong, *Kim Il Sung*, Vol. 2 (Tokyo: Miraisha, 1970), p. 31; and Cumings and Kim, op. cit., p. 17.
26. *History of the North Korean Army*, p. 17.
27. Shijuo Mitani, "North Korea and Sino–Soviet Relations," in *Guimusho Chosa Geppo* [Japanese Foreign Ministry Monthly], 1965, nos. 2–3, pp. 45–74.
28. *New York Times*, "Korea Skeptical on Soviet Exodus," by Richard J. H. Johnston, January 1, 1949, p. 7.
29. *History of the North Korean Army*, p. 17.
30. Translated by General Headquarters, United States Far East Command, Military Intelligence Section, April, 1952.
31. *Kyodo Tsunshin* (the major Japanese news agency), Tokyo, May 11, 1950, p. 8.
32. Moscow Radio, March 17, 1949.
33. *Hanguk Chŏnjaeng-sa* [Korean War History], Vol. 1 (Seoul: War History Compilation Committee of the Ministry of National Defense, 1967), p. 711. See also Kim Chum-Kon, *The Korean War* (Seoul: Kwangmyong Publishing Co., 1973), p. 51.
34. *China Times* (Shanghai), May 5, 1949, p. 2; See also *New York Times*, "China Reds Reported in North Korea Pact," May 6, 1949, p. 7.

Economic Report from Vice-Minister Ko Hi-man, Department of Industry, D.P.R.K., to Vice-Premier Kim Ch'aek, January 10, 1950

Items Exported to the USSR in 1949

No	Export Item	Unit of Measure	Price per Unit	Planned Amount in 1949		Total Delivered to NK Govt for Export		Total Exported in 1949		Percent	Stock on Hand by Trade Control Bureau
				QUANTITY	VALUE	QUANTITY	VALUE	QUANTITY	VALUE		
1	Electric Copper	Ton	2,512 (20)	300	753,660	800	2,009,760	803 (196)	2,017,788 (99)	100	
2	Electric Lead	Ton	1,749 (60)	4,000	6,996,000	4,500	7,870,500	4,381 (084)	7,662,533 (40)	97	496,716 (284T)
3	Electric Zinc	Ton	1,600	5,450	8,723,270	5,850	9,363,510	5,364 (550)	8,586,498 (73)	92	720,270 (450T)
4	Cadmium	Ton	23,320	24	59,680	24	559,680	27	629,640 (50)	113	
5	bismuth	Ton	23,320 (30)	9	209,880	7	165,572	3 (844,147)	89,645	54	
6	Tantalum	Ton	16,355	5 (2)	85,047	5 (2)	85,047 (56)	4 (710)	77,033 (46)	91	26,170 (1,600)
7	Barium	Ton	5,300	23 (2)	122,860	28	132,500	45 (540)	241,362	182	
8	Concentrated Mg Ore	Ton	5,300	300	1,590,00	7,000	37,100,000	5,732	30,379,600 (91)	82	1,098,690 (2,073)
9	Concentrated Zinc Ore	Ton	530	14,000	7,420,000	17,000	9,010,000	17,359 (747/413)	9,200,665 (91)	102	
10	Fe-W (TN Tungsten)	Ton	16,377 (80)	450	7,369,650	550	9,007,350 (40)	630	10,324,273 (70)	115	
11	Fe-Si (TN Silicon)	Ton	879	6,750	5,738,650	4,063	3,574,627	4,233 (836)	3,724,928 (88)	104	
12	High-speed Steel	Ton	11,130 (66)	1,250	13,812,500	1,250	13,912,500	1,304 (815)	14,522,590 (95)	104	
13	Special Tool Steel	Ton	3,156 (10)	1,800	5,681,881	1,800	5,681,880 (10)	1,539 (811)	4,860,567 (40)	86	422,393 (234)
14	Carbon Tool Steel	Ton	1,805	5,000	9,025,500	3,471	6,265,502	1,838 (941)	3,319,472 (·32)	53	
15	Steel Rod	Ton	485 (10)	2,200	1,067,000	2,000	970,000	2,384 (130)	1,156,303 (05)	119	
16	Plate	Ton	461	24,800	11,135,280	22,800	10,513,080	19,681 (841)	9,075,296 (88)	86	

Economic Report from Vice-Minister Ko Hi-man, Department of Industry, D.P.R.K., to Vice-Premier Kim Ch'aek, January 10, 1950

[THIS TABLE CONTINUES THROUGH PAGE 47.]

No	Export Item	Unit of Measure	Price per Unit	Planned Amount in 1949		Total Delivered to NK Govt for Export		Total Exported in 1949			Stock on Hand by Trade Control Bureau
				QUANTITY	VALUE	QUANTITY	VALUE	QUANTITY	VALUE	Percent	
17	Pig Iron	Ton	265	40,000	10,600,000	50,000	13,250,000	800 51,332	13,603,192 03	103	
18	Angle Steel No 130	Ton	469			1,300	609,700	725 1,644	771,376 55	126	
19	Angle Steel No 150	Ton	469 66			1,500	703,500 20	498 3,492	1,637,981 06	233	
20	Angle Steel No 65–75	Ton	469	2,400	1,127,184	2,570	1,207,026	870 2,781	1,306,533	108	7,097
21	Fertilizer	Ton	318 50	81,000	25,758,000	111,000	35,298,000	103,903 540	33,041,154 77	100	2,256,845
22	Carbide	Ton	450	26,700	12,028,350	14,000	6,307,000	18,461 400	8,316,923	132	
23	Acetylene Black	Ton	1,060 50	1,960	2,077,600	1,000	1,060,000	1,021	1,082,684	102	
24	Arsenic Acid	Ton	715	740	529,470	740	529,470	270 670	193,185 50	36	
25	Lead Oxide	Ton	2,650	180	477,000	180	477,000	200	531,775	101	
26	Zinc Oxide	Ton	1,592 20	100	159,200	100	159,200	124	197,408	124	
27	Ammonium Nitrate	Ton	280 20	400	112,360	400	112,360	400	112,360	100	
28	Alundum	Ton	1,346	900	1,211,580	1,000	1,346,200	1,025	1,379,855	103	
29	Fuses	KM	61 72	1,200	871,320	12,000	871,320	12, 00	871,320	100	
30	Percussion Primers	3 10	55 71	600	429,300	600	429,300	600	429,300 30	100	6,000
31	Cement	T	65 55	30,000	1,669,500	30,000	1,669,500	27,402 210,550	1,524,921 57	111	330,900
32	Silk	Ton	26,500	40	1,060,000	70	1,855,000	71	1,887,079	100	

No.	Name of Item	Unit of Measure	Price per Unit	Planned QUANTITY	Planned VALUE	Delivered QUANTITY	Delivered VALUE	QUANTITY	VALUE	Percent
33	Washing Soaps	Ton	1,590 (80)	3,000	4,770,000	3,000	4,770,000	3,000	4,770,000	100
34	Iron Ore	Ton	31 (40)	50,000	1,590,000	30,000	954,000	30,000	954,000	100
35	Magnesite	Ton	95 (50)	10,000	954,000	12,000	1,144,800	8,747 (190)	834,481 (92)	73
36	Talc	Ton	79 (90)	2,300	182,850	3,500	278,250	4,036 (900)	320,862 (61)	115
37	Perlite	Ton	116 (70)	6,000	701,400	850	993,650	9,336 (900)	1,091,483 (61)	110
45	Acetone	Ton	1,107 (90)	420	465,234	420	465,234			
46	Starch	Ton	757 (80)	3,000	2,273,700	3,000	2,273,700			100
47	Fluorite	Ton	137 (60)			3,000	413,400	3,192 (070)	439,867 (24)	106
48	Kaolin	Ton	63 (80)			2,100	133,560	1,430 (670)	90,948 (76)	68
49	Sodium Hydroxide	Ton	429	2,160	928,368	2,160	428,368	2,166	931,234	100
50	Ammonium Nitrate Explosives	Ton	1,060			10	10,600	10	10,600	100
51	Cables 15 T	33cm	10,600	129	1,367,400	129	1,367,400	67	710,200	52
52	Cables 45 T	33cm	32,860	35	1,150,000	35	1,150,100	35	1,150,100	100
53	Barium Chlorate	T	2,978			30	89,340	30	89,340	100

Comparative Chart with Listings According to Control Bureau and Suboffice in 1949

1. Chemical Control Bureau

Location of Enterprise	Name of Item	Unit of Measure	Price per Unit	Planned Amount		Delivered to NK Govt for Export		Percent	Stock on Hand by the Trade Control Bureau	Remarks
				QUANTITY	VALUE	QUANTITY	VALUE	Percent		
CHUNSU Chemical	Carbide	T	450 (50)	5,000	2,252,500	7,005 (800)	3,156,112 (90)	140		
CHUNSU Chemical	Acetylene Black	T	1,060	300	318,000	321 (400)	340,684	107		

1. *Chemical Control Bureau*

Location of Enterprise	Name of Item	Unit of Measure	Price per Unit	Planned Amount QUANTITY	Planned Amount VALUE	Delivered to NK Gov't for Export QUANTITY	Delivered to NK Gov't for Export VALUE	Percent	Stock on Hand by the Trade Control Bureau	Remarks
CHUNSU Chemical			80		2,570,500	520	3,496,796	155		
			90							
BONKUNG Chemical	Fe–Si	T	879	1,140	1,002,972	1,256	1,105,486	113		
			50			740	21			
							87			
BONKUNG Chemical	Carbide	T	450	9,000	4,054,500	11,455	5,160,810	103		
BONKUNG Chemical	Acetylene Black	T	1,060	700	742,000	700	742,000	100		
			80			670	76			
BONKUNG Chemical	Sodium Hydroxide	T	429	2,160	928,368	2,166	931,234	103		
BONKUNG Chemical	Alundum	T	1,346	1,000	1,346,200	11,025	1,379,855	103		
			20							
BONKUNG Chemical	Acetone	T	1,107	420	465,234		92	109		
			70							
					8,539,274		9,319,386			
HÜNGNAM Fertilizers	Fertilizer	T	318	111,000	35,298,000	103,903	33,041,154	100		
HÜNGNAM Fertilizers	Washing Soaps	T	1,590	3,000	4,770,000	3,000	4,770,000	100		
HÜNGNAM Fertilizers	Concentrated Mg Ore	T	5,300			100	530,000		7,097T	101%
									2,256,846	
					40,068,000		38,341,154	96	7,097T	
									2,256,846	
HÜNGNAM Powders	Ammonium Nitrate	T	280	400	112,360	400	112,360	100		
			90							
HÜNGNAM Powders	Fuses	KM	72	12,000	871,320	12,000	871,320	100		
			61							
			55							
HÜNGNAM Powders	Percussion Primers	10³	71	600	429,300	600	429,300	100		
HÜNGNAM Powders	Nitrate Explosives	T	1,060	10	10,600	10	10,600	100		
HÜNGNAM Powders	Barium Chlorate	T	2,978	30	89,340	30	89,340	100		
					1,512,920		1,512,920	100		
							82			
Total					52,690,694		52,670,257	100	2,256,846	104%

2. Control Bureau for Building Materials

Location of Enterprise	Name of Item	Unit of Measure	Price per Unit	Planned Amount		Amount Delivered to NK Govt for Export		Percent	Stock on Hand by the Trade Control Bureau	Remarks
				QUANTITY	VALUE	QUANTITY	VALUE			
CH'UNNE-Ni	Cement	T	65 55	30,000	1,669,500	27,402	30 1,524,921	81	333,900	111%

3. Control Bureau for Colored Metals

Location of Enterprise	Name of Item	Unit of Measure	Price per Unit	Planned Amount		Amount Delivered to NK Govt for Export		Percent	Stock on Hand by the Trade Control Bureau	Remarks
				QUANTITY	VALUE	QUANTITY	VALUE			
KUMDOK Mine	Concentrated Zinc Ore	Ton	530	17,000	9,010,000	747 17,359	91 9,200,665	102		100%
CHULSAN Mine	Concentrated Mg Ore	Ton	5,300	7,000	37,100,000	5,411	28,678,300	77	Stopped 1,239 6,566,700	
TANNOK Mine	Tantalum	Ton	30 16,355			470 1.	29 24,042			
TANNOK Mine	Barium	Ton	5,300			390 24.	129,267			
YUNKOK Mine	Tantalum	Ton	30 16,355			240 3.	17 52,991			
YUNKOK Mine	Barium	Ton	5,300			350 1.	7,155			
SONCH'ON Mine	Fluorite	Ton	80 137	1,500	206,700 56	950 1,650	91 227,500	101		
Total		Ton			46,534,247		28 38,319,922	86	6,566,700	100%

43

4. *Light Industry Control Bureau*

Location of Enterprise	Name of Item	Unit of Measure	Price per Unit	Planned Amount QUANTITY	Planned Amount VALUE	Amount Delivered to NK Govt for Export QUANTITY	Amount Delivered to NK Govt for Export VALUE	Stock on Hand by the Trade Control Bureau Percent	Remarks
CHORWON Silk Reeling	Silk	T	26,500	29	768,500	1299 / 29	35 / 771,942	100	
HAMHŬNG Silk Reeling	Silk	T	26,500	41	1,086,500	08065 / 42	22 / 1,115,137	103	
PYŎNGYANG Silk Reeling	Starch	T	90 / 757	3,000	2,273,700	3,000	57 / 2,273,700	100	
Total					4,128,700		99 / 4,160,779	101	
HŬNGNAM Refinery	Electric Copper	T	2,512	800	2,009,760	196 / 803	2,017,788	100	
HŬNGNAM Refinery	Electric Lead	T	1,749	1,830	3,200,670	840 / 1,915	16 / 3,350,804	105	
HŬNGNAM Refinery	Concentrated Mg Ore	T	5,300			221	15 / 1,171,300		
					5,210,430		24 / 6,539,893	126	
MUNP'YŎNG Refinery	Electric Copper	T	1,749	2,670	4,669,830	254 / 2,465	24 / 4,311,729	92	
MUNP'YŎNG Refinery		T	23,320	1 / 7	165,572	844,147 / 3.	50 / 89,645	54	
MUNP'YŎNG Refinery	Lead Oxide	T	2,650	180	477,000	670 / 200	50 / 531,775	112	
					5,312,402		24 / 4,933,150	93	
NAMP'O Refinery	Electric Zinc	T	60 / 50 / 1,600	5,850	9,363,510	550 / 5,364	73 / 8,586,498	91	
NAMP'O Refinery	Arsenic Acid	T	7.5	740	529,470	270	193,185	36	
NAMP'O Refinery	Zinc Oxide	T	1,592	100	159,200	124	177,408	124	
NAMP'O Refinery	Catorium	T	23,320	24	559,680	27	73 / 629,640	113	
					10,611,860		9,606,731	91	

(TN [Table Note] Discrepancies in totals appear in original document.)

44

5. Control Bureau for Machinery Industry

Location of Enterprise	Name of Item	Unit of Measure	Price per Unit	Planned Amount QUANTITY	VALUE	Amount Delivered to NK Govt for Export QUANTITY	VALUE	Percent
CHUNGJIN Shipbuilding	Cables 15 T	33 cm	10,600	129	1,367,400	67	710,200	52
WONSAN Shipbuilding	Cables 45 T	33 cm	32,860	35	1,150,100	35	1,150,150	100
					2,517,500		1,860,300	74

6. Control Bureau for Metal Industry

Location of Enterprise	Name of Item	Unit of Measure	Price per Unit	Planned Amount QUANTITY	VALUE	Amount Delivered to NK Govt for Export QUANTITY	VALUE	Percent
HŬNGNAM Refinery	Electric Copper	T	2,512	800	2,009,760	196 803	99 2,017,788	100
HŬNGNAM Refinery	Electric Lead	T	1,749	1,830	3,200,670	840 1,915	16 3,350,804	105
HŬNGNAM Refinery	Concentrated Mg Ore	T	5,300			221	1,171,300	
					5,210,430		15 6,539,893	126
MUNP'YŎNG Refinery	Electric Copper	T	1,749	2,670	4,669,830	254 2,465	24 4,311,729	92
MUNP'YŎNG Refinery		T	23,320	1		844,147	50	54
			80	7	165,572	3. 862	89,645 18	
PURYUNG Metallurgy	Fe–Si	T	879	2,600	2,287,480	862 2,626	2,311,113	101
SUNGJIN Steel	Fe–W	T	16,377	550	9,007,350	413 630	95 10,324,273	115
SUNGJIN Steel	High-Speed Steel	T	11,130	1,250	13,912,500	815 1,304	14,522,590	104
			60					
SUNGJIN Steel	Special Tool Steel	T	3,156	1,800	5,681,880	811 1,539	40 4,860,567	81

6. Control Bureau for Metal Industry

Location of Enterprise	Name of Item	Unit of Measure	Price per Unit	Planned Amount		Amount Delivered to NK Govt for Export		Percent
				QUANTITY	VALUE	QUANTITY	VALUE	
SUNGJIN Steel	Carbon Tool Steel	T	1,805.10	3,471	6,265,502.10	1,838.341	3,319,472.39	53
SUNGJIN Steel	Steel Rod	T	485	900	436,500	981.376	475,967.39	109
					35,303,732.10	800	33,502,871.80	95
HWANGHAE Iron	Pig Iron	T	265	50,000	13,250,000	51,332	13,603,192	103
HWANGHAE Iron	Plate	T	461.10	22,800	10,513,080	19,681.841	9,075,296.88	87
HWANGHAE Iron	Angle Steel	T	469	2,800	1,313,200	5,137.223	2,409,357.58	185
					25,076,280.40	454.46	25,087,846.46	100
KANGSUNG Steel	Fe-Si	T	879.80	323	284,175	350	308,329.42	108
KANGSUNG Steel	Steel Rod	T	485	1,100	533,500	1,402.754	680,335.169	127
KANGSUNG Steel	Angle Steel	T	469.66	2,570	1,207,026.20	2,781.870	1,306,533.06	101
					2,024,701.60		2,295,198.17	113
Total					85,826,885.70		84,276,804.73	98

46

7. *Control Bureau for Black Metals*

Location of Enterprise	Name of Item	Unit of Measure	Price per Unit	Planned Amount QUANTITY	VALUE	Total Amount Delivered to NK Govt for Export QUANTITY	VALUE	Percent
MUSAN Mine	Powdered Iron Ores	T	80 31	30,000	954,000	30,000 190	954,000 92	100
NAMKAE Mine	Magnesite	T	40 95 50	12,000	1,144,800	8,747	834,481	73
KUMHWA Mine	Talc	T	79 90	3,500	278,250	4,036 900	320,862 61	116
KUMHWA Mine	Perlite	T	116	8,500	993,650	9,336 800	1,091,483	109
KUMHWA Mine	Barium	T	5,300		1,271,900	19. 61	104,940 1,517,285	120
HASUNG Mine	Fluorite	T	80 137 50	1,500	206,700	120 1,541	61 33 212,366	105
IWON Mine	Silicon	T	185			360	66,780	
CHUNGHAK Mine	Bulb Lead	T	318			60	19,080	

(TN [Table Note] Discrepancies in totals appear in original document.)
Translated by the *United Nations and United States Far East Command, Intelligence Summary* (Tokyo), no date.

3

China Leans to
One Side

The story of China's subjection to semicolonialism, with the economic and political exploitation that this entailed, has been often told and need not be repeated here. It is important to remember, however, that the Chinese leaders who came to power in 1949 had not forgotten the "century of humiliation" that their nation had just endured. Their primary concern was for their motherland to recoup the losses incurred as a result of intrusions by the Great Powers. Their search for alignment partners was propelled by this preoccupation with national reconstruction and the desire for national independence.

The past tendency of students of the People's Republic of China (PRC) has been to view the new state's foreign policy as being created largely *ex nihilo*. One such observer described the PRC's thinking on foreign policy as "distorted," caused by the "isolation and misinformation" of the Chinese leadership.[1] It was thus natural, under this interpretation, for the new Chinese regime, in a fervor of anti-Westernism, to turn to an alignment with the Soviet Union.

Furthermore, a substantial harmony of interest is often assumed to have existed between the PRC and the Soviet Union in the period 1949–50, partly because of the fact of the shared ideology of Marxism-Leninism and partly because of the belief that the Chinese Communist Party (CCP) in this period was naive in matters of maneuver among the Great Powers. The im-

pression of a totally successful partnership between China and
the Soviet Union was reinforced by such factors as Soviet support of the PRC's claim to a seat in the United Nations (to be examined below), vociferous Chinese support for the idea of a
united international communism under the leadership of the
Soviet Union (allegedly exemplified by Mao Tse-tung's celebrated "lean-to-one-side" speech of 1949), Soviet aid to the
PRC, and, finally, the two states' professed cooperation during
the Korean Civil War.

Was this evaluation valid? A University of Chicago scholar,
Tang Tsou, has pictured China's self-image of the late 1940s as
one of growing self-confidence:

> In the light of the dynastic cycles characteristic of China,
> the present confusion of China could be easily seen as an
> interregnum after which a period of restored greatness and
> glory was sure to come. . . . It could be interpreted as
> twilight before the dawn of a new era in which the tradi-
> tional grandeur of the Middle Kingdom was to project itself
> through the power of a modernized, industrialized and
> democratic China. [2]

Within this context of a resurgent nation-state, summarized in
Mao Tse-tung's 1949 declaration that "China has stood up, "
relations between China and the Soviet Union, adjoining countries with historically often conflicting interests, would tend to
have a likelihood toward strain. [3]

It is the contention of this chapter that the view of the new
regime's foreign policy as being "distorted" in the direction of a
monolithic alliance with the Soviet Union is itself distorted, and
that the leadership of the CCP, although certainly laboring under
the burden of some of the perceptual distortions with which
crisis-oriented movements are usually encumbered, was vigor-
ously interested in maintaining diplomatic and economic contacts with the West.

(It might be noted that a distinction should be made between those communist governments which came to power by

their own strength, such as Yugoslavia, China, North Vietnam, and, perhaps, Cuba, and those which were largely imposed externally by the force of Russian arms, such as the regimes of Eastern Europe. The former type has evidenced more flexibility in their international orientation than the latter.)

During the two decades before its accession to power, the CCP gradually gained experience in external dealings and created what was essentially an alternative foreign ministry. Under the leadership of the sophisticated and urbane Chou En-lai, the CCP possessed a complex communications network to the outside world, particularly from 1942 to 1949. Its newsmen served as envoys in Hong Kong and Chungking. Its diplomatic dealings with the KMT of Chiang K'ai-shek resembled those of a government-to-government relationship. In contrast to most other nationalist movements, which gained power with little such practical experience, the CCP early on developed an awareness of its place in the world political environment.[4]

CCP–United States Relations Before 1949

It was to be expected that the victorious CCP would find an enemy, at least in the short run, in the United States—the main prop of the KMT in the three-decade-long Chinese Civil War. Although American observers were to comment later mainly on the ineffectualness of America's economic and military aid to the KMT, the CCP has understandably dwelled more on its bitter fruits. For example, American exports to China, excluding aid, comprised 57.2% and 48.4% of China's total imports in 1946 and 1948, respectively. China's total exports to the U. S., meanwhile, were less than one-quarter of her imports from the U.S. in any given year between 1945 and 1949.[5] U.S. aid to China from V.J. Day to March 21, 1949, was valued by Washington at $1,986.3 million, and military aid in the same period was cited as $1,100.7 million. These figures are not necessarily an accurate accounting, however, because much of the military equipment was sold to the KMT at large discounts, while some of the "economic" assistance was used, in reality, for political or military support of the KMT regime.[6]

Although, as shall be noted below, relations between the CCP and the Soviet Union were not entirely harmonious, the CCP waged its civil war with the largely factual perception that the United States was indeed the friend of its enemy. A second factor (aside from the many basic philosophical values which the CCP did, in fact, share with the Soviet Union) in China's "leaning to one side" was the traditional technique of "using barbarians to control barbarians." Historically, a weak China had sought to survive foreign penetration by allying itself with some groups in order to balance economic and/or territorial incursions by other threats. Similarly, the new Chinese regime in 1949 was eager to maintain its national independence and to begin national reconstruction. It needed the military and economic help of the Soviet Union, as well as the international legitimacy which it felt that an alignment with the Soviet Union might offer, in contrast to the recent American economic and political predominance.

There were also indications, however, that the CCP leadership in the 1944–45 period was seeking some flexibility in its dealings with the two giants in its international world. During World War II, there appeared to be significant pro-American feelings within the CCP; July 4, 1944, for example, was celebrated in Yenan with enthusiasm. Later that same month a small team of American advisors arrived to analyze the military potential of the People's Liberation Army (PLA). The Chinese Communists asked for American military help and aircraft; the plea almost succeeded. "Impressed with the Communist battle claims and their plans for the future provided they received American fighters and bombers, the U.S. mission suggested that Chiang K'ai-shek share some of his supplies with his old foes. The result was an immediate crisis between the United States and the Nationalist government. The plan was dropped."[7]

Shortly thereafter, the CCP leadership was again rebuffed in an attempt to expand its dialogue with the United States. In early 1945, Mao Tse-tung and Chou En-lai vainly sought passage to Washington in order to discuss with President Roosevelt the potential for improved relations between the United States and the CCP.[8]

An American foreign service officer, John Stewart Service, later recounted that he had been impressed during his extended discussions with CCP leaders in 1944–45 with "the depth and conviction of a desire for American friendship and cooperation with China."[9] Mao Tse-tung at this time, Service recalls, wanted American economic and military support and thought that Russian help was "a practical liability."[10] On August 23, 1944, Mao told Service that "the United States will find us more cooperative than the Kuomintang. We will not be afraid of American influence—we will welcome it."[11] On March 13, 1945, Chairman Mao declared:

> America is not only the most suitable country to assist the economic development of China: she is also the only country fully able to participate. For all these reasons, there must not be any conflict, estrangement or misunderstanding between the Chinese people and America.[12]

The CCP prevailed upon Chiang K'ai-shek to appoint a senior CCP official, Tung Pi-wu, as one of ten Chinese delegates to the spring, 1945, San Francisco conference of the United Nations (reviewed below)—the first time that a CCP notable had taken part in a non-communist-organized conference outside of China. Tung spent most of his time in America cultivating Americans. He published a thirty-one-page English-language pamphlet explaining the CCP's position.[13] Tung traveled widely in America and was officially welcomed to New York City by the

Mayor and the City Council. He finally returned to Yenan in December, 1945.

The CCP Attempts to Join the U.N.

Consistent with its interest in a resurgence of China's national strength and stature, the CCP looked forward to China joining "a new League of Nations built on a basis of democracy."[14] This marked a change from the statement signed by Mao, Hsiang Ying, and Chang Kuo-t'ao and issued twelve years before, after the Lytton Commission had published its report on the Japanese invasion of Manchuria. At that time, the Kiangsi Soviet had denounced both the report and the League of Nations, described as "a League of Robbers by which the various imperialisms are dismembering China."[15] Now, in 1945, the CCP said that it was a great honor for the Chinese people that the Big Three had asked China to cosponsor the San Francisco conference. The invitation, explained as editorial of *Chieh-fang Jih-pao* [Liberation Daily], was the result of the Chinese people's resistance to the Japanese, especially behind the Japanese lines in the liberated areas. The editorial called, therefore, for two-thirds of China's delegates to the San Francisco conference to come from the liberated areas.[16]

On February 16, 1945, the day before this editorial appeared, a meeting of the trade union delegates in South Shansi had adopted a resolution calling for one-third of the Chinese delegation to San Francisco to come from the CCP.[17] On February 18, Chou En-lai wrote to the American ambassador in Chungking, Patrick J. Hurley, claiming that Hurley had previously told him that the Chinese delegation to San Francisco should consist of CCP, KMT, and Democratic League members, and stating that a delegation without this $\frac{1}{3}$-$\frac{1}{3}$-$\frac{1}{3}$ ratio would "never be in a position to settle any problem in the conference on behalf of China."[18] Hurley answered in a letter dated February

20, declaring that the delegation was to be a national one, not merely a grouping of parties.[19]

Thereupon, in a letter of March 9, Chou En-lai informed Hurley that Yenan had suggested to the KMT the inclusion of himself, Tung Pi-wu, and Ch'in Pan-hsien in the delegation.[20] After Chou's letter, Yenan radio broadcast a number of reports of resolutions and statements from various parts of North China demanding either that the KMT be limited to one-third of the delegation, that a separate delegation be chosen from non-KMT elements, or that the whole dispute be laid before the plenary conference in San Francisco.[21] There were also reports that telegrams demanding that KMT representation be limited to one-third of the delegation had been sent to Churchill, Stalin, and Roosevelt.[22] Nonetheless, the CCP did accept the appointment of only one CCP official on the Chinese delegation. Mao stated the party's official position in his political report to the Seventh Party Congress on April 24: "The Chinese Communist Party welcomes the conference of the United Nations in San Francisco. It has sent its own representative to join the Chinese delegation to this conference in order to express the will of the Chinese people."[23]

This position appears to have reflected a compromise between the Mao-Chou group and others within the CCP over the strategic interest of the party in keeping contacts with the West open; and it was a concession which probably inflamed the "hardliners." A British citizen, then resident in Yenan, later reported that "Mao Tse-tung and Chou En-lai . . . seriously risked their positions and influence in accepting American mediation, and in hoping that civil war could be avoided by compromise." Michael Lindsay also reported that many people in Yenan in 1945 "were critical of this policy and openly said that American imperialist power could never serve as an honest broker."[24] If this account is accurate, it would help to explain—in conjunction with Washington's refusal to welcome a CCP delegation—Mao's later bitterness and his strong reaction against American influence in China when the United States actively aided the KMT and the "hardliners" were proved correct. The seal on a negative U.S. attitude toward the CCP was placed by Ambassador Hurley, who, on April 2, 1945, unequivocally announced that America would give aid only to the KMT.[25]

CCP–Soviet Relations Before 1950

While the CCP did turn toward the Soviet Union as its ideological and economic mentor, it had good reason to chafe at the direction given by the Russians. In the Byzantine power struggles which characterized Mao's rise to power, he had been almost consistently opposed by Stalin. It is by now well documented that Stalin's orders impaired the success of the CCP.[26] As late as July, 1948, it was widely rumored that "Stalin urged through Liu Shao-ch'i that the Chinese Communists continue guerrilla war and refrain from pushing their victory to a decisive conclusion."[27]

The Soviet Union's arrogant and harsh behavior in Manchuria in 1945–46 was not that of a fraternal ally. The young Chinese state remembered the seizure of whole factories and vast amounts of equipment after World War II. The American Pauley Commission estimated the Soviet Union's removal of stockpiles of food, machine tools, power generators, and other equipment at $858 million, and the total destruction caused by Soviet forces in Manchuria at over $2 billion.[28]

In 1945, Stalin had told American envoy Averill Harriman that he had recognized the Chinese Nationalists instead of the CCP as the government of China because he desired to avoid "exorbitant demands for the industrialization of China." "Such demands," he added, "Soviet Russia could not meet."[29] Indeed, the CCP had long expected territorial and financial largesse from its "fraternal ally." For example, Mao had stated in 1936 that "when the people's revolution has been victorious in China, the Outer Mongolian Republic will automatically become a part of the Chinese Federation at their own will."[30] Mao's expectations were formally supported by the Soviet Union; in 1925, for example, Soviet Foreign Minister Gregori Zinoviev had stated that Outer Mongolia would "return to China when the Chinese will liberate themselves from their oppressors."[31] On May 31, 1924, the Soviet Union, in an official statement, had declared that "the government of the USSR recognizes that Outer Mongolia is an integral part of the Republic of China, and respects Chinese sovereignty therein."[32] But the CCP's hopes were, of course, to be disappointed; Outer Mongolia remained firmly within the Soviet sphere of influence after 1949, despite the fact that one of Mao Tse-tung's earliest proposals to Stalin in the first days of the new PRC was that Outer Mongolia revert to China. One informed observer has related that

> Premier Tsedenbal of Outer Mongolia has told me that one of Mao's first acts on coming to power was a request to Stalin for the return to Chinese suzerainty of Outer Mongolia. Stalin refused this request and tightened his control of this strategic area with its 1500 mile frontier on China. . . . [33]

The emergent PRC was to have other unfortuante territorial problems with the Russians that would indicate a less-than-harmonious relationship. In 1948, the Soviet Union endeavored to absorb Inner Mongolia into Outer Mongolia. The Chinese resisted Soviet manipulations by stationing units of the PLA in Inner Mongolia before they "succeeded in outmaneuvering Stalin" without resort to arms.[34] In 1949, as the PLA advanced upon the northwest province of Sinkiang (an area in which the Russians had traditionally tried to exert their influence), the Soviets established their own political/military presence in the vicinity. They then unsuccessfully attempted to proclaim the automony of Sinkiang from China, but were foiled by a PLA agreement with the local warlord.[35] From the period of its establishment, then, the PRC has had ample cause to doubt the goodwill of its neighbor.

Stalin observed the growth of the CCP under Mao's leadership with "serious reservations."[36] There are some indications that Stalin in the 1946–50 period was trying to extend his influence on the CCP by tying the vital industrial province of Manchuria to the Soviet Union as a client substate. Stalin—in all of his dealings—did not want to become involved in situations which he could not control, and Mao had long taken independent positions.

After World War II, in economically strategic Manchuria, P'eng Chen was chairman of the Politburo of the CCP's Northeast Bureau, Lin Feng was chairman of the Northeast Administrative Committee set up in early 1946, and the regional Party Secretary was Kao Kang, with whom Stalin apparently had developed close relations. The Russians were later to charge that the Central Committee of the CCP in 1946 *"was forced* to condemn the 'mistakes' of the group of P'eng Chen and Lin Feng. This group maliciously distorted the role of the Soviet Union, and spread slander about the USSR. But the resolution on the P'eng Chen–Lin Feng group was not made available to Party organs." New charges were made again in 1949: "But this time things again went no farther than the formal condemnation of nationalistic anti-Soviet tendencies."[37] The question then presents itself: did Stalin "force" the Central Committee of the CCP to admit its "mistaken" attitude toward Soviet machinations in Manchuria?

In July, 1949, while not yet overtly dealing with Mao Tsetung, Stalin negotiated a treaty with Kao Kang, as head of the "People's Government of the Northeast," in Moscow, and granted him substantial financial (and therefore political) benefits.

It is reasonable to presume that Stalin schemed to acquire organizational footholds in China, as he had in Eastern Europe. Perhaps he intended to do so by capturing the economy of China. Manchuria was rapidly being turned into the bastion of the Chinese economy, with a man in control who most likely was linked with the Soviets. The CCP could not be captured, for the men of Yenan had built up the Party as their one great organizational instrument. But the system of economic administration could be infiltrated, and perhaps also the military. [38]

Kao Kang was purged by Mao shortly after the end of the Korean Civil War in the year of Stalin's death. Perhaps the latter two events facilitated the first? Peking may have been referring to these events in a spring, 1956, declaration on de-Stalinization when it claimed that Kao Kang's antiParty activity had represented "reactionary forces at home *and abroad*." [39] The official charges against Kao Kang, elaborated by CCP Secretary-General Teng Hsiao-p'ing in April, 1955, pointed toward Kao's collaboration with the Russians. His "independent kingdom" of Manchuria was accused of "being an agent of imperialism." While this would seem to refer to Western contacts, the year given for Kao's treachery was 1949, the year when he traveled to the Soviet Union to conclude a trade agreement. Mao Tse-tung, "with his own record of resistance to Moscow's direction and advice, and seeing Kao Kang apparently enjoying Moscow's favor, may have looked on Kao as a potentially dangerous, Soviet-backed rival." [40] A remark by Krushchev in 1960 would appear to bolster the impression of a Stalin–Kao collaboration; Khrushchev suggested that Kao's only crime had been to oppose the CCP's incorrect policy vis-à-vis the Soviet Union. [41]

Harrison Salisbury notes that in the middle 1960s, when the "Sino–Soviet alliance" had largely disintegrated, "Kao blandly reappears in the Soviet history of relations with China, with no suggestion that he was not the most honorable of men. It is an insult comparable to calling the notorious Soviet police chief, Lavrenti Beria an honorable colleague of Party Secretary Brezhnev." [42]

Mao himself has hinted at these developments in a speech given to the CCP's Tenth Party Plenum of October, 1962:

Even after the success of the revolution, Stalin feared that China might degenerate into another Yugoslavia and that *I might become a second Tito.* I later went to Moscow and concluded the Sino-Soviet Treaty Alliance. Stalin did not wish to sign the Treaty Alliance. Stalin did not wish to sign the Treaty; he finally signed it after two months of negotiations. *It was only after our resistance to America and support for Korea that Stalin finally came to trust us.* [43]

During its swift seizure of power (a rapidity unanticipated by either the Soviet Union or the CCP[44]), there was apparently considerable resistance within the CCP to a close coalition with the Soviet Union. This becomes readily understandable if it were indeed the case that the Soviet Union was actively supporting a domestic rival to Mao Tse-tung. In a manner reminiscent of the North Korean political situation, an intruding Great Power was seeking to manipulate domestic politics by throwing some-—although not all—of its weight behind one faction. P'eng Chen, the same man who had only shortly before been accused by the Soviet Union of slandering it in Manchuria, referred in the third person to a distrust of the Soviet Union:

> We can still remember that for a short time after the liberation of Peking, many people still had obscure ideas about the Soviet Union because of all the slanderous, twisting and arbitrary propaganda that the KMT reactionary clique had spread for so long along with an "anti–Soviet Union" atmosphere engendered by the counter propaganda of the enemy. But now faced with the iron facts, and with people realizing more and more the truth, the counter propaganda has been smashed. [45]

China Leans to One Side (Cautiously)

American publicists tried to encourage China's feelings of dissatisfaction with the Soviet Union in a campaign that was to reach its height with Secretary of State Acheson's speech of January 12, 1950, declaring that the Soviet Union was seeking to subjugate and detach northern parts of China. *Shih-chieh Chih-shih* [World Culture], a weekly, semiofficial publication of the PRC's Foreign Ministry, explained the new regime's position in August, 1949, at a time when U.S. aid and supplies were still flowing to the KMT:

> American imperialism realizes that the Chiang bandits can no longer be exploited as a means for the enslavement of the Chinese people. The complete collapse of the Chiang clique being a foregone conclusion, it is now attempting to create dissenting factors from within the ranks of New China. . . . It is true, from a certain point of view, that China's victory is the Soviet Union's, and vice versa. But this significance is different from that which the imperialists try to convey to the world . . . . the victory of one member [of the camp] is also the victory of another.[46]

Here, between the lines, the Foreign Ministry was apparently admitting two things: 1) there were differences of opinion within the CCP leadership over the wisdom of alignment with the Soviet Union; 2) since communism has always treated the enemy with respect, while at the same time being prepared to take advantage of his weaknesses, and given the fact of some pro-American feeling in the CCP, if the KMT collapse were "a foregone conclusion," then the new China should come to terms with the Americans, who had just as ambivalent feelings toward the CCP as the CCP had toward the United States.

Mao Tse-tung, while believing that China must essentially align itself with the Soviet Union against the hostile United States, tried to keep the door to the West ajar in his speech of June 30, 1949, entitled "On the People's Democratic Dictatorship." This speech apparently was an attempt by Mao to juggle the various alignment preferences among the CCP leadership. The Chairman first stated the well-grounded beliefs that: 1) the new PRC would need foreign financial, economic, and military aid, and 2) since the U. S. had actively supported the KMT, it could not be trusted. However, rather than being a black-and-white presentation of reality,[47] the speech then masterfully went on to try to create what was actually a middle road between wholeheartedly joining with the seemingly logical ally (Russia) and rejecting it in favor of Western aid:

> "We need help from the British and U. S. governments." This, too, is a naive idea in these times. Would the present rulers of Britain and the U. S., who are imperialists, help a people's state? Why do these countries do business with us and, supposing that *they might be willing to lend us money on terms of mutual benefit in the future*, why should they do so? Because their capitalists want to make money and their bankers want to earn interest to extricate themselves from their own crisis—it is not a matter of helping the Chinese people. The Communist parties and progressive groups in these countries are urging their governments to establish trade and even diplomatic relations with us. This is good-will, this is *help*, this cannot be mentioned in the same breath with the conduct of the bourgeoisie in these same countries.[48]

This speech consequently welcomes Western aid with the caveat—apparently a bow toward the "hardliners" within the CCP with whom Mao had had to contend with in the past—that one must accept such aid cautiously and with the realization that it is not given altruistically. Similar advice was undoubtedly being given by Mao with reference to Soviet maneuvers in Manchuria, Inner Mongolia, and Sinkiang.

The foreign ministry organ published an important interpretation of Mao's speech which outlined China's firm but flexible stance toward the U.S. (this deserves full citation—and careful reading—for it delicately recognizes a middle road):

> Any country or any nation today must stand on the side of either one or the other of these two camps. Which side, then, should China choose?

When the political authority of China was held in the hands of the Kuomintang reactionaries headed by Chiang K'ai-shek, China had necessarily to lean to the imperialist and antidemocratic front. For the Chiang K'ai-shek regime represented the interests of the big bourgeoisie and the feudal influences, and these interests were inseparable from those of the imperialists.

But when the political authority of China falls into the hands of the people, our diplomatic policy must undergo a complete change. We must adopt the course of peace, the course of the people's democracy, the course of Socialism—in short, the course of "leaning to one side" as stated by Chairman Mao Tse-tung, leaning, however, to Socialism, and not to imperialism.

The reason is simple. The revolution carried out in China today is a revolution of the New Democracy, a necessary factor for the further step in the march toward Socialism. Thus in our diplomatic relations we must also adopt the diplomatic policy of the people's democracy in coordination with the needs of the New Democracy. The revolution of China is a part of the world proletariat revolution. Since international imperialism is the greatest enemy of the Chinese Revolution, we naturally cannot adopt the diplomatic policy of following the imperialist course and lean to the side of our enemy.

Since we cannot lean to the side of imperialism, and since there is no "third road" to follow, there remains only one course—the course of international peace, the course of the people's democracy, and the course of Socialism.

The official announcement of the policy of "leaning to one side" has brought about the anxieties and fears of certain quarters. These have all been due to a failure to recognize the basic development of the postwar world situation and the basic nature of the Chinese Revolution. Some of those fears and reactions may be briefly discussed.

In the first place, there are those who think that dependence on both sides is better than leaning to one side. They consider that by pursuing a diplomatic policy of depending on both sides, we may move between the two major world camps and thereby achieve our objective of independence and sovereignty. Such a conception is erroneous because of the failure to recognize the acute antithesis between the two camps, and to realize that the future of the Chinese Revolution is the realization of Socialism via the New Democracy. Indeed, factual developments in the past have shown that the theory, propounded by certain so-called progressives in the past, of befriending both the Soviet Union and the United States only tended to reveal the advocates to be irresponsible parties.

Others entertain the doubt that once we adopt the policy of leaning to one side, we are to abandon relations with such countries as Britain and the United States, and to terminate our dealings with the various peoples of the world. Such a view is obviously mistaken. What we want to expel is American and British imperialism, and not the peoples of America and Britain. Much less than abandoning them, we must strive to win over the innocent peoples and the progressive forces in the imperialist countries. Of course such people should not include those who implement imperialist aggressive policies or entertain imperialist aggressive ideals.

Then there are others who fear that once we lean to one side, we shall cease all trade relations with such countries as Britain and the United States. This is also a mistaken view. In his statement on July 1, Chairman Mao clearly stated: "We want to do business. We only oppose domestic and foreign reactionaries who hamper us from doing business. . . . Unite all forces at home and abroad to smash domestic and foreign reactionaries and there will be business, and the possibility of establishing diplomatic relations with all foreign countries on the basis of equality, mutual benefits, and mutual respect for territorial sovereignty."

There are also those who consider foreign aid necessary for China's revolution and the reconstruction of New

China, and that such aid will be withheld from us if we lean to one side. It is indeed true that the success of China's revolution calls for foreign assistance. The crux of the problem, however, is: Who can help the Chinese Revolution? Can American imperialism help China's Revolution? This is a ridiculous thought. American imperialism under certain conditions will help China, that is, help China's reactionaries, as was done in the past few years. But if we are to succeed in the revolution, to succeed in the expulsion of imperialist influences, American imperialism will not aid us, and we do not want this aid. The Chinese Revolution can get the international aid it needs, and is actually getting such aid—aid given in various ways by the international revolutionary forces.

And still there are others who agree that the policy of leaning to one side is correct, but point out that in the implementation of our diplomatic policy, we should exploit the inherent contradictions within the American, British, and other imperialisms, so that we may succeed in breaking down individually the aggressive designs of all. This view is a correct one. "Leaning to one side" is our basic policy and course, but it does not call for the abandonment of the proper employment of diplomatic strategy. But one point deserves careful recognition, and that is that any strategy employed must not exceed the bounds of the basic principle of "leaning to one side." If strategy is used in such a way as to replace the basic principle, it would be most absurd.

Another problem which is related to the issue of "leaning to one side" is the question of the blockade of Shanghai and other coastal districts carried out jointly by the imperialist countries and China's remnant reactionary forces. Some people who do not know the facts consider that following the official advocacy by Chairman Mao of the policy of "leaning to one side," the imperialist countries became disillusioned over New China, and so joined forces with the remnant reactionaries to exercise the blockade. This view seems to consider that the present blockade has been the direct result of the official cart before the horse. The imperialists basically do not want to see the success of the Chinese Revolution, and have resorted to all measures to thwart its progress, especially since the liberation of Shanghai. As early as in the beginning of June, the rumor was spread of the mining of the waters at the mouth of the Yangtze. It was with the exposure of this rumor that the Kuomintang reactionaries, with the support of the imperialists, announced the blockade of the coast as from June 25. The blockade of the imperialists in conjunction with the Kuomintang reactionaries was thus carried out prior to the official announcement of the policy of "leaning to one side."[49]

Welcome to the Soviet Union

During the PLA's rapid march southward in 1948–49, the Soviet ambassador, in a move certainly not calculated to endear the Soviet Union to the CCP, was the only major foreign representative to follow the peripatetic government of Chiang K'ai-shek. Khrushchev later revealed that Sino–Soviet relations were so strained in 1949–50 that the two countries "came to the verge of a split."[50] The Russians had been negotiating agreements which were financially and territorially unfavorable for China right up to the very moment when Chiang was forced to flee the Mainland. On May 11, 1949, for example, the Soviet Union and the Chinese Nationalist government extended their agreement, advantageous to the Soviet Union, on joint rights in Sinkiang for five more years. In a 1965 interview with André Malraux, Mao acidly remembered that the Russian ambassador's "good wishes were reserved for Chiang K'ai-shek. When Chiang fled from China, the Soviet ambassador was the last to take leave of him."[51]

Then, in a classic display of tactlessness, this same Russian ambassador suddenly was declared to be the Soviet envoy to the new PRC government. The new regime noted the recycled ambassador's arrival in Peking with a sardonic editorial in the CCP newspaper, *Jen-min Jih-pao:*

> The Chinese people know Ambassador Roschchin very well. He was sent to China in the capacity of a military attaché during 1939–41. Following the Soviet victory in the war against Germany, Mr. Roschchin was for a time the Soviet ambassador to China. He had, representing the Soviet government, persisted in carrying out to the end the great Stalin's foreign policy and exerted all-out effort to help the Chinese people to triumph over the Japanese brigands. But China at that time was still the old China under the reactionary rule of the imperialists and its lackey, the KMT bandit clique. [52]

It was evident to both the Chinese and the Russians that the Soviet Union had not hesitated to make its peace with "the old China under the reactionary rule of the imperialists and its lackey, the KMT bandit clique."

In order to explain the need to maintain its ties to the Soviet Union as its chief military, economic, and ideological patron, and at the same time to account for the value of keeping the door open for the imperialists—who could not be trusted, but whose economic aid and trade would be of great help (and who could potentially serve as a counter to sole dependence upon the greedy Soviet Union)—the Chinese leadership sought a historical analogy to indicate that the doors to the West, while necessarily guarded due to the imperialists' evident hostility, could be nudged open. It was this need, in part, which apparently gave rise to increasingly numerous references to the T'ai-p'ing Rebellion.

An article in the first issue of *Hsueh Hsi* [Study], the intraparty theoretical journal, demonstrated the contemporary value of the analogy: "From 1853 to 1860, foreign nations adopted a policy of 'neutrality' toward the war between the Manchus and the T'ai p'ings. This neutrality was maintained, of course, to allow time to determine the best side to take." [53] Even if not pleased the West must now acknowledge, such an analogy would imply, that the time for "neutrality" was over; the PRC was an established fact and the West, ever in search of profits, must accommodate itself to the new situation. This article echoed the mid-August *Shih-chieh Chih-shih* advice to the West, in which Chiang Kai-shek's fall was labeled a "foregone conclusion."

The CCP's isolation in the Ching Kan Mountains in the 1930s had sensitized it to the need for allies, while the traditional Chinese practice of using "barbarians to control barbarians" had given the party an image of national independence based upon balancing Great Power intrusions. As victory in the Civil War grew closer, Peking detected a possibility of detente with the West. The Republican candidate in the U. S. presidential election of 1948 seemed to strongly support Chiang K'ai-shek's requests for additional American aid.[54] After Truman's victory in that campaign, there were widespread rumours in the CCP press that Chiang had spent a great deal of money to assist Governor Dewey's presidential hopes—the implication being that the Truman administration, contrariwise, might now be more amenable to increased contacts with the CCP. Several articles in the Hong Kong English-language Communist weekly, *China Digest* (precursor of both *People's China* and *Peking Review*; all three were meant for western readers) referred to the KMT's desire that Truman lose the November, 1948, election. For example:

> It has been generally accepted by the Kuomintang that the Republicans seemed much more vigorous in supporting Chiang and a bigger foe of "Communism in China" than the Democrats. . . . This impression has become so dominant that Chiang Kai-shek is led to expect the victory of Dewey in the impending American presidential election as one of his last saviours to salvage his tottering rule.[55]

After the election, *China Digest* printed an editorial which seemed to be a sigh of relief:

Nanking was openly stunned by Dewey's defeat in the American presidential election. According to KMT inside information, the Central News Agency, anticipating Dewey's election, had prepared two long articles entitled "Dewey, the Man in White House in the Next Four Years" and "Dewey's Foreign Policy." They had been distributed to the Agency's offices throughout KMT China for release pending the outcome of November 2. The United Press reported from Nanking on November 4 that Chiang Kai-shek sat out the night on November 3 waiting for hourly reports from S. F. Tsao, his secretary, who was listening to the radio. The support-Dewey parade in Peiping had been constituted of children and feeble old men. They were paid for the occasion. This tragi-comical performance, however, expressive of Nanking's burning desire for Dewey's success, will remain a laughing stock throughout the world.

What did Dewey promise to help Nanking which Truman had not given? America's China policy has been bi-partisan for the last two years. Why should Nanking prefer one to the other?

To the Nanking officialdom, Dewey stood for direct military intervention in China and an early World War III. In their public statements, the Republican politicians have never concealed their war hysteria. Military and economic assistance in the present form no longer meets the emergency demand of a tottering regime. Nanking wants an American government which would plunge headlong into a world conflagration. Only then could KMT count on the large scale and direct American armed intervention which it sorely needs in its dying agony. Nanking hopes that in a world-wide war, it would be considered by the USA as the eastern front of the American military position. Whatever responsibility it has shouldered up to now in its war against the Chinese people, would then automatically become the job of the Americans. It could therefore sit out the war, hoping to pick up another easy victory.[56]

On May 13, 1949, less than a month after Communist troops captured the Nationalist capital of Nanking, a key Communist diplomat, Huang Hua, asked the United States ambassador, J. Leighton Stuart, to visit Peking to discuss future relations with Mao Tse-tung and Chou En-lai. Writing in an unpublished diary, Mr. Stuart welcomed the move as a possible "beginning of better understanding," but his requests for authorization to make the trip went unanswered by the State Department until July 2. By then, Chairman Mao Tse-tung had proclaimed that China would "lean to the side" of the Soviet Union, and the department responded with instructions that the envoy turn down the invitation. [57]

Jen-min Jih-pao, in an article on October 8, 1949, summarized the Chinese attitude toward potential relations with the West, using phrases which probably also reflected hopeful expectations of ever-closer contacts with the Soviet Union, which at the time still recognized and negotiated with the KMT:

> On November 21 of last year, the Chinese Communist Party Central Committee issued a statement . . . declaring "the CCP, the People's Democratic Government in the liberated areas, and the Chinese PLA are willing to enter into equal and friendly relations with any foreign nation, including the U.S.A. . . . provided China's territories are kept intact and immune from aggression." On April 30 of this year the spokesman of the Chinese PLA Command, General Li Tao, also mentioned this point in a statement. "Any foreign government which is willing to consider establishing a diplomatic relation with our country should cut off its relations with the KMT remnant power, and also withdraw its armed forces from China." What we oppose is only imperialism as an institution and its intrigues and plots against the Chinese people. As for a diplomatic relationship based upon equality, mutual benefit and mutual respect for territorial sovereignty . . . a the rulers of countries like the U.S. and Britain . . . only need to cut off their relations with the KMT reactionary clique and adopt a genuine, and not hypercritical, amicable attitude towards New China and then we shall be willing to negotiate. [58]

In February, 1947, the Central Committee of the CCP had declared that it considered invalid all of the treaties, agreements, and loans previously concluded by the KMT. On October 10 of that year the PLA had reiterated those points. [59] In light of this policy, it is noteworthy that *Shih-chieh Chih-shih* in mid-October of 1949 indicated that the new regime would be willing to renegotiate or even maintain the agreements that the deposed KMT had concluded earlier with the United States:

> New China naturally must reexamine the various treaties which implied the betrayal of China's national interests, such as the Sino–American Commercial Treaty of November 1, 1946; the Sino–American Air Pact of October 20, 1946; the Sino–American Bilateral Agreement of July 3, 1947; and the Sino–American Naval Pact of December 8, 1947. *Some of them* may have to be abbrogated, and others revised or reconcluded. [60]

In November, 1949, the Chinese media explained to its readers that history had vididly demonstrated the possibility of the U.S. pragmatically seeing that the time for "neutrality" was over, that the world's chief imperialist power was capable of opening relations with Communist countries, to the advantage of the latter. A Shanghai newspaper, for example, stressed this historical trend, which seemed to favor the PRC much more strongly than it had the Soviet Union a quarter of a century before: "Even the stubborn United States resumed relations with the Soviet Union in 1933, and admitted that past treaties should be invalidated. The Soviet Union has thus established a precedent which smashes the designs of the imperialists and helps to restore the true significance of the underlying principle of international law." [61]

This comparison with the Soviet Union's previous diplomatic experience—underlining the favorable position of the PRC in its seeking of international legitimacy—was elaborated by *Shih-chieh Chih-shih* in mid-January 1950:

The diplomatic weapon of "nonrecognition," which the imperialists had previously applied without success against the Soviet Union, is all the more futile if applied against New China today. . . . This is why Great Britain, which took six years to make up its mind to establish foreign relations with the Soviet Union two and one-half decades ago, has now presented a request for relations with New China only ninety-eight days after the foundation of the People's Republic. [62]

There were indications in early 1950 that the PRC was nervous about what it considered to be the overly bellicose nature of the Soviet Union. Belonging to a "camp" was one thing, especially since the opposing side was increasing its hostile signals, such as forming a "defensive" arc around China via Japan, the Philippines, Indochina, and perhaps Taiwan. [63] At this time, however, China was mostly eager to settle down to the work of national reconstruction. *Jen-min Jih-pao* of May 1, 1950, printed an article which clearly expressed the PRC's aversion to armed conflict with the West:

Warmongers have a good deal of tricks for agitation. They always utilize "naive" people to propagate vicious "arguments" to hinder the struggle of the defenders of world peace. For instance, in Britain and the various Scandinavian countries, some people have remarked that they didn't believe in the existence of the danger of a new world war. . . . Another "argument" which is most widespread in the U.S.A. and also most dangerous says that war is inevitable . . . . the most vicious "argument" is spreading in the colonies and satellite countries. This "argument" says, "Well, look, the first world war produced the Soviet Union. The second world war produced many new democratic countries. Then, the third world war will definitely result in the liberation of all the colonies and satellites. The peoples of colonies and satellites, let's welcome the third world war!"[64]

This criticism of the "warmongers of the West" takes on added significance when put into its probable context. Soviet Foreign Minister Molotov had made a speech in praise of Stalin the previous week that was reprinted in *Jen-min Jih-pao* of May 4. Molotov's speech sounds remarkably similar to what *Jen-min Jih-pao* had criticized just a few days before. Molotov seemed to argue for precisely the militant, provocative attitude regarding the benefits of a new world war that the Chinese had so recently denounced: "If the imperialists launched a new world war, the peace-loving peoples of different countries and the whole of the peaceful camp would inevitably be compelled to take the counter offensive. The counter offensive would result not only in the defeat of certain aggressor countries, but also in the extinction of the whole system of imperialism."[65] The Chinese leadership, then, was apparently signaling to the Soviet Union that it did not wish to gamble its barely-won power on the chance to "extinguish the whole system of imperialism."

In the early days of the new regime, the PRC maintained the refrain, in its comments on Sino–Soviet relations, that the Soviet Union was willing to abide by the new government's requirements of respect for equality and territorial noninterference. Yet, the PRC's references to the necessity for other states to break connections with the KMT must have aroused bitter memories of the Soviet's continued contacts with that regime up until September 30, 1949. The celebrated "Sino–Soviet Treaty of Friendship, Alliance, and Mutual Assistance," concluded only after ten weeks of what must have been extremely hard bargaining, was an indication of the strains between the two neighbors. Although formalizing their closer relations, it nonetheless suggested the existence of unresolved dissension.

As a result of the February, 1950, Sino–Soviet Treaty, the Soviet Union granted China a loan of $300 million at 1 percent interest. To place this loan in perspective, it must be remembered that the Soviet Union shortly before had extended a similar loan to Poland—of $450 million at no interest. The Chinese were reportedly very disappointed at their lack of success in negotiating more favorable terms. [66] Before the conclusion of the Sino–Soviet treaty, the Chinese strongly implied an expectation of large-scale Russian aid, which was to be "unconditional and asks for nothing in return."[67] After the signing of the treaty in Moscow on February 14, 1950, however, emphasis on the economic assistance that could be expected from the Soviet Union was dropped: "The Chinese people are brave and industrious, China is a country of vast territory, plentiful resources and a huge population. Through hard struggle under the leadership of the Chinese Communist Party, in addition to the favorable conditions of assistance from the Soviet Union, the great People's Republic of China is certain to be swiftly transformed into a strong, prosperous and industrialized country."[68]

A *Pravda* editorial of February 14, 1950, noting the successful conclusion of the treaty talks, declared that "the decisive victory of the Chinese people became possible in consequence of the defeat of German fascism and Japanese imperialism, a defeat in which the Soviet Union, led by the great Stalin, played a decisive role." Chou En-lai, perhaps in a pique at the lack of credit given to the Chinese leadership itself, explained a day later that "the victory of the Chinese people has brought about radical changes in the situation. The Chinese people, under the leadership of Chairman Mao Tse-tung, have set up the People's Republic of China and made possible the sincere cooperation between our two states."[69]

The economic export-import agreements which China and Russia signed at about this time were also disadvantageous to the PRC, since the exchange rate between the rouble and the yuan "greatly overvalued the rouble."[70] The establishment of joint stock companies (mining, railroad, airline), actually an extension of a similar practice by the Russians under the weak KMT government, also did not work to China's advantage. These were Soviet-controlled, since the Chinese had almost no capital to contribute.

For all these reasons, the PRC was repeatedly constrained to issue assurances to its people that the Sino–Soviet treaty was in China's best interests, such as the following:

> The ultranationalists may raise objections as to why the handling over of the installations Port Arthur and Dairen should not take place immediately. It must be pointed out that though the victory has been scored in the liberation war, reconstruction of China has only just commenced, and national defense measures have not yet been consolidated. The evacuation of Soviet troops just now from Port Arthur will give the American and Japanese reactionaries an opportunity for encroachment, and therefore it must await the peace treaty with Japan. . . . This provision, made after the fullest consideration of the situation, is in the interests of both China and the Soviet Union, particularly those of China.[71]

China's Stance

The CCP came to power nursing vivid images of the past exploitation of China, while holding with a general recognition of the need for an alignment with the Soviet Union. At the same time there was a desire for maintaining contacts with the West, as a continuation of the traditional "barbarians-to-control-barbarians" policy and as an outgrowth of a basic, historically conditioned distrust of the Soviet Union. There were, apparently, disagreements among the leadership regarding contacts with the West, while the Soviet Union seemed to be actively cultivating Kao Kang in Manchuria. In brief, the subsequent alliance of the PRC—in need of economic assistance and international legitimacy with the Soviet Union—was not inevitable. Chapter 4 will explore this point from another perspective.

We have said that China's alliances had not hardened before June, 1950. It should be noted, however, that several of the quotations introduced are not unambiguous in their interpretation. For example, Mao Tse-tung, in 1944 undoubtedly was speaking favorably of the United States partly in an attempt to isolate the Kuomintang and to gain support for the CCP along the lines on which Tito was then receiving Western aid. Moreover, Mao's public views toward the United States in the mid-1940s were, understandably, by no means uncritical. Segments of Mao's speeches can be read as efforts to prevent previously noncommunist bourgeoisie from welcoming a return of pervasive capitalist influences. With these caveats in mind, however, it seems clear that the newly successful CCP, aware of its past bitter experiences at the hands of both the West and the Soviet Union, was keenly desirous of now becoming completely dependent on neither—while recognizing that much of its future aid would come from Moscow.

In general, it seems that when a new revolutionary state "arrives" in the international system, the system's image of the intruder's disequilibrium tendencies are stronger than that which the state holds of itself (e.g., Cuba). Within the context of Peking's foreign policy, in an upward spiral of expectations, a process of mutual reinforcement takes place; as contacts to the West were not taken up, the PRC moved closer to the Soviet Union.

Notes

1. Allen S. Whiting, *China Crosses the Yalu: The Decision to Enter the Korean War.* (New York: Macmillan Co., 1960), p. 9
2. Tang Tsou, *America's Failure in China, 1941—1950* (Chicago: University of Chicago Press, 1963), p. 35–36.
3. One frequently overlooked, or at least underemphasized, cause of strain is race. Both the Russians and the Chinese share hostility perceptions of the other based on racial fear. See Harrison E. Salisbury, *War Between Russia and China* (New York: Bantam Books, 1969), especially pp. 15–23.

4. See Ishwer C. Ojha, *Chinese Foreign Policy in an Age of Transition: The Politics of Cultural Despair* (Boston, Beacon Press, 1971), p. 23. On the pre-1949 "Foreign Ministry" of the CCP, see Donald W. Klein, "The Management of Foreign Affairs in Communist China," in China: *Management of a Revolutionary Society,* ed. John M. H. Lindbeck (Seattle: University of Washington Press, 1971), pp. 305–13.

5. Yu-kwei Cheng, *Foreign Trade and the Industrial Development of China* (New York: Frederick A. Praeger, 1956), pp. 180–82.

6. First published in 1949 by the United States State Department; reissued as *The China White Paper, August, 1949,* introduction by Lyman P. Van Slyke (Stanford: Stanford University Press, 1967), pp. 969–75, 1043–44.

7. Richard M. Bueschel, *Chinese Communist Air Power* (New York: Frederick A. Praeger, 1968), p. 12.

8. John Gittings, "The Origins of China's Foreign Policy," in *Containment and Revolution,* ed. David Horowitz (Boston: Beacon Press, 1967), p. 192.

9. John S. Service, *The Amerasia Papers: Some Problems in the History of U. S.—China Relations* (Berkeley: China Research Monograph, 1971), p. 175.

10. Ibid., pp. 182–83.

11. Ibid., p. 173.

12. Ibid., p. 175.

13. *Memorandum on China's Liberated Areas* (San Francisco, May 18, 1945). No publisher listed.

14. Interview with Mao Tse-tung, July 14, 1944. In Gunther Stein, *The Challenge of Red China* (New York: McGraw-Hill, 1945), pp. 448–49.

15. Telegram of October 6, 1932. Cited in Stuart Schram, *The Political Thought of Mao Tse-tung* (Baltimore: Penguin Books, 1963), pp. 266–67.

16. "The Achievements of the Crimea Conference," cited by Yenan Radio in *Foreign Broadcast Information Service,* February 17, 1945.

17. Yenan Radio, in *Foreign Broadcast Information Service,* March 7, 1945.

18. *The China White Paper,* p. 576.

19. Ibid., p. 577.

20. Ibid., p. 85

21. *Foreign Broadcast Information Service;* contained in issues dated March 17, 19, 23, and 24, 1945.

22. *New York Times,* "Chinese Reds Seek World Policy Role," March 24, 1945, p. 13.

23. *Selected Works of Mao Tse-tung,* vol. 3. Peking: Foreign Languages Publishing House, 1961), p. 256.

24. Michael Lindsay, "China: Report of a Visit," *International Affairs* (January, 1950), p. 17

25. Warren J. Cohen, *America's Response to China* (New York: John Wiley, 1971), pp. 174–78.

26. The Chinese have also noted this strained history: "in the late 1920s, the '30s, and the early and middle 1940s . . . Comrades Mao Tse-tung and Liu Shao-ch'i resisted the influence of Stalin's mistakes." "Kuan-yu Sze-ta-lin wen-t'i" [On the Question of Stalin] *Jen-min Jih-pao* [People's Daily], September 13, 1963, p. 1.

27. C.P. Fitzgerald, *Revolution in China* (London: Cresset Press, 1952), p. 164. See also Milovan Djilas, *Conversations with Stalin* (New York: Harcourt, Brace and World, 1962), p.182, for Stalin's advice to the CCP at the end of World War II to form a coalition government with the KMT.

28. Harry Schwartz, *Tsars, Mandarins, and Commissars* (Philadelphia, J.P. Lippincott, 1962), p. 147.

29. "Industrialization of China Bogs Down in Russian Relations," in *Christian Science Monitor,* (March 25, 1953), p. 8.

30. Klaus Mehnert, *Peking and Moscow* (New York: Mentor Books, 1964), p. 264.

31. David J. Dallin, *Soviet Foreign Policy After Stalin* (Philadelphia: J.P. Lippincott, 1961), p. 75.

32. G.M. Friters, *Outer Mongolia and Its International Position* (Baltimore: Johns Hopkins University Press, 1951), p. 130.

33. Harrison E. Salisbury, "Image and Reality in Indochina," *Foreign Affairs* (April, 1971), pp. 383–84.
    In July, 1964, Mao charged that "in accordance with the Yalta Agreement the Soviet Union, under the pretext of securing the independence of Mongolia, actually placed the country under its domination. . . . " Cited in Edward E. Rice, *Mao's Way* (Berkeley and Los Angeles: University of California Press, 1972), p. 216.

34. Mehnert, op. cit., p. 264.

35. Allen S. Whiting and General Sheng Shih-ts'ai, *Sinkiang: Pawn or Pivot* (East Lansing: Michigan State University Press, 1958), pp. 117–18. See also James Harrison, *The Long March to Power,* (New York: Frederick A. Praeger, 1972), pp. 380–82.

36. Harold Hinton, *Communist China in World Politics* (Boston: Houghton Mifflin Co. 1966), p. 19.
37. "Proletarian Internationalism is the Banner of the Working People of All Countries and Continents," editorial in *Kommunist* (Moscow), no. 7 (1964). Cited in John Gittings, *Survey of the Sino—Soviet Dispute* (New York: Frederick A. Praeger, 1969), p. 41. Emphasis added. See also Harrison, op. cit., p. 383.
38. Franz Schurmann, *Ideology and Organization in Communist China* (Berkeley and Los Angeles: University of California Press, 1966), p. 344.
39. *The Historical Dictatorship of the Proletariat* (Peking: Foreign Languages Publishing House, 1959), p. 8. Emphasis added.
40. Rice, op. cit., p. 130. This would integrate the two views in notes 38, 41, and 43.
41. O. Edmund Clubb, *China and Russia, the Great Game* (New York: Columbia University Press, 1971), p. 406.
42. "War Between Russia and China?" *New York Times Sunday Magazine,* July 27, 1969, p. 56.
43. Cited in Gittings, *Sino—Soviet Dispute,* pp. 43–44. Emphasis added. For a somewhat different interpretation which emphasizes personal-political factors, as opposed to Soviet influence, in Kao Kang's ouster, see Frederick C. Teiwes, "A Review Article: The Evolution of Leadership Purges in Communist China" in *The China Quarterly* (January–March, 1970), especially pp. 122–26.
44. Molotov told British Prime Minister Anthony Eden that the Russians had not expected the CCP to establish themselves in power so quickly. Anthony Eden, *Full Circle* (Boston: Houghton Mifflin Co., 1960), p. 131. John Gittings believes that "there is no doubt that victory came to the communist leadership much earlier than expected . . . ." John Gittings, *The Role of the Chinese Army* (London: Oxford University Press, 1967), pp. 18–19. Gittings thinks that a slower communist victory would have resulted in less anti-American feeling.
45. "P'eng Chen t'ung-chih tsai Pei-ching Chung-Su yu-hao hsieh-hui chih k'ai-mu tzu" [Comrade P'eng Chen's Opening Address at the Meeting of the Sino–Soviet Friendship Association in Peking], *Jen-min Jih-pao,* October 11, 1949, p. 1.
46. Chiang Hseuh-jo, "New Schemes Engineered in the White Paper," August 19, 1949. Translated in *Chinese Press Survey* (Shanghai), September 1, 1949, pp. 1–3. A former instructor in a school of the Chinese Foreign Ministry in the early 1950s, Mr. C.

Tam, in an interview in September, 1971 with this writer, said that "almost all of the articles published in *Shih-chieh Chih-shih* were written by officials of the Foreign Ministry and then signed by pseudonyms." *Shih-chieh Chih-shih* was for distribution to CCP cadres within China.

47. For an interpretation of Mao's 1949 speech as an expression of rigid anti-United States and pro-Soviet Union feelings see Peter Van Ness, *Revolution and China's Foreign Policy: Peking's Support for Wars of National Liberation* (Berkeley and Los Angeles: University of California Press, 1970), p. 11.

For a recent article that closely analyzes the kinetic relationship between the CCP and the United States of this period, see Donald S. Zagoria, "Choices in the Postwar World (2): Containment and China," in *Caging the Bear: Containment and the Cold War*, ed. Charles Gati (Indianapolis and New York: The Bobbs-Merrill Co.), 1974.

48. *Mao Tse-tung*, vol. 4. (Peking: Foreign Languages Press, 1961), p. 417. Emphasis added.

49. *Shih-chieh Chih-shih*, "Why Must We Lean to One Side?" by Chang Ming-yang, August 5, 1949; translated in *Chinese Press Survey*, August 11, 1949, pp. 106–7.

50. Salisbury, *The Coming War Between Russia and China*, pp. 106–7.

51. Cited in Gittings, *Sino—Soviet Dispute*, p. 14. Remember that the above quote from *Shih-chieh Chih-shih* noted that China had leaned to the imperialist side under Chiang K'ai-shek.

52. "Huan ying Lo shen ta shih" [Welcome Ambassador Roshchin], October 11, 1949, p. 1.

53. Hu Chen, "T'ai-p'ing T'ien-kuo yü tzu-pen chu-i wai-kuo ti kuan-hsi" [The Relations Between the T'ai-p'ing T'ien-kuo and the Capitalist Nations], *Hsueh Hsi*, September 20, 1949. Translated in *Chinese Press Survey*, November 1, 1949, p. 19. The rebellion, of course, had been cited frequently before this time, but it now was mentioned both more frequently and with this particular slant of relevance regarding international recognition.

54. See McGeorge Bundy, *The Pattern of Responsibility* (Boston: Houghton Mifflin Co., 1952), p. 179.

55. "U. S. New President and China Policy," by Allan Chang, November 1, 1948, p. 2. See also Edward Friedman, "Problems in Dealing with an Irrational Power," in *America's Asia*, ed. Edward Friedman and Mark Selden (New York: Pantheon Books, 1971), p. 213.

56. "Dewey's Defeat," *Chinese Press Survey*, November 16, 1948, p. 10.
57. Seymour Topping, *Journey Between Two Chinas* (New York: Harper and Row, 1972), pp. 83–85.
58. "These Principles Remain Valid," p. 1.
59. Tang Tsou, op.cit., p. 516.
60. Chang Ming-yang, "The Foreign Policy of New China," October 21, 1949, Translated in *Chinese Press Survey* (November 1, 1949), p. 11. Emphasis added.
61. "The Examination of China's Existing Treaties," *Kuan Ch'a* [Observer] (Peking), November 16, 1949, p. 3. Translated in *Chinese Press Survey*, December, 1949, p. 3.
62. Ssu Mu, "The Fight for and against Righteousness at Lake Success," January 20, 1950. Translated in *Chinese Press Survey*, February 1, 1950, p. 97. Pursuing this campaign, *Jen-min Jih-pao* of May 21, 1950, printed an interview which Lenin had held with a *New York Evening Post* reporter in 1920, previously unpublished in the Chinese press:

> *Question*: What is the basic condition for peace with the U.S.A.?
> *Answer*: If the capitalists don't bother us, we won't bother them. We are even prepared to purchase from them, with gold, their machinery and equipment for our transportation and production. Not only with gold, but with raw materials, too. . . .
>
> *Question*: Is Russia prepared to have relations with the U.S.A.?
> *Answer*: Of course, just as she is prepared to do with any country. The peace treaty which we have signed with Estonia (on this matter we have made great concessions) can prove that we are prepared to pursue such a goal. Under certain conditions, we will even lease our enterprises.

It might have done the United States well to have studied the Soviet Union–Estonia precedent.

63. Chiang K'ai-shek flew to the Philippines to pay a state visit to President Quirino on July 10, 1949. They agreed to hold a larger conference to organize an anticommunist alliance. Chiang then visited South Korea in early August, where he and President Rhee repeated this proposal. General MacArthur, meanwhile, was apparently coordinating military strategy between American forces in Japan with Taiwan, the Philippines, and South Korea. See Tang Tsou, op. cit., pp. 503–10.

The United States started giving military aid to the French in Indochina in the spring of 1950. On May 8, 1950, Secretary of State Acheson promised "economic aid and military equioment" to the pro-French Bao Dai regime on the grounds that neither "national independence nor democratic evolution exists in any area dominated by Soviet imperialism." Royal Institute of International Affairs, *Survey of International Affairs, 1949-1950* (London: Oxford University Press, 1951), p. 609.

64. Hsiao San, "Ch'ing-chu shih-chieh ho-p'ing chih jih" [The Day of Struggle for World Peace], p. 11.

65. Molotov, "Sze-ta-lin te ling-tao" [The Leadership of Stalin], p. 5.

66. David Floyd, *Mao Against Khrushchev.* (New York: Frederick A. Praeger, 1964), p. 12. Floyd suggests that the Chinese received only 10 percent of what they requested in aid from the Soviet Union.

67. Liu Shao-ch'i, in New China News Agency (NCNA) dispatch, October 10, 1949.

68. NCNA editorial, February 15, 1960, noting the conclusion of the treaty talks.

69. Cited in Gittings, *Sino–Soviet Dispute*, p. 209.

70. Kang Chao and Feng-hwa Ma, "A Study of the Rouble–Yuan Exchange Rate," *China Quarterly* (January–March 1964), p. 193.

71. Meng Hsien-cheng, "Chung-Su t'iao yüeh ho Jih-pen wen-t'i [The Sino–Soviet Treaty and the Japanese Issue], *Kuan Ch'a,* March 4, 1950, p. 1.

4

The Soviet Union Freezes China Out of the United Nations

Chapter 9 of this book analyzes the generalized concept of coalitions by dividing interstate ties, in stages of increasing intensity, into the (nonexclusive) categories of association, alignment, and alliance. For the purposes of this chapter, it is worthwhile to note that while crisis points are the thresholds of events *between* alignments and alliances, the major determinants of the developing ties *within* an alignment are preconditions, such as historical memories, geographical proximity or natural barriers, and trade patterns. All play an important part in the likelihood of an alignment forming between two states. As important as these factors are, however, the formation and development of an alignment, because it is a *process*, depends to a great extent upon the range of options that seems to be open to each partner. Oftentimes, the process proceeds step-by-step in a series of mutually reinforcing perceptual expectations. This seems particularly to apply to new revolutionary regimes. The international system is usually not receptive to an accommodation with the self-proclaimed revolutionary goals of a feared new actor (e.g., the cases of Cuba, North Vietnam,

China). The status quo members of the system tend to react rigidly to the perceived threat. Frequently, as an unfortunate consequence, opportunities for compromise are missed because of a spiraling overreaction on the part of each of the antagonists. The inertia, then, probably will start with the historical and geopolitical preconditions, but it is this shared feeling of constantly closing options toward perceived enemies that commonly binds the partners together.

Countries enter *alliances* for reasons other than the most common one of the simple aggregation of military force. Other reasons, which, of course, may overlap, are that state X may want to deny to other states the resources of state Y. Ideology and a reciprocal need for legitimacy may also play a part. This is particularly true when state Y is a weak, new revolutionary regime, seeming to menace the international system at the same time that it itself feels acutely threatened. At this point, its "natural" allies will be those states with whom it shares similar (although not, it should be added, identical) perceptions of the world. When state Y is both weaker than the status quo powers that seek to effect the manner of its survival and also possesses fragile ties to the outside political world, it will find itself becoming more dependent upon state X for both its sense of legitimacy and economic aid.

In this case study, X and Y are the Soviet Union and the PRC respectively. In brief, the dialectic inertia in the relationship runs: Y feels weak relative to X and vulnerable toward the rest of the international system. If X can cultivate this sense of threat by minimizing Y's opportunities for peaceful contact with the international system, then each thwarted contact makes it more likely that Y will turn toward X, and that Y will increasingly adopt X's attitudes and perceptions. The outside world thereupon feels justified in its initial hostility toward Y, since X is already an international pariah and X and Y are now seen to be drawing closer together. This mutually reinforced "vicious circle" is difficult to break.

The Russians were probably aware of the exponential potential of this inertia process, and in late 1949 were apparently looking for a means to utilize this principle to bind China closer to the Soviet Union. Moscow also presumably appreciated the inherent ambiguity of the Russian–Chinese–American triangle at this time. China was suspicious—justly so—of Russian designs upon her territory, resources, and political system. The Soviet Union, in turn, didn't trust the consistently independent stance behind Mao's policies; she also held the traditional Russian fear of the "Yellow Peril." The CCP, as indicated in the last chapter, had tried to keep its options to the West open. For their part, the Americans, due largely to domestic political considerations, were unwilling to recognize the PRC until all of the KMT's cards had been played out. Even at that point, Washington's plans called for a ring of bases around China's perimeter.

The components of this triangle were a largely frozen anticommunist position on the part of the United States, which was unwilling to initiate a compromise with the PRC but prepared to become more flexible under the pressure of imminent events (e.g., the fall of Taiwan); a PRC perceiving itself to be incrementally "boxed in" by U.S. hostility, although more than willing to employ western states as counters to Russian influence; and a Soviet Union anxious to solidify its somewhat shaky influence over the PRC—via either Manchuria or Peking.

The Soviet Union and the United Nations

The logical battleground for the PRC's attempted entry into the international system was the United Nations, although the United States at the time seemed to miss much of the conflict between the strategies that were being employed by China and the Soviet Union:

In 1950 prospects seemed bright for the admission of communist China to the U.N. . . . . Under the circumstances, if the Soviet delegation had been more tactful, it might have succeeded in leading the Peking government into the United Nations. . . . Instead of escorting its friend through the main entrance, which might have yielded to a few gentle knocks, it had chosen to shoot its way in and thrust its friend through a narrow side window, which, by the way, was closed.[1]

Almost immediately after the beginning of the Korean Civil War on June 24, 1950 (June 25 Korean time), the United States was able to utilize the United Nations Security Council in order to mobilize legitimized force and public opinion against North Korea and its Russian ally. American actions in the Security Council were quickly successful, largely because of the Soviet Union's absence from the Council.

Two explanations have been advanced to account for the absence of the Soviet delegates after June 24. One is that the Soviet Union wished to avoid the embarassment of having to defend the actions of North Korea in the world body. The other, frequently held view is that the Soviets disdained the influence of the United Nations, and did not consider it necessary to be present in such an impotent body at moments of crisis. Oftentimes these two arguments are presented together, a fair indication that a great deal of uncertainty remains.[2] Two other ideas are sometimes raised to explain the Russians' absence: 1) there may have been a lack of coordination within the Russian bureaucratic structure and hence a critical delay in Russia's return to the Security Council; and 2) the Russians might have considered their absence as having the effect of a veto on the Security Council's actions. Neither of these explanations has validity, however, when considered against the many similar situations in which Soviet diplomacy had found itself before June 25.[3]

One section of Secretary of State Acheson's famous speech of January 12, 1950, foresaw an American appeal to the United Nations in the event of a crisis outside of his "perimeter":

> Should such an attack occur . . . the initial reliance must be
> on the people attacked to resist it, and then upon the com-
> mitments of the entire civilized world under the Charter of
> the United Nations, which so far has not proved to be a
> weak reed to lean upon by a people who are determined to
> protect their independence against outside aggression. [4]

In short, regardless of any definitive contingency plans for
the military defense of the "free world," Washington did expect
to utilize the United Nations as—at the least—an instrument
with which to mobilize world public opinion in the event of any
"aggression." An indication of the widespread belief, at the time
of the North Korean attack, that the United States would at the
least go to the United Nations to accuse the North Koreans of
aggression was an A.P. dispatch from New York dated June 25:
"Aside from an appeal to the U.N., the United States may consider
sending more arms and equipment to the South Koreans. It
seems unlikely that the United States would go beyond that." [5]
    In previous situations in which the Cold War had been
moved to the front burner (Iran, 1946; Germany, 1947–48;
Greece, 1947), the Russians had engaged in harsh debates in the
United Nations. Why should they absent themselves now that
an established satellite was being attacked with the support and
approval of the U.S.? From American public speeches made
before June 25, 1950, which proclaimed the intention to use the
U.N. in just this way as a legitimizer of American actions, the
Soviet Union might well have anticipated that at least an American oral response in the United Nations would have been involved in the aftermath of the June 25 crisis.
    Because of the scanty nature of the available evidence, a
categorical answer to the question of why the Soviet Union was
absent from the Security Council in June, 1950, remains elusive.
A tentative answer to this still-perplexing problem will be presented in chapter 5. First, however, the basic question presents
itself of why the Soviet Union walked out of the United Nations

in January, 1950. What caused the original Russian boycott, which was eventually to culminate in their absence on June 25?

The Soviet Boycott

The usual interpretation of the Soviet walkout and boycott of the United Nations six months before the beginning of the Korean Civil War is that it was caused by the defeat of the Soviet proposal that China be seated in the U.N. A rereading of the available data, however, indicates that the Soviet's original absence from the United Nations was more likely occasioned by the desire to keep the PRC *out*. Such an exclusion would cut off potential PRC contacts with the West, inhibit the new state's sense of having "arrived" in the international system, and increase China's dependence upon her Soviet "patron" for both economic and ideological support.

At the beginning of January, 1950, five out of eleven members of the Security Council (the Soviet Union, India, Yugoslavia, Great Britain, and Norway) had already recognized the PRC. Two other members, France and Egypt, were expected to extend recognition soon.[6] Conditions looked very favorable for the PRC's early admission: India recognized the PRC on December 30; Britain on January 5, 1950, and Israel on January 9.

On December 23, 1949, the United States State Department had sent a "top secret" memorandum to its embassies around the world concerning Taiwan's future; it declared that "the fall of Formosa is widely anticipated," and suggested public relations–type statements which the embassies could make in order to deemphasize this final defeat for the KMT. Quotations from this document (apparently leaked by General MacArthur's headquarters in Tokyo) were published on January 3, 1950, in an A.P. dispatch from Tokyo. The incident seemed to indicate that the United States did not consider the PRC's rival delegation, then seated in the United Nations, to be more than a temporary obstacle of the new regime's achieving its goals.

While Washington appeared to be taking a "let the dust settle" (Acheson's phrase) attitude, its position was ambiguous enough to cause considerable concern to the PRC. President Truman declared on January 5, 1950, that

> the United States has no desire to obtain special rights or privileges or to establish military bases on Formosa *at this time*. Nor does it have any intention of utilizing its armed forces to interfere *in the present situation*. The United States will not pursue a course which will lead to involvement in the civil conflict in China. Similarly, the United States government will not provide military aid or advice to Chinese forces on Formosa. [7]

That same afternoon, Secretary of State Acheson, in an elaboration of Truman's remarks, explained that "in the unlikely and unhappy event that our own forces might be attacked in the Far East, the United States must be completely free to take whatever action in whatever area is necessary for its own security." [8]

The PRC understood that U.S. military forces, and American military aid—regardless of President Truman's disclaimers—were still on Taiwan, and could serve as a "trigger" for further hostilities between the U.S. and the PRC. For example, NCNA on January 2, 1950 accurately charged that the United States had agreed to give sixteen naval vessels, radar installations, and arms and equipment for five divisions to the KMT forces on Taiwan. The Democratic administration in Washington, a minority government, was balancing several factors that would affect any final decision on Taiwan: its vulnerability to Senator Joseph McCarthy's charges of being "soft on communism" and of having "lost China"; a desire to cut its losses with the apparently doomed KMT; and the domestic political framework established by the Marshall Plan and the Truman Doctrine, which encouraged an activist opposition to an assumed monolithic, expansionist communism. Peking correctly saw that, although chances appeared good that the U.S. would stand relatively aloof from a Chinese invasion of Taiwan, this was still only one of several options seen by Washington as being worthy of active consideration. NCNA continued its charges of U.S.–Taiwan collusion throughout the winter and spring of 1950. Hence, the view that Peking "took at face value President Truman's disclaimer"[9] of interference in China's plans vis-a-vis Taiwan is not completely accurate.

In this context, Acheson's speech of January 12, 1950, takes on a different light. Taiwan also was left out of his famous "defense perimeter," while the United States was deliberately obfuscating what its reaction would be to an attempted change in the East Asian status quo. The Chinese recognized this ambiguousness, and were outraged. For example, on February 9, 1950, NCNA lashed out at the United States, blaming it for the heavy KMT air raids of the previous week, which almost completely destroyed the American-owned Shanghai Power Company and caused more than 1,000 deaths and injuries. The Chinese claimed that: 1) the planes and bombs were supplied by the U.S., despite Truman and Acheson's disclaimers. 2) the planes were flown by American and Japanese "volunteers"; 3) the U.S. State Department must have given tacit permission before the KMT "dared to single out the American-owned Shanghai Power Company plant, Shanghai's largest power supplier."[10] Peking was also nervously apprehensive about the possible resurgence of a Japan which had made a separate peace with the Western powers.[11] General MacArthur seemed to be calling for a rearmed Japan, declaring in his 1950 New Year's message that Japan had "the inalienable right of self-defense against unprovoked attack."[12]

Consequently, the PRC in the first half of 1950 had ample cause to both puzzle over and fear possible actions by the West against her territory. The year itself, however, began on an auspicious note. The PRC was both eager and optimistic about being seated in the United Nations, its major potential vehicle for the opening of contact with the West. Membership in the world organization would: 1) legitimize the end of the long, bitter Chinese Civil War and herald the symbolic arrival of the PRC as the equal of the other four Great Powers; 2) open an avenue for economic and cultural contacts with the West; 3) give China an opportunity to take an active part in the shaping of a peace treaty with its recent, and still very much feared, enemy, Japan.

Although conditions did seem favorable for the PRC's entrance in January, there was one major drawback: the President of the Security Council for that month was Dr. Tsiang Ting-fu, the representative from Taiwan. Contemporary observers believed, therefore, that

> it would be difficult to bring about the debarment of Dr. Tsiang during January, since he will preside over all Council meetings this month, and it is believed that the Soviet Union will wait until February, when Dr. Alberto L. Alvarez of Cuba will become President of the Security Council under the system of alphabetical rotation, or longer, before making a serious move in this direction. [13]

On January 7, U.N. Secretary-General Trygvie Lie made the admission of the PRC easier by stating that each major organ of the United Nations would have to make its own decision on which Chinese delegation was to be represented on that particular organ. This would lead, Lie explained, to a "natural solution" [14] since smaller, functional groups might be expected to admit the PRC quickly; the "natural solution" appeared to auger well for the smooth entrance of the PRC into the United Nations at quite an early date. The day after Lie's announcement, it was widely reported that France and Egypt were about to recognize the PRC government. Still, the *Times* reported that "it is generally anticipated that the Soviet Union will not pass the question until the 7 votes are assured." [15]

On January 8, 1950, PRC Foreign Minister Chou En-lai sent a telegram to Trygvie Lie and the Security Council declaring that the KMT "reactionary remnant clique" was seated illegally and demanding its expulsion. This telegram was highly similar to one which Chou had sent on November 15, 1949. This time, however, the Soviet delegate took the opportunity to introduce a draft resolution demanding the immediate expulsion of Dr. Tsiang. The United States then declared that it was not "irreconcilably opposed" to the admission of Peking and did not consider the question to be a vetoable one. [16] It noted that it would vote against the draft resolution of the Soviet Union, but declared that it considered this to be a procedural, rather than an "important," question. The U.S. delegate further mildly declared that his government would "accept the decision of the Security Council on this matter when made by an affirmative vote of 7 members." [17] On January 13, the Soviet draft resolution was defeated by a vote of 6 to 3, with Britain and Norway abstaining, and the Soviet Union began its celebrated boycott—"although it would certainly be accepted within a few weeks." [18]

The nature of the Soviet walkout leaves many loose ends to be resolved. For example, the Soviet Union previously had announced that it would not recognize the election of Yugoslavia by the U.N. General Assembly as the representative of Eastern Europe on the Security Council. Yet, on the same day that the Soviet Union first walked out (January 10, returning on January 13 to vote for its obviously doomed resolution), it did not challenge Yugoslavia's credentials. One explanation of this, of course, is that the Soviet Union was, understandably, concerned only with the unjust treatment of the PRC. A second explanation, however, seems to accord better with our available knowledge: viz., that the Soviet Union was engaged in a deliberate attempt to exclude the PRC from the United Nations in order to solidify the Sino–Soviet relationship. The Russians' walkout assured that the question of PRC representation in the U.N. would become a bitter Cold War issue (without being diluted by debate over the Yugoslav question), thus foreclosing the PRC's possibility of "sneaking" into the various organs of the United Nations.

Trygvie Lie later wrote that Sir Alexander Codogan, the permanent British delegate to the 1950 United Nations session, had told him at the time that "Soviet policy was based on a calculated policy of discouraging rather than encouraging recognition, therefore more effectively placing China in isolation from the West and more under the Soviet Union's domination."[19] Secretary-General Lie concurred with this idea. In speaking with the Chinese ambassador to Russia, Wang Chia-hsiang, in Moscow in May of 1950, he said:

> The Russian boycotts and walkouts . . . have not made it any easier to seat the Peking government in the various U.N. organs. Instead of helping, they have actually made things more difficult for you. . . . The ambassador seemed to have difficulty in grasping the situation, perhaps he did not want to grasp it.[20]

It is perhaps not too cynical to suggest that the Chinese were apprehensive that this conversation, significantly held not in the Chinese embassy but in a Moscow hotel room, was "bugged," and that they were therefore leery of rashly agreeing with Lie. The Secretary-General also expressed his view to Soviet Foreign Minister Molotov, who "merely smiled."[21]

Later treatment of Lie in the Chinese media strongly suggests that China was aware of, and appreciated, his earlier efforts to gain its admission to the U.N. For example, after the beginning of the Korean Civil War, when the Chinese were criticizing Lie for what they considered to be his pro-American actions, they remembered that "Lie once exerted great efforts on the Chinese representation issue and he did not seem too bad then."[22]

China's Cut-Off Contacts

Two further events of January, 1950 seemed to increase China's isolation from the world community. These generally have been viewed as calculatedly hostile acts on the part of a frenzied, ideological PRC, intended to express its disregard for the sensitivities of the (Western-dominated) international system. In retrospect, however, and especially in light of our subsequent experience of analogous actions on the part of other revolutionary mass-movement regimes, the Chinese seizure of American, French, and Dutch consular property in Peking on January 14 does not seem to have been a purely antagonistic act. In fact, this was the act of a newly successful strongly nationalistic government, symbolically declaring its integrity and independence.

This first incident marked the third major confrontation between the new, revolutionary PRC and the United States. In July, 1949, the U.S. Vice-Consul in Shanghai, William B. Olive, had been arrested and beaten by Chinese police. In October, the U.S. Consul-General in Mukden, Angus Ward, and four of his staff had been put under house arrest, which was to last a year. The third confrontation, the seizure of consular property, involved no personnel, which may be attributed to an increasing appreciation of Western reactions on the part of the PRC. As noted previously, the Central Committee of the CCP in February, 1947 had declared that it would consider invalid all of the treaties, agreements, and loans concluded by the KMT. Therefore, this last Chinese action should not have come as a complete surprise to the United States.

More to the point, PRC seized only one of three American buildings, and based its action upon what it considered to be a legal stature. The PRC stated that only those lands were seized upon which former barracks of imperialist militarism were situated. As the PRC saw it, foreigners' rights to maintain troops in Peking had derived from the West's exploitation of China (as expressed in unequal treaties) and for that reason had been abrogated.

Peking explained its position on January 18, 1950, in an NCNA editorial: "We have confiscated only the barracks situated on the sites. Moreover, our people's government is going to adopt a new measure to solve the estate problems engendered by our reclaiming these lots."[23] The editorial emphasized several times the fact that the only seized buildings were those which had been used as military barracks by these intruding powers under the terms of unequal treaties. This might well have been meant both as a means to signify the initial PRC position in negotiations with the United States over the latter's properties in China, and as a message to the Russians, with whom prolonged negotiations were then going on in Moscow, that the PRC did not wish to endure continued unequal treaties with their "fraternal" neighbor. Moreover, Peking indicated the possibility of negotiating a financial settlement for the seized properties.

The French and the Dutch thought these measures inconsequential enough so as not to constitute an impediment to their relations with the new PRC. Secretary of State Acheson, however, saw this incident as cause to order the complete withdrawal of U.S. consular and diplomatic personnel from China. A *New York Times* correspondent writing from Hong Kong commented that "it was implied that the Peiping Government had envisaged paying compensation for the requisitioned properties and that measures would be announced later to solve the questions arising from the requisitioning."[24] He also cited diplomats in Hong Kong as saying that the American overreaction to the PRC's seizure of property was "unwise and precipitate." Here again, the PRC's action was viewed by the Chinese themselves as moderate nationalism, and by the Americans as evidence of unremitting, intensely ideological, hostility.

There is a different, highly intriguing, hypothesis which relates the seizure of the consular properties to an anti-Mao faction in the CCP. Taking advantage of Mao's absence from China while he was in Moscow negotiating with Stalin, this faction, according to this explanation, sought to eliminate potential American influence by this provocative act.[25] This hypothesis, is, of course, unverifiable, but from what is known of past CCP leadership divisions regarding the correct stance to take toward the West, it *is* conceivable. Whatever the cause of the seizure of the American property, it does seem likely that it weakened Mao's overall negotiating position in Moscow, because Peking was now further isolated from possible contact with the West.

In the second incident (December, 1949), the puppet Bao Dai regime in Vietnam signed a pact with France which granted internal independence for Vietnam. This attempt to legitimize the position of the Bao Dai group as a national government prompted Ho Chi Minh to officially seek support in the international community.

China recognized Ho Chi Minh's government, an incident that seemed to suggest that the PRC was acting in the international arena out of a spirit of revolutionary *animus* which hotly disregarded all potential contacts with the West. For its part, Washington, in the first week of January, 1950, announced that it planned recognition of the Bao Dai government, along with economic aid.[26] It was also widely predicted that the United Kingdom was soon to recognize that government. If England can recognize Bao Dai and still have financial and diplomatic relations with us, the PRC may well have argued to itself, what should inhibit our relations with both Ho Chi Minh and the U.S.?

The crux of the problem of the PRC's handling of these two incidents lies in the timing. In the latter case, why the usual query runs, would the PRC alienate France, when the crucial French vote was needed to seat the PRC on the U.N. Security Council? The answer would seem to be that by the time the PRC recognized the Ho Chi Minh government in Vietnam, the matter of how France would vote on the PRC's admission to the United Nations had receded into the background.

As noted earlier in this chapter, by making the PRC's admission to the United Nations a crucial test of ideological will

and leverage, rather than a matter of a "natural solution" which
time would take care of, the Soviet Union had prompted a rigid
division in the U.N. on January 13. After that date, the possibility of rapid PRC entrance sharply diminished. Ho Chi Minh's
government had requested China's official recognition on
January 14, 1950. It is noteworthy that recognition was requested
at the same time that China was losing its potential membership
in the U.N. Peking did not grant official recognition until
January 18—a lapse of time which exceeded that characterizing
China's other diplomatic exchanges, particularly with communist regimes. Did the fiercely nationalistic Ho Chi Minh
cause the PRC an awkward moment by requesting recognition at
such an inopportune moment? Did the Russians (who waited
until January 30 to extend their own diplomatic recognition)
assure the Chinese that they would move on the matter of diplomatic recognition toward Ho at the same time as the PRC and
then delay, thus causing Peking to appear even more rigidly
ideological? These are two possibilities.[27] What we do know is
that the PRC delayed its recognition of the Ho Chi Minh government until its probable effect of alienating the French vote in
the United Nations Security Council no longer had a bearing
upon its admission.

Peking's relations with the Vietnamese communists were
supportive; the CCP had declared that the Chinese revolution
was now to serve as a model for the colonial and semicolonial
countries. But Peking's relationship with Vietnam suggests that
she was not anxious to form official ties with her which would
jeopardize China's future relations with the West. The lag of four
days between Vietnam's request and Peking's granting of recognition becomes even more interesting when the fact is noted that
Ho Chi Minh had sent a personal message to Mao Tse-tung on
December 5, 1949, signaling his imminent official request:

> Brotherly relations have existed between the Vietnamese
> and Chinese nations during thousands of years of history.

Henceforth these relations will be even closer for the developments of the freedom and happiness of our two nations, as well as for the safeguard of world democracy and lasting peace.[28]

On January 14, 1950, Vietnam stated that it wished to establish relations with all friendly nations. The formal four-day delay, therefore, was in reality a longer one. A further indication of China's reluctance to become deeply involved in Vietnam's problems is that Peking did not receive a Vietnamese "representative" until April 28, 1951 (an ambassador did not officially take up his post until October 10, 1952), while China did not send an envoy to Vietnam until September, 1954.[29]

China's Reactions

Both of these actions, then—China's increasingly militant posture toward the U.S. and her recognition of Ho Chi Minh—rather than being irrational or impulsive actions generated by ideological machismo, were in fact calculated moves by the PRC, which were assessed in terms of probable costs and benefits.

Jen-min Jih-pao [People's Daily] did not print an editorial endorsing the Soviet Union's walkout from the United Nations until January 17, and then it was rather mild. On January 20, Chou En-lai announced the appointment of Chang Wen-t'ien as the PRC's representative to the United Nations Security Council. Chang had been a student at the University of California's Berkeley campus from 1921 to 1923. On February 2, Chou appointed Chi Chi'ao-ting as the PRC's representative to the United Nations Economic and Social Council. Chi held a 1936 Ph.D. in Economics from Columbia University, and had been with the Economics Ministry of the KMT before 1949. Both representatives were thus ones who would be acceptable to the West.

China maintained her interest in the United Nations through the first half of 1950. The preamble to the Sino–Soviet Treaty of Friendship, Alliance, and Mutual Aid of February 14, 1950, for example, stated that the two neighbors were entering into this pact "in conformity with the aims and principles of the United Nations Organization. . . . " Until the beginning of the Korean Civil War, the PRC repeated its requests to both the U.N. General Assembly and its specialized agencies for admission. However, Russia's continuing boycott solidified the West's opposition to that admission. There were strong indications that the PRC was anxious that the Soviet Union end its boycott and return to the United Nations, which might, it was thought, increase China's chances for entrance:

> No matter how unscrupulous the acts of American imperialism may be, so long as the United Nations will exist, *especially that United Nations which is joined by the Soviet Union* and the People's Democratic countries, American imperialism will inevitably feel it as an obstacle.[30]

Such was the ambivalent situation of Peking in the world community at the beginning of the Korean Civil War, an event which was to catapult China into an alliance with the Soviet Union.

Notes

1. Henry Wei, *China and Soviet Russia* (New York: D. Van Nostrand, 1956), p. 283.
2. Alexander Dallin has combined these two strands of thought. Because "the Soviet Union did not take the United Nations seriously" there had been no coordination between Soviet plans for Korea and those for the U.N. *The Soviet Union and the United Nations* (New York: Frederick A. Praeger, 1961), p. 36.
3. "Nothing has been of more basic importance to the Soviet Union than the use and defense of the veto." Rupert Emerson and Inis L.

Claude, Jr., "The Soviet Union and the U.N.: An Essay in Interpretation," *International Organization* (February, 1952), p. 8. If this were the case, would the Russians remain out of the Security Council during a crisis when it could most effectively utilize its veto power? Her absence from the Security Council did not in itself constitute a veto. "By a long chain of precedents dating back to 1946 a resolution of the Security Council was valid even though one or more of the permanent members had abstained from voting. Russia itself had accepted resolutions passed in this way. It had been laid down specifically by a President of the Council—and not challenged—that to abstain was not to veto." Guy Wint, *What Happened in Korea: A Study in Collective Security* (London: Batchworth Press, 1954), p. 31. For an indication that both the Russians and the Americans realized the importance of these precedents, see Thomas J. Hamilton, "Malik Action Held Not Shackling U.N.," *New York Times*, January 12, 1950, p. 12. As for the question of coordination among Soviet bureaucracies during crisis periods, the Berlin Airlift of 1947–48 provides an example of quick Soviet reaction to Western moves.

4. *New York Times*, January 13, 1950, p. 1. There are two interesting sidelights to the timing of this speech, unfairly much maligned due to a careless reading, in which Acheson had, in fact, cleverly fudged the actual American commitment. First, the speech, accusing the Russians of nefarious designs in Northern China, probably strengthened the PRC's bargaining hand in the negotiations that were then going on in Moscow. Secondly, John Foster Dulles chose that exact date, four years later, to declare that the United States had learned its lesson and announce his policy of "massive retaliation." The timing was perhaps not a coincidence.

5. *South China Morning Post* (Hong Kong), "War in Korea," June 26, 1950, p. 12. Emphasis added.

6. Tang Tsou, *America's Failure in China, 1941–1950* (Chicago: University of Chicago Press, 1966), p. 524.

7. *Department of State Bulletin*, Washington, D.C., January 16, 1950. Emphasis added.

8. *New York Times*, January 6, 1950, p. 1. The ambivalent American posture, one of compromising with the new PRC only if all other options seemed closed, was clear to a defensive PRC, worried about both American and Japanese military threats. For example, the U.S. Congress voted $58 million for construction of land and air bases on Okinawa in October, 1949.

9. Allen S. Whiting, *China Crosses the Yalu: The Decision to Enter the Korean War* (New York: Macmillan Co., 1960), p. 22.

10. This was only one of numerous KMT air, land, and naval raids from 1948 on that the PRC blamed on KMT–American collusion.

11. See, for example, *New York Times*, "Japan Premier for Separate Pact," by Lindsay Parrott, November 12, 1949, p. 1.

12. *New York Times*, "Japan Has Right of Defense, MacArthur Says in Message," by Lindsay Parrott, January 1, 1950, p. 1.

13. *New York Times*, "U.S. Path Is Eased on U.N. China Shift," by Thomas J. Hamilton, January 5, 1950, p. 18.

14. *New York Times*, January 7, 1950, p. 5.

15. *New York Times*, "No Message Received," by Thomas J. Hamilton, January 9, 1950, p. 1

16. See Tang Tsou, op. cit., p. 523.

17. *United Nations Security Council Official Records*, 460th meeting, p. 6. Also see David Brook, *The United Nations and the China Dilemma* (New York: Vintage Press, 1956), pp. 60–69.

18. *New York Times*, "Malik in Walkout," by Thomas J. Hamilton, January 11, 1950, p. 3.

19. Trygvie Lie, *In the Cause of Peace* (New York: Macmillan Co., 1954), p. 250.

20. Ibid., pp. 267–68

21. Ibid., p. 268

22. "P'ing-lün: Ko-lo-mi-ko te mu-piao shih cheng-ê, yü-yen shih ching-ting te" [Commentary: Just Is the Cause and Stern the Words of Gromyko], *Shanghai Ta Kung Pao*, July 6, 1950, p. 2.

23. *Hsin-hua Yueh-pao* [New China Monthly], Peking, February 15, 1950, p. 854.

24. *New York Times*, "Peiping Maintains Seizures Justified," by Tillman Durdin, January 19, 1950, p. 2.

25. O. Edmund Clubb, *China and Russia: The "Great Game"* (New York: Columbia University Press, 1971), pp. 381–82. On January 24, 1950, Secretary of State Acheson, in an executive session of the U.S. Senate Committee on Foreign Relations, noted that "there is some reason to believe, from the sort of gossip that flies around Peiping, that the PRC really thought that this was a bluff, and I think that they are in a somewhat difficult situation." Cited in *Economic Assistance in China and Korea: 1949–50* (Washington: U. S. Government Printing Office, 1974), p. 206.

26. *New York Times* "U.S. Plans Aid Programs to Push Recovery in Asia," by James Reston, January 6, 1950, p. 1. Reston was known as

a particularly "authoritative" reporter. That Washington held an active interest in the survival of the Bao Dai regime *before* the beginning of the Korean Civil War was accurately perceived by the PRC. For example, the U.S. Seventh Fleet arrived in Saigon on March 16, 1950, and stayed a week, with overflights of American fighter aircraft, as a demonstration of support for the French-sponsored regime.

27. One scholar has argued that it was Ho himself who delayed in asking for Chinese recognition, in fear that this might prompt attacks by remnant KMT forces. This claim, however, is followed by quotes from Ho pointing up his publicly militant praise of the PRC, apparently weakening the assertion of Ho's caution. See King C. Chen, *Vietnam and China, 1938–1954* (Princeton: Princeton University Press, 1969), pp. 228–29.

28. Cited in Melvin Gurtov, *The First Vietnam Crisis* (New York: Columbia University Press, 1967), pp. 7–8.

29. Ibid., p. 9.

30. "American Imperialism Intends to Spurn United Nations," *Ta Kung Pao* (Shanghai), May 9, 1950; translated in *Chinese Press Survey*, May 21, 1950, p. 56. Emphasis added.

5

A Hypothesis on the Origins of the Korean Civil War

The precise nature of the coordination existing between Moscow and the Chinese and the North Korean governments at this time remains obscure.[1] (1953)

Why did Stalin order the invasion of South Korea? Indeed, did he? Though hypotheses abound, conclusive historical evidence is lacking for any objective assigning of responsibility.[2] (1960)

We should be honest enough to admit that we simply do not know enough about this period to reach any confident conclusion.[3] (1969)

Concealed within the still-obscure origins of the Korean Civil War lies a hinge of the Sino–Soviet relationship. Vitally important to an understanding of the schism between these two neighbors in the late 1950s are the lessons which each learned from its experiences in the war. The full significance of these lessons, however, can be grasped only if the origins of the war are known. So far, well over two decades after the events, these beginnings remain shrouded in uncertainties.

The literature of the Korean crisis of the summer of 1950 has customarily described it as occurring in the context of a tight, bipolar world. The predominant view of the causes of the war has been that the Soviet Union completely controlled the North Korean invasion of June 25.[4] A much less accepted variant of the bipolar concept states that the responsibility for the North Korean attack rests with the PRC.[5] Neither hypothesis, however, is sufficient to explain satisfactorily the events of the summer of 1950 and their consequences.

Most observers of this period have seen the North Korean regime as a satellite of the Soviet Union, and Kim Il-sŏng as a mere hireling of the Russians. Stalin, so this version runs, pulled the trigger that started the war. Such a metaphor, of course, neglects the "gun" itself: viz., the government in P'yŏngyang.[6] Because the origins of the war have been placed in Moscow, research on its Korean paternity has been largely neglected. Chapter 2 briefly examined the factional divisions within the P'yŏngyang government which had an immediate bearing upon the initiation of the war. In this chapter we pursue this discussion and conclude that the Kim Il-sŏng regime of 1950 was neither a passive "gun" for an itchy Soviet trigger finger, nor a monolithic system subservient to Moscow. Hence, analysis of its own internal factional components is necessary in order to explain the origins of the war.

Although the Russians certainly armed the North Koreans, and did expect a war, this chapter contends that the *timing* of the war—which was primarily a *civil* conflict—can best be understood in terms of the indigenous conditions on the Korean peninsula.

All Koreans were united in their urgent desire for an early reunification. However, the specific timing of the June 25 invasion was caused by intense intra–Korean Worker's Party (KWP) rivalry in the north, combined with appeals from South Korean–based guerillas who had powerful supporters in the north. These pressures forced Kim Il-sŏng into a war date earlier than the one which his Soviet mentors and he had probably agreed upon. This hypothesis, based upon a fresh reconstruction of the available evidence, leads to conclusions which more satisfactorily account for previously unresolved enigmas, viz.: 1) the nature of the triangular bonds between Peking, P'yŏngyang, and Moscow; 2) the reactions of China and the Soviet Union to the North Korean attack; and 3) the effect of the Korean Civil War on the Sino–Soviet relationship.

The Democratic People's Republic of Korea (DPRK)

The DPRK declared itself an independent state on September 9, 1948, with Kim Il-sŏng as Premier. Soon thereafter, the southern regime of Syngman Rhee carried out a stringent purge of the South Korean Communist Party; many of the party's leaders, foremost among them Pak Hŏn-yŏng, fled to the north. This was followed by the fusion of the North and South Korean Communist Parties into the Korean Workers' Party on June 24, 1949 (one year plus one day before the beginning of the war, Korean time). Because of his de facto control of the north, Kim Il-sŏng remained as Premier; according to one scholar, the merger "appeared more like an incorporation of the Workers' party of the South into the Workers' Party of the North than a unification of the two."[7] Pak, however, still enjoyed widespread support among the newly unified KWP. His arrival in the north undoubtedly spurred North Korean irredentist feelings toward the south. Both as a symbol of the repression in the south and as a respected spokesman voicing the view that the Rhee government could be easily overthrown, Pak encouraged a drive south.

On June 25, 1949 (one year to the day before the war's initiation), Pak helped organize the Democratic Front for the Unification of the Fatherland (DFUF), which carried out guerrilla activities in the south. Concurrently, he was also the supervisor of the Kang-Dong Political Institute, on the outskirts of P'yŏngyang, which trained the guerillas sent to the south. From

these two positions, he monitored and encouraged revolution-
ary actions in the south. Accordingly, his influence in the north
rose and fell largely according to how well the anti–Syngman
Rhee movement was doing in the south. (In a loose analogy,
Pak's position is reminiscent of Le Duan's situation in North
Vietnam between 1954 and 1964.) Pak was also concurrently the
Vice-Chairman of the KWP, a Vice-Premier of the DPRK, and its
Foreign Minister.

Both the DPRK's ambassador to Peking, Yi Chu-yŏn, and
the ambassador to Moscow, Chu Nyŏng-ha, had been comrades
of Pak Hŏn-yŏng. Through them Pak was both quickly aware of
thinking in those two capitals of the DPRK's allies and was also
able, perhaps, to speak to those allies on his own authority. Pak
accompanied Kim to the Moscow conference between Russian
and Korean leaders in March, 1949, and took part in the meetings
with Stalin. In short, although Pak Hŏn-Yŏng occupied positions in the DPRK below Kim Il-sŏng, his very important posts
and connections ensured his continued prestige and potential as
a rival to Kim.

In July, 1949, the DFUF called for nationwide elections for
September 15, 1949, but this demand was simply dropped on
that date.[8] That this attempt at a September reunification
aborted was probably due to the south's largely successful policy
of obstructing the DFUF's guerillas. This failure of the DFUF was
undoubtedly a setback for Pak within the factional maze of
P'yŏngyang.

Another possible explanation is that the DPRK was prohibited by its allies from attempting a drive south in September,
1949. U.S. Senator H. Alexander Smith later recounted that during a fall, 1949, inspection trip to South Korea he had been told
that:

the north Koreans had endeavoured to enlist the aid of the
Chinese Communists in order to take over and conquer the
South Koreans, but the Chinese Communists turned them

down on the grounds that they had too many responsibilities in other parts of China. . . . They also tried to get
the Russians to intervene directly in taking over South
Korea but the Russian reply was that they did not wish to
initiate World War Three by creating an incident in a minor
area like Korea."[9]

On June 7, 1950, the DFUF abruptly released an appeal for
reunification combined with a proposal for nationwide elections
to be held on August 5–8. A national conference would be held in
either Haeju or Kaesŏng on June 15–17 to discuss the mechanics
of carrying out the election. The all-Korean legislature resulting
from these elections would then meet in Seoul on August 15, the
fifth anniversary of liberation from Japanese rule. This appeal,
however, was issued not by the government of the DPRK but
rather by the DFUF, indicating, perhaps, that this plan was
under the immediate direction of Pak Hŏn-yŏng. That the Russians were aware of the importance of the August 15 date is
suggested by an *Izvestiya* article of June 10, 1950, which declared
that "on the fifth anniversary of the liberation of Korea, the
people of South and North Korea can and should mark this day
by celebrating it in the folds of one united, democratic state."[10]

On June 19, 1950, P'yŏngyang made another proposal, this
one originating from the Supreme People's Assembly of the
DPRK government. Directed toward the South Korean National
Assembly, it suggested the merging of the South and North
Korean parliaments into one all-Korean legislative body, the
reorganization of the Korean military bodies into one unit, and
an agreement that the Korean United Nations Commission leave
South Korea. These three measures were to be completed by
August 15.

Why would the anti–Syngman Rhee program now be transferred from the DFUF to the Supreme People's Assembly? There
are at least two, partially contradictory, hypotheses. Both
hypotheses emphasize the domestic determinants of the Korean
Civil War. Although there was certainly some congruence of

plans made in Moscow and P'yŏngyang, the final stamp on the war nonetheless reads "made in Korea."

The first conjecture is that the Kapsan faction, either with or without Soviet approval, launched the invasion under the charter authorized by the Supreme People's Assembly, the Kim Il-sŏng group thus outmaneuvering Pak Hŏn-yŏng by weakening the DFUF's claim to the authorship of the liberation of South Korea. What we know of Kim's personal predilections would seem to support this idea:

> Those of the Kapsan faction, directly under Kim Il-sŏng, were principally guerilla fighters and underground organizers. The members of all these groups were essentially revolutionaries accustomed to small group activities and to destructive operations rather than to orderly, structured functioning. Those from the Soviet Union, on the other hand, were born and raised in a relatively stable and highly bureaucratic environment where affairs of the Party were routinized. In short, the men from the Soviet Union already belonged to the second generation.[11]

On the other hand, of course, this description of the Kapsan faction also largely fits Pak's Domestic faction, since it had also operated as a guerrila and clandestine organization during the long, harsh Japanese occupation. In contrast, the above description would argue, the Soviet faction would both be cautious about the actual beginnings of the Korean Civil War and would most likely be opposed by both Kim and Pak's factions as not being truly representative of revolutionary Korean interests. Indeed, by June, 1950, the Soviet–Korean faction was beginning to be displaced by Kim and Pak's men within the KWP:

> Although the Soviet–Koreans held key posts, by the start of the war they were no longer proportionately a very large number in a party numbering 750,000, or an army of 198,380 men. This meant that their position was vulnerable if opposition on the part of other party members could

be galvanized against them. *This is in fact what happened during the Korean War.* [12]

The launching of the war as a *nationalist* crusade (rather than merely as a product of Soviet foreign policy) would thus benefit both Kim and Pak's factions. The first hypothesis, then, concludes that Kim launched the invasion in order to preempt his major rival, Pak, who was calling for an early invasion of the south. Kim Il-sŏng's credentials to legitimacy rested upon his nationalist claims, his "guerilla-hero" status. When he had returned to Korea in 1945, his first public speeches had been not about communism but rather about the nationalist aspirations held by all Koreans, for the reunification of an independent Korea. In 1950, this young (aged 38) leader, in a nation where age is thought to be correlated with respect and wisdom, needed to present himself as out-nationalizing any political rival, particularly Pak Hŏn-yŏng, who held most impressive nationalist credentials and was urging the early reunification of the Fatherland.

Kim's pre–June 25 actions toward the weakened South Korean Communist Party would seem to validate the idea that he might have planned to use the invasion to undermine Pak's position in the south. Since Pak's main strength remained in the south, Kim Il-sŏng, a few weeks before the invasion, sent Kapsan-faction personnel south to take control of the remaining apparatus of the South Korean Communist Party. It was Kapsan men who were now to run the southern party; Kim, aware of Pak's residual strength in the south, which might coalesce to form an active opposition, acted to control it before Pak could reactivate his followers after June 25. [13]

The second hypothesis relating to the switching of the North Korean program toward the south from the DFUF to the Supreme People's Assembly in mid-June suggests that it was Pak himself who triggered the invasion with Kim's reluctant consent, which the last-minute approval by the Supreme

People's Assembly might indicate. Because Pak's nationalist credentials within the KWP were stronger than Kim Il-sŏng's—and because Kim himself was a fervent believer in the desirability of an early Korean reunification—this view postulates that Pak outflanked Kim by questioning his independence from his Russian supporters. "What kind of leader is this," Pak may have asked the KWP, "who waits upon the word of his Masters before giving the signal for the quick and inevitable overthrow of the corrupt Syngman Rhee regime?"

Pak was in a pivotal position to influence the tactical judgment to initiate hostilities by virtue of his near-monopoly of information on conditions in the south. Information on favorable dates for an invasion and the likelihood for the success of an attack was funneled to the KWP by virtue of Pak's position both as head of the guerrilla training school which sent agents south and then collected military/political data from them, and concurrently as de facto head of the remaining communist apparatus in the south. That Pak utilized these positions to press for an early invasion date is indicated by the charges which were publicly brought against him on the day after the signing of the armistice in July, 1953. Item no. 5 of the indictment stated: "In the June 25 war, he indulged in circulating a false report that in South Korea the South Korean Labor Party had an underground organization of 500,000 members, who were ready to take action in concert with the north." North Korean agents who went south, it was charged, returned with reports that these 500,000 were most eager for the war's beginning. "This was a major reason why the Kapsan faction decided to attack South Korea."[14]

One knowledgeable observer of what happened during this period summarized conditions within the KWP in June, 1950 as follows:

Pak thought that the party members he had left in South Korea would be saved only by a war, and that if all Korea were unified, he would be sure to win much more support

than Kim Il-sŏng in view of his popularity with the people.
Since his entry into the north, he had been asking Kim
Il-sŏng to invade the south. As a condition for an absolute
victory, he emphasized that the 500,000 South Korean
Labor Party members were standing by to fight, and as
evidence he presented reports from the agents trained at
Kumgang School [Kang-Dong Political Institute]. He
preached that the south should be invaded as soon as
possible . . . and thought that the time had ripened for the
invasion of the south. He calculated that the whole of Korea
would be completely liberated in two months or even that
the day of liberation would be August 15. In regard to Pak
Hŏn-yŏng and the South Korean Labor Party, he thought
that he would be victorious over them even after reunification so long as he controlled the Party's main-current faction and the People's Army. [15]

Kim Il-sŏng and Pak Hŏn-yŏng (as well as Syngman Rhee)
shared a moral imperative to reunify the nation. It appears likely,
however, that some of the tactics of the civil war, and particularly
the timing of it, were dictated in part by the Kim–Pak rivalry.

The leaders of the DPRK (and of the Republic of Korea)
remembered their history: intruding powers on the peninsula
could not be completely trusted. Although there were factional
divisions within the leadership, all of the groups agreed on the
desire for an early Korean reunification. The Russians, who had
operated an unpopular occupation policy, did not control this
irredentist urge. In sum, an understanding of the war must take
into consideration both the "images" which all of the participants held of the significance of the peninsula, and the domestic
factional infighting which led to the war.

The Republic of Korea (ROK)

In September, 1947, the United States Joint Chiefs
of Staff, reacting to the dispersal of American troops around the

world, recommended the withdrawal of American forces from South Korea, and added that Korea was not essential for the security of the United States.[16] General MacArthur, in a March, 1949, newspaper interview, traced an American line of defense which left out both Taiwan and Korea, on the assumption that in an all-out war (the expected type) they would be strategic liabilities.[17] In his famous speech of January 12, 1950, which was a summary of accepted Washington wisdom on the topic, Secretary of State Dean Acheson also left Taiwan and South Korea out of the American vital defense perimeter—although, as noted before, Acheson's celebrated speech was more ambiguous in its strategic implications than his later critics would allow. In late April, 1950, Senator Tom Connally, the Chairman of the Senate Foreign Relations Committee, reiterated the American public position: "Korea is not an essential part of America's defense strategy, and Russia could overrun it whenever it takes a notion."[18]

However, the speeches, as messages in and of themselves to the North Koreans and their allies were superfluous pronouncements. The repeated cuts in U.S. troop deployments and defense budgets were sufficient signals. Of particular significance to the Korean peninsula was the fact that the American military occupation force in Japan was both understrength and "soft."

There seemed to be little doubt that the peninsula was ripe for irredentist impulses from both sides. After the cancellation of the DFUF-sponsored elections of 1949, Kim Il-sŏng wrote to United Nations Secretary-General Trygvie Lie an assurance of his determination to continue his labors:

> The Korean people will not abandon the struggle and will reserve for itself the right to continue by any maneuvers at its disposal the struggle . . . for the final unification of the country by its own forces into a unified democratic state.[19]

There were constant and sizeable armed clashes and border incursions between the north and the south for over a year before the final crisis. A U.S. State Department official in April, 1950, stated that "the boundary at the 38th parallel . . . is a real front line. There is constant fighting. . . . There are very real battles, involving perhaps one or two thousand men."[20] Koreans were accustomed to the fighting; each side believed that an early reunification was worth a war. The south was as intense in this yearning as the north.

Syngman Rhee, even as he apparently planned to mount an invasion of the north, consolidated his control of the south, his regime becoming increasingly autocratic. The judiciary, for example, was an "instrument of executive predominance, not the defender of rights or instrument of balance of forces. . . . [It] became even more active than under colonial rule."[21] In 1946 the north had redistributed 2.3 million acres of land to 600,000 households; over 50% of North Korea's land and 70% of its farm families were affected. The P'yŏngyang government profited in popularity. Seoul, however, did not carry out land reform until 1950; its regime was less popular and there were sporadic revolts.

Between September 4, 1948, and April 30, 1949, over 80,710 people were arrested in the south. During this same period, more than one-third of the officers of the South Korean army were discharged as procommunists. By October of 1949, 7 percent of the South Korean National Assembly had been jailed by Syngman Rhee's police.[22]

At the end of October, 1949, the South Korean Defense Minister was quoted as saying: "If we had our own way we would, I'm sure, have started up already. But we had to wait until they [the Americans] are ready. They keep telling us, 'No, no, no, wait. You are not ready.'"[23] Washington, aware that Rhee might attempt to begin a war and then entangle the United States in it, was leery of granting arms. William Sebald, State Department representative in Japan during this time, later wrote of Rhee's belligerency: "It was feared that, properly armed for offense, Rhee promptly would punch northward across the 38th parallel."[24] While it has frequently been remarked in military histories of the war that the North Korean army possessed greater firepower than the south, and that some blame should therefore be attached to the United States for failing to protect its client state, the official history of the American advisor force in Korea presents a supplementary view of why heavy tanks and more powerful artillery were not supplied to Seoul. Rather than an apprehension about Rhee's northern intentions, "it is much more likely that terrain factors and dollar limitations were actually responsible for the United States' failure to supply this type of equipment."[25]

Although Washington was not parsimonious in its financial support of Seoul, it was wary of granting arms. The Syngman Rhee regime received $495.7 million in military and economic aid between the end of World War II and the beginning of the Korean War: $53.7 million was economic assistance, while the rest was military.[26] Moreover, the American army maintained a 482-man military assistance mission in South Korea. Under the guidance of this permanent American military advisor mission, Syngman Rhee in 1949–50 was in the process of rapidly expanding his military forces. At the end of 1948 the South Korean army had consisted of 60,000 men, when the war began it had grown to approximately 100,000.[27] The American advisors were attached to thirteen military training schools.

Rhee's air force also began to increase. The Korean Military Advisory Group's (KMAG) semiannual report of December 31, 1949, requested forty F-51 fighter aircraft, ten T-6 trainers, two C-47 cargo planes, and $225,000 for supporting equipment.[28] It is, of course, true that Rhee's air force was not a solid weapon as of June 25, 1950. It appears, however, that in not very much time it would have become a potent force. During the first months of 1950, for example, the air force rapidly expanded from a few hundred men to 1,865 officers and men.[29] Before the war began, Rhee reportedly was seeking a ninety-nine plane air force.[30]

In April of 1950 Rhee decided to create twenty-one combat police battalions with 1,200 men in each. Meanwhile, the U.S. Congress had on March 15, 1950, voted a grant of $10,970,000 in additional aid for Seoul. Consequently, although by June 25 neither Rhee's air force nor his police battalions had been operationalized, it seemed only a matter of time before they would be. After the war began, United States Army Brigadier General William L. Roberts, head of the American advisor mission, was quoted as saying: "The only real flaw in KMAG's plan [in preparing the South Korean military] was that time ran out."[31] Considering the rapid growth of the South Korean military, this view is understandable. In fact, less than three weeks before the war began, General Roberts assured Seoul that "the passage of military aid to the Republic of Korea looks slow because it was extended by appropriations of many committees in the U.S. However, the earnest [sic] aid will be extended from July."[32]

As it was, the North Korean army actually invaded the south with a numerically smaller force than the one Seoul commanded. The south controlled a 95,000-man army and a national police force of 48,000 that was essentially an arm of the military. P'yŏngyang, on the other hand, invaded with an army of 103,800 infantry and 18,600 police.[33] Probably a contributory factor in P'yŏngyang's decision to invade was a desire to disarm Rhee's military machine before—as seemed likely to happen in the near future—it became too powerful to contend with. Two scholars, noting that the North Korean army had not been fully mobilized by June 25, and that the South Korean elections held three weeks before had returned an anti–Syngman Rhee National Assembly, suggest the possibility that Kim Il-sŏng meant only to take Seoul and then "open negotiations with the new assembly on favorable terms."[34] In short, the North Korean victory was caused not by the size of its invading force, but rather by a combination of superior fire power (tanks, artillery, and planes), the element of surprise, and a greater morale.

Events in South Korea seemed to augur increasingly well for a successful invasion from the north. The black market in Seoul in January, 1950, listed the *won* at 4,200 to one U.S. dollar;

the official rate was 600 *won*.[35] The price of rice in the south jumped 30 percent in the first three weeks of June, 1950.[36] The elections of May 30, 1950, to the South Korean National Assembly (postponed by the unpopular government and conducted only under pressure from Washington) resulted in a massive display of discontent with the Syngman Rhee regime: out of 210 seats in the National Assembly, only 47 were now held by Rhee supporters. Guerillas were active, and South Korean dislike for American G.I.'s was very much in evidence.[37]

It was this combination of anti–Syngman Rhee sentiment and widespread desire for reunification that led one responsible observer to declare that:

> Considering the relative strength and combat readiness of the forces that faced each other across the thirty-eighth parallel in June 1950, it was a miracle that the North Korean armies were delayed at all in their desire to overrun all of South Korea. . . . it was as if a few troops of Boy Scouts with hand weapons had undertaken to stop a panzer unit.[38]

Seoul apparently held similar expectations with regard to a quick triumph over its enemy. It was also anxious to engage in hostilities, and felt restrained only by the Americans' limited grant of armaments. In March, 1950, Syngman Rhee promised an early armed reunification: "even though some of our friends across the sea tell us that we must not cherish thoughts of attacking the foreign puppet who stifles the liberties of our people in the North. . . . We shall respond to the cries of our brothers in distress."[39]

In a private letter dated June 14, 1950, to his chief adviser, Dr. Oliver, President Rhee said:

> I am going to say a few words about the Korean situation. I think now is the best time for us to take on the offensive to mop up the guerrillas in P'yŏngyang. We will drive Kim Il-sŏng and his bandit to remote mountains and make them

starve there in order to make the Tumen and Yalu rivers our defense line. . . . Our people are desiring for an action against the north. And Koreans in the north are also fervently looking forward to our action. . . ."[40]

A South Korean scholar comments that "a look at President Syngman Rhee's letter indicates that he had a foray into the north in mind, while his top Army commander was fully prepared to translate his design into action."[41]

For its part, P'yŏngyang, listening to Seoul's provocative rhetoric and observing the burgeoning capabilities of the ROK's military, must have been concerned about Rhee's martial plans. Professor Robert Jervis has described a phenomenon of perception relevant to the manner in which a regime such as P'yŏngyang's would probably assess the situation:

> The evidence from both psychology and history overwhelmingly supports the view (which may be labeled hypothesis 1) that decision-makers tend to fit incoming information into their existing theories and images. Indeed, their theories and images play a large part in determining what they notice.[42]

From P'yŏngyang's perspective, then, its invasion *may have been* launched as a preemptive strike in the expectation of an early South Korean attack.

Prelude to June 25

Although it is certain that the Soviet Union armed the North Korean army, there is evidence that the North Koreans were not as well armed in June as they would be in late July. In fact, until the end of 1949 the North Korean army had been, to quote an official U.S. military history of the war, a "defensive-type army." This military history further stated that it was only when Seoul's army began to bulge, and Rhee loudly announced his intentions of marching north in the not-too-distant future, that P'yŏngyang began receiving large amounts of weapons from the Soviet Union.[43] Indeed, the North Korean army had not reached its war mobilization level in June:

> The North Korean Army had not carried out its mobilization plan at the time the war began on June 25, but now, despite heavy losses, has raised its strength to about 200,000 men, a spokesman for the American intelligence staff (in Tokyo) said today. He asserted that only six full divisions had been ready for combat when the invasion started, although the North Korean war plans called for thirteen to fifteen.[44]

Of course, an alternative interpretation might argue that mobilization might have tipped the north's hand, thus losing the element of surprise. Moreover, mobilization may have been thought unnecessary, given the perceived vulnerability of the south. As indicated below, I consider these suggestions less persuasive than the interpretation which sees the north as having speeded up its invasion date. There are also strong indications that the Russians themselves were not prepared to work with their ally in the field in July of 1950:

> Over a period of four weeks, systematic investigation into what went on in Seoul and the conquered areas during the Communist occupation has not revealed more than a handful of lesser Russian military officials or any political agents seen by South Koreans. . . . this, coupled with the reportedly confused and disorganized interim in Seoul while the Communists held power, is taken as indicating either that *the Russians had not as much control over the Korean Communists as supposed* or had not intended to move in until the military conquest of South Korea was complete."[45]

Since the conquest was expected to take a matter of days, however, the Russian advisers reasonably would have been present with their organizational plans and advice. Their absence suggests that they were surprised by the early date of the invasion.

On the day of the invasion, Lee Sang-jo, Chief of North Korean Military Intelligence, was in Moscow.[46] It would seem unlikely that a Soviet-planned attack with a definite June 25 date would take place while this vital official was outside of the peninsula; he would presumably have been stationed in North Korea, monitoring data on the rapidly changing situation.

There were 100,000 North Korean troops in the ranks of the Chinese People's Liberation Army (PLA) in 1949. Only 12,000 of them had been returned to North Korea before June 25.[47] It is reasonable to assume that the bulk of these battle-hardened 100,000 would have been returned to North Korea before the invasion as a core of the invasion force, if the invasion had taken place as scheduled on a previously planned date.

A "harder" indication that June 25 was not the prearranged date is the fact that in late April, 1950, at a conference of the communist Korean League in Japan, a North Korean invasion was spoken of in these terms: "To facilitate the achievement of this objective, we will engage in guerrilla activities directed at the destruction of imperialistic industry. Our operations are scheduled, until further notice, for August."[48] At least as late as the end of April, then, Koreans in Japan anticipated an August invasion. All of these factors indicate that the decision for war was made rather suddenly by the P'yŏngyang leadership.

We dealt earlier with the pressures bearing on Kim Il-sŏng to initiate an invasion of South Korea as early as possible. It seems that the initiative for the war lay with Kim, rather than with Stalin. Nikita Khrushchev, for one, allegedly later declared: "I must stress that the war wasn't Stalin's idea, but Kim Il-sŏng's. Kim was the initiator."[49]

Part of the basis for the general belief that Stalin could closely monitor the thoughts and actions of Kim Il-sŏng, and would thus be aware of all of the developing plans for the beginning of the war, is the fact that a key influential adviser to Kim was a Soviet Major General, Rebezev, who "followed Kim Il-sŏng like a shadow, living, eating, and sleeping in the same house."[50] Rebezev, however, was posted to Kim Il-sŏng's staff *after* the war began; he was undoubtedly *then* a factor in North Korea's diminished political autonomy.

There is also the possibility that the Russian proconsul in North Korea, operating under what he considered to be general orders from Moscow (a "blank check"), collaborated with Kim's timing for the invasion, while keeping Moscow only loosely informed. The war, after all, was expected to be brief and successful. A former Lieutenant Colonel in the Russian internal police later wrote that it was Colonel General and Ambassador to P'yongyang, Terenty F. Shtykov who sold Stalin on the idea of the war. Shtykov therefore held a proprietary interest in the strategy of the invasion; since there were few Soviet advisers in North Korea, he probably held a free rein in his communications with Moscow. In 1951 Shtykov was deprived of rank and sent to a Russian province in disgrace for low-level work.[51]

Interestingly, the Americans had a potentially analagous situation with respect to General MacArthur. *If* the United States had given Rhee a "blank check" for the invasion of the north, *if* Rhee's victory had seemed assured, and *if* communications between the White House and MacArthur had been lax, one wonders whether the General would have insisted that Rhee wait for an invasion date six weeks hence when all conditions on the peninsula itself said "go." (In fact, while the analogy must necessarily be loose, General MacArthur did have a somewhat similar experience of operating on his own authority, without Washington's knowledge, in drafting and proclaiming the Japanese constitution in 1946.)[52]

A Hypothesis

Would it have been physically possible for P'yŏngyang to have begun the attack earlier than the Soviet Union expected? The usual assumptions regarding Soviet control of North Korea and its influence on the beginnings of the Korean Civil War would deny this possibility. As suggested above, however, what is known about the factional infighting within the North Korean regime casts doubt upon these assumptions. Moreover, weapons for the invasion were still coming through the Soviet "pipeline" in June, which would indicate an invasion plan for sometime later than June 25, when all of the military preparations would have been completed. The absence of Soviet military advisers with the North Korean army also indicates Soviet unpreparedness. (A less likely explanation would be the Russian hesitation to become involved. Given the Russian mistrust of the North Koreans and Moscow's behavior in similar crises, however, it would seem more likely that the Soviet Union would have been quite anxious to supervise directly the actions of its client state.)

"But," an objection to this hypothesis might be voiced, "surely the Russian advisers attached to the North Korean army prior to June 25 would have prevented an unauthorized attack." The surprising rejoinder is that as of the June 25 invasion date there were very few Russian advisers present to counsel against an independent North Korean decision. In 1948 there were 150 Soviet advisers in each North Korean army division (approximately one per company); in 1949 this number was reduced to 20 per division; by the spring of 1950 there were only between 3 and 8 per division.[53] An alleged Russian defector who served in North Korea shortly before the Korean Civil War began later stated that the Soviet Union's military adviser group numbered only 40 before June 25.[54] With such a small group of Russians posted to the North Korean army, it is entirely possible that events could have taken place without Moscow's foreknowledge. Not only the Russians but much of the North Korean leadership itself were apparently prevented from learning intimate details of the invasion:

Top secret work plans of the Standing Committee of the Labor Party headquarters dated January–June 1950 make

> absolutely no reference to the forthcoming invasion, although covering in some detail all other aspects of government policy. Second, a number of fairly highly placed North Korean officers that were interviewed, including the Chiefs of Staff of two divisions, stated that they had only the barest presentiment of the coming of hostilities, and that they were given no concrete indication of their onset until approximately one week before the invasion took place. [55]

This would suggest, again, that the initiation of hostilities came as a rather precipitous move on the part of the inner core of the P'yŏngyang government.

So far, three elements are evident in the puzzling story of the origins of the war: 1) the underlying assumption in almost all Western accounts is that the war was caused by external machinations, within which the role of the North Koreans themselves was minimal; 2) despite the American occupation of P'yŏngyang in the fall of 1950 and the interrogation of high-ranking North Korean and Chinese prisoners throughout the war, we have no "hard" data to back up this assumption; and 3) there are a number of circumstances from which one can tenably argue that it was the North Korean government which chose the actual June 25 invasion date. [56]

Does it in fact make any significant difference whether or not the Korean Civil War was expected by the Russians to begin on June 25? Perhaps the best way to answer this question is to propose an alternative expected date: given the information available, that date would have been about August 7. It will be remembered that the June, 1950, election proposals put forward by P'yŏngyang, and endorsed by Moscow, called for those elections to have been completed by August 8, with the resultant all-Korean legislature to meet in Seoul on August 15, the fifth anniversary of Korea's liberation from Japanese rule. [57]

Russian and American foreign policy had at least one characteristic in common: a compulsion for legitimacy. Stalin, regardless of his tactical moves on the international chess board, was intensely interested in garbing his actions in an aura of legitimate behavior. Following this pattern, it would have suited Stalin's style to have called for an election which he knew would be forbidden by the Syngman Rhee regime in South Korea. Then, at the very moment when these "rightful" elections had been scheduled to have taken place, the people in the south, in righteous indignation and anger at this refusal of the their basic right to peaceful all-Korean elections, would rise up against the dictator. At this point, such a scenario would run, their North Korean compatriots would feel compelled to aid their brothers in the south to gain victory over the hated dictator and reunion with the north. The people of the world would, of course, recognize reunion as a popular and inevitable development; the corrupt Rhee regime would, in effect, have condemned itself by refusing to listen to the will of the people in elections and reunification would follow as a natural result, with a little help from the north.

As we have seen (see p. 86), one section of Secretary of State Acheson's January 12 speech foresaw an American appeal to the United Nations in such a crisis as the Korean Civil War. Consequently, the Soviet Union could have anticipated that an American response to the beginning of the war, at least for the purpose of legitimizing any U.S. actions in aiding South Korea—and such actions were expected to be mostly propagandistic—would have involved the United Nations.

In previous crises of the Cold War, regardless of the West's ordering of priorities or perception of provocation, the Soviet Union had not hesitated to engage in vitriolic debate in the United Nations (e.g., the Northern Iran and Greek Crises of 1946–47).

Why should they absent themselves now that an established satellite was being attacked with the approval of the United Nations?

In fact, the Soviet Union issued no public pronouncements, not even *pro forma* declarations in support of its ally, for thirty-six hours after the beginning of the war. Moreover, the first full official statement of Russian attitudes was not released until July 4.[58] There were no mass meetings in support of North Korea, even though the Soviet Union was at this time in the midst of a major "world peace campaign" which would have lent itself ideally to such demonstrations, until July 3. Moscow Radio's domestic service commented on July 2 that "the most important event which has had great influence on the international situation during the last week is the collection of signatures for the Stockholm Peace Appeal which has been started in the Soviet Union." The Soviet Union's public reaction may well have been testimony to its surprise at the timing of the invasion.

If the fiction of the action being a *South* Korean invasion were to be created and maintained, the Soviet government should logically have addressed notes of protest to the U.S. and the U.N. immediately after the beginning of the war. But no such messages were delivered; instead, in its June 29 reply to an American note of June 27 the Soviet Union disavowed any responsibility, merely indicating instead that its information was that it was South Korea who had been the aggressor. This mild Soviet note could just as easily have been issued on June 25. Subsequently, the Soviet government elaborated its response to the fluid situation on the Korean battlefield only after some delay. Until July 3, the news from Korea was tucked in the back pages of the Soviet press. Nothing suggested to the Soviet reader that a major world crisis had just erupted.[59]

In looking for an analogous situation, one notes that during the 1948 Berlin Blockade, Soviet response to each American action was very rapid.[60] While a detailed knowledge of the P'yŏngyang–Peking–Moscow relationship in the summer of 1950 remains unobtainable, a review of the available evidence suggests that the reason that the Soviet Union was absent from the United Nations during the early stages of the Korean Civil War was its surprise at the actual event of June 25.

By regular rotation, the Soviet Union was scheduled to have its delegate assume the president's seat in the United Nations Security Council in August. It had been boycotting that body since January, 1950, ostensibly in protest against the Council's failure to seat the PRC (see chapter 4); but on August 1 it resumed its seat on the Council. As president for the month, it was able to prevent any U.N. business concerning Korea from being accomplished.

The inference which may be drawn from these circumstances is that the Soviet Union—if it had had control over the beginning of the Korean Civil War—would have "scheduled" it for a date after it was to assume the Council presidency and after South Korea had, as expected, prohibited the all-Korea elections that had been proposed for August 5–8.

China, Taiwan, and the United Nations

The hypothesis of an approximate August 7 invasion date would also easily accommodate itself to another vexing problem raised by the actual June 25 date: why did the Korean Civil War (a provocative incident in the Cold War context) begin before the taking of Taiwan by the PRC (a nonprovocative event, as Washington had previously stated that it would not assist the KMT in actively defending the island)? The Chinese must have been surprised and displeased by the June 25 date, which effectively prevented the liberation of Taiwan.

Peking had apparently completed its invasion preparations before the beginning of the war. Reference to the U.S. State Department's "top secret" memorandum of December 23, 1949 (leaked in early January) stating that the "fall of Taiwan is widely anticipated" has already been noted. Further warnings of Taiwan's fall continued; Western military attachés and diplomatic representatives on Taiwan in May, 1950, expected it to fall "by July 15, 1950."[61] U.S. Secretary of Defense Louis Johnson later testified that between June 10 and June 24 "the troops opposite Formosa had been increased from more than 40,000 to about 156,000.[62] In a dispatch from Taiwan, the Associated Press reported at the end of April that the PRC's invasion, "it is generally believed here, will be delivered in July."[63] At the end of May, the United States Consulate-General in Taiwan "strongly advised" all Americans to leave Taiwan as soon as possible, predicting a "communist invasion within the next three months. The attacking force will be the Third Field Army, whose commander is Ch'en Yi. Last week's ignominious Nationalist collapse on Hainan has led even the most optimistic observers here to suspect that Formosa cannot long stand up under attack once the Communists are ready."[64]

One high official described June 15 as "the deadline by which the buildup and invasion were to be completed. Reports here indicate the preparations have been completed, and that another 'pushbutton decision' between now and the start of the typhoon season in August could launch the invasion attempt."[65] Secretary of State Acheson, at an Executive Session of the U.S. Senate Foreign Relations Committee on March 29, 1950, stated that the early fall of Taiwan was "probably . . . inevitable. . . . Under the present circumstances, the Communists would be criminally crazy if they did not put an end to it [the KMT regime] just as soon as possible."[66]

As suggested in chapter 4, the PRC likely did not take "at face value President Truman's disclaimer"[67] of interference with its plans in relation to the taking of Taiwan. The Americans were still sending military and economic aid to Taiwan and forging a surrogate league against the PRC made up of Taiwan, Japan, South Korea, Indochina, and the Philippines, and had made their assurances to the PRC sufficiently vague as to be less than reassuring. Moreover, there was a vocal and influential conservative minority in Washington that was pressing for more active opposition to the PRC and additional support for the KMT. In such a situation, the PRC must have understood that its best chance to acquire Taiwan without American resistance lay in a relatively quiescent military situation in the Far East. If, as seems likely from the available contemporary indications, the PRC did expect to take Taiwan by the middle of July, then the logic of the June 25 North Korean invasion becomes even more questionable. It was certainly in the PRC's interest to have the Korean Civil War begin in August, after it had successfully completed its own civil war, rather than in June, when there would be the likelihood of American reaction—not in Korea itself, but in Indochina and Taiwan, where America had already demonstrated its qualified interest in maintaining an active anticommunist stance.

There is an additional reason why the PRC would have been vitally interested in an August invasion date by the North Koreans. Peking, as seen earlier, was extremely interested in joining the United Nations. After her exclusion on account of the Russians' clumsy/clever actions of early January, China continued her quest of a U.N. seat. It was reliably reported in March that the PRC had put considerable pressure on the United Kingdom, as part of the conditions for better PRC–U.K. relations, to actively support Peking's claims to a U.N. seat. [68] In April, a leading American strategist and then adviser to the State Department, John Foster Dulles, published a widely noted book in which he declared that there was no real barrier to China's admittance to the United Nations. [69] In late May, Egypt, one of the states which had voted against the PRC's admission to the U.N. in January, let it be known that it was considering recognition of China. [70] Even more importantly, the "swing" French vote seemed to be oscillating.

China's chances for admission to the United Nations improved as the spring of 1950 turned into summer. In late May, in Paris diplomats were predicting that France would not stand in China's way. [71] At the United Nations itself, in early June, the French chief delegate to the U.N., Jean Chauvel, hinted in a radio broadcast that France "might vote to oust the Chinese Nationalists from the Security Council." [72] What gave these various reports, and others like them, particular substance was the fact that if the U.N. were to move on the China question it had to do so soon. Secretary-General Trygvie Lie reminded the members of the need for quick action: "He pointed out that U.N. rules will call for Security Council action on certain issues by sixty days before the General Assembly meets. The Assembly meets on September 19 and that would make the deadline July 19."[73]

By mid-June, then, the PRC was acutely aware of two facts: 1) its invasion of Taiwan, in order to be definitely unopposed by the United States, must take place before the Americans were provoked into a more activist anticommunist stance; and 2) the elimination of the Taiwan regime as an alternative Chinese government would probably assure Peking's entrance into the U.N. by Lie's July 19 "deadline." As a corollary to this second point, the fall of Taiwan by mid-July, before the Korean Civil War's hypothetically slated beginnings, would be accepted by the United States as a *fait accompli*. Put another way, an invasion of Taiwan *after* the Korean War began could have been expected by the Chinese *at that time* (pre-June 25) to have drawn some form of military repercussions from the United States somewhere. The Chinese, eager to begin their invasion of Taiwan without American obstruction, must have expected that the Korean Civil War would begin *after* their attack on Taiwan.

One supposition that may have occurred to Peking at the time was that Moscow might have encouraged the war's early beginning in order to continue to freeze China out of the United Nations and perpetuate its dependence upon the Soviet Union. In this scenario, why wouldn't Soviet policy makers calculate that China's exclusion from the U.N. would be less important than confronting Western propaganda on the war? Moreover, if the summer months of 1950 seemed most propitious for a Chinese invasion of Taiwan (a topic explored further below), why not provoke a confrontation in the Far East that would, perhaps, blunt China's efforts? Regardless of the Soviet Union's actual role in the timing of the war, it is probable that its beginnings added further strain to the Moscow–Peking relationship.[74]

In sum, the hypothesis of an expected August 7 (approximately) beginning of the Korean Civil War would seem to answer satisfactorily a number of previously unresolved questions:

1) Why was the Soviet Union absent from the United Nations at the beginning of the Korean Civil War? 2) Why did both the Russians and the Chinese propaganda machines respond so sluggishly to the beginning of the war? 3) Why, according to available indications, were the North Koreans not completely prepared for the war on June 25? 4) Why did the PRC not attack Taiwan before the more incendiary Cold War event of the Korean Civil War? Finally, as shall be shown in chapter 7, this hypothesis also helps to explain why the Russians refused to help the North Koreans on a scale which the DPRK required, and why the Chinese were also slow in offering assistance.

A DPRK Note

In late July, 1950, a leading North Korean newspaper, published an article which, apparently using a "mirror image" interpretation, lends credence to this chapter's contention that P'yŏngyang "jumped the gun":

> A meeting of high American military officials in Tokyo discussed time and methods for conducting war in Korea and the question of legalizing the occupation of Taiwan. According to MacArthur's plan, the American troops were to have taken Formosa before the end of July. Thus the war in Korea had to start earlier, since this was to be the means for occupying Formosa. . . . There was no rice on the market and everywhere the populace was critical of the Syngman Rhee government. Dulles concluded that without rice and other goods it would be impossible to carry out any policy, and in the final analysis the U.S.A. would be blamed for the situation. Therefore, Dulles informed Syngman Rhee that the U.S.A. agreed to the beginning of the civil war."[75]

P'yŏngyang here acknowledged the expectation of Taiwan's expected change of status "before the end of July." The article notes the ripe conditions for a North Korean attack upon

South Korea, and then slyly declares that the Great Power would be blamed for the war anyway (so the timing is not too important). It concludes that the war is a *civil* war, to which the Great Power had given its assent. This may suggest that the North Koreans were reminding their Russian allies that since the war was "civil" it was up to them to decide the timing and nature of its beginning. The article accurately assesses the intertwining of the Taiwan and Korean questions within the context of the Cold War. However, the comment that "the war in Korea had to start earlier, since this was to be the means for occupying Formosa" makes no sense from either an American or a Chinese point of view, because the American signals on this very topic prior to June 25 had been directly opposite. Thus, in "mirror image" fashion, this may well have been an admission on the part of P'yŏngyang that its early start of the war foreclosed the PRC's taking of Taiwan. One further North Korean statement which could be interpreted as an admission of its responsibility for an early beginning of the war will be discussed in the next chapter.

Accepting the hypothesis of P'yongyang's beginning the Korean Civil War six weeks earlier than its two allies expected lends a particular perspective to the alliance: that of increased suspicions and tensions between the three states. This aspect will be explored throughout the remainder of this book, but at present it may be germane to ask if this type of situation has been unknown in our history books. The response, of course, is no. For example, the impression remains even today that the much weaker Austria was a "puppet" of the omniscient, manipulating German Kaiser. Actually, the Austrians were encouraged by the German "blank check" of July 5, 1914, and went farther and faster than their German allies expected or wanted. "The 'puppet' got out of hand. Like much of history, this series of events was largely a matter of sheer thoughtlessness and failure to communicate. Germany can be blamed not so much for malice or for dreams of world conquest as for ordinary carelessness. She should have tried sooner and harder to stop Austria."[76]

Even with a great deal of historical information at hand, however, intellectual inertia still operates to prolong the belief in a German-caused World War I. This indicates the tremendous staying power of a simplistic "devil theory" of crises, and should prompt a reexamination of unquestioned assumptions concerning the beginnings of the Korean Civil War. In addition, the World War I example demonstrates the very real possibility of a client state feeling encouraged by its stronger partner to undertake actions on its own, especially when it has a narrowly focused perception of the pressures and priorities which work upon it. Similarly to 1914 Austria, the North Korea of 1950 felt strongly impelled by its desire for reunification with the south and militarily bolstered by a "blank check" from the Soviet Union. That "blank check" was Moscow's approval of an imminent war; analogously to the 1914 situation, P'yŏngyang felt that a quickening of its strategy would not be greeted by disfavor by its Great Power ally.

Notes

1. Max Beloff, *Soviet Foreign Policy in the Far East, 1944–1951* (London: Oxford University Press, 1953), p. 183.
2. Alvin Rubenstein, *The Foreign Policy of the Soviet Union* (New York: Random House, 1960), p. 251.
3. John Gittings, "The Great Power Triangle and Chinese Foreign Policy," *The China Quarterly* (July–September, 1969), p. 48.
4. Among other things, the North Korean invasion was a "Soviet war plan" (David Rees, *Korea: The Limited War* [Baltimore: Penquin, 1964], p. 19), which Stalin "planned, prepared and initiated" (David Dallin, *Soviet Foreign Policy After Stalin* [Philadelphia: J. B. Lippincott, 1961], p. 60). An exception to this simplified version, with a great deal of valuable data which underlines the complexities of contemporary North Korean factional politics, is Robert A. Scalapino and Chong-sik Lee, *Communism in Korea: The Movement* (Berkeley and Los Angeles: University of California Press, 1972), especially pp. 382–452.
5. Harold Hinton believed that the North Koreans wanted to attack

South Korea but the Soviet Union originally vetoed the idea. The North Koreans then took their case to the Chinese, who thereupon convinced Stalin to allow the North Korean attack. *Communist China in World Politics* (Boston: Houghton Mifflin Co., 1966), p. 206. Prof. Hinton reversed this position in his next work, *China's Turbulent Quest* (New York: Macmillan, 1970), pp. 41–43.

　　Marshall Shulman saw an even more marked Chinese influence in the genesis of the war: "It seems probable that the Soviet Union was faced with a situation in which the Chinese were prepared to drive ahead with or without the Russians. This put the Russians in a painful dilemma: even if they preferred to be cautious they would lose whatever influence they hoped to exercise over the Chinese revolution and, specifically, they would lose their dominant position in North Korea." *Stalin's Foreign Policy Reappraised* (Cambridge: Harvard University Press, 1963), p. 141.

　　The evidence is against this latter formulation. Allen Whiting, for example, states that the PRC lacked responsibility for the war's initiation (*China Crosses the Yalu* [New York: Macmillan Co., 1960], p. 46). John Gittings notes that "whatever were the fundamental causes behind the Korean War (and *that* is still an open question) there is no evidence that it was instigated by the Chinese." Gittings, op. cit., p. 48; italics in original.

6. See Wilbur Hitchcock's article "North Korea Jumps the Gun" in *Current History* (March, 1951), pp. 136–44, which early on disputed this conventional belief: "Stalin may have loaded the gun, but it was Kim Il-sŏng who seized upon it and pulled the trigger."

7. Dae-sook Suh, "North Korea: Emergence of an Elite Group," in *Aspects of Modern Communism*, ed. Richard F. Starr (Columbia, S.C.: University of South Carolina Press, 1968), p. 326.

8. See Pak Hŏn-yŏng, "Heroic Struggle of the People of South Korea for the Unity and Independence of the Country," *For a Lasting Peace, For a People's Democracy (Bucharest), March 24, 1950, pp. 3–5*.

9. *Hearings on the Military Situation in the Far East* (MacArthur Hearings), 82d Congress. (Washington, D.C.: U.S. Government Printing Office, 1951), p. 3320.

10. *New York Times*, "North Korean Plan Bared Seventeen Days Ago," by W. H. Lawrence, June 27, 1950, p. 3.

11. Chong-sik Lee and Ki-wan Oh, "The Russian Faction in North Korea," *Asian Survey* (April, 1968), p. 285.

12. Joungwon Alexander Kim, "Soviet Policy in North Korea," *World Politics* (January, 1970), p. 242. Emphasis added.

13. Recounted by Mr. Kim Nam-shik, former high-ranking cadre in the South Korean Communist Party, in an interview with the author on January 20, 1971, Seoul, South Korea.

14. "The North Korean Labor Party's Internal Factions," originally published in the Japanese monthly *Jiyu*. Written anonymously by "The Neighbouring Countries Research Institute." Translated in *The Selected Summaries of Japanese Magazines* (U.S. Embassy, Tokyo, June 26–July 3, 1967), p. 4

    Also see Roy U. T. Kim, *The Sino-Soviet Dispute and North Korea*, unpublished Ph.D. dissertation, University of Pennsylvania, 1967, pp. 65–75.

15. "The North Korean Labor Party's Internal Factions," op. cit., p. 11.

16. John Spanier, *The Truman–MacArthur Controversy and the Korean War* (Cambridge: Harvard University Press, 1959), p. 120.

17. *New York Times*, March 2, 1949, p. 22.

18. *U.S. News and World Report*, May 5, 1950, p. 23.

19. *New York Times*, October 18, 1949, p. 20.

20. Phillip Jessup in the *Department of State Bulletin*, (Washington), April 24, 1950, p. 627.

21. Gregory Henderson, *Korea, The Politics of the Vortex* (Cambridge: Harvard University Press, 1968), p. 163.

22. Ibid., p. 166.

23. *New York Herald Tribune*, November 1, 1949, p. 5.

24. William Sebald, *With MacArthur in Japan* (New York: Norton: 1965), pp. 180–81.

25. Robert K. Sawyer, *Military Advisors in Korea: KMAG* [Korean Military Advisory Group] *in Peace and War* (Washington, D.C.: Office of the Chief of Military History, 1962), pp. 100–101.

26. *United States Congressional Record*, 81st Congress (Washington, D.C.: U.S. Government Printing Office, 1950). Statement by Senator Millard Tydings, August 16, 1950, p. 12589.

27. Sawyer, op. cit., p. 98

28. Ibid., pp. 94–95.

29. Ibid., p. 92.

30. Joyce and Gabriel Kolko, *The Limits of Power: The World and United States Foreign Policy*, 1945–54 (New York: Harper and Row, 1972), p. 573. For an exchange about this study see William Stueck, "Cold War Revisionism and the origins of the Korean Conflict: The Kolko Thesis"; and Joyce and Gabriel Kolko, "To Root Out Those Among Them—A Response," in *Pacific Historical Review* (November, 1973), pp. 537–75.

31. Sawyer, op. cit., p. 90.
32. Seoul Radio, in Korean, June 8, 1950.
33. Sawyer, op. cit., pp. 105–6.
34. Kolko and Kolko, op. cit., p. 578.
35. *New York Times*, March 30, 1950, p. 7.
36. *New York Times*, June 29, 1950, p. 3.
37. P'yŏngyang claimed that there were 77,000 guerillas in South Korea: Rees, op. cit., p. 16. On the roots of South Korean anti-Americanism see, for example, Allen Raymond, "Robbing So Widespread That American Personnel Has Become Anti-Korean; Looting Found to Be Big Business Done by Highly Organized Groups," *New York Herald Tribune*, February 1, 1948, p. 9.
38. Matthew Ridgway, *The Korean War* (New York: Doubleday and Co., 1967), p. 17. Hanson Baldwin summarized North Korean expectations of a mopping-up operation by noting that June 25 must have seemed to the north to be "the *coup de grace* against a nation of people weakened by internal subversion, economic distress and political instability." *New York Times*, June 27, 1950, p. 10.
39. *South China Morning Post* (Hong Kong), Reuter dispatch, Seoul, March 2, 1950, p. 10.
40. Lee Chong-Hak, "Historical Review of Korean War," *Korea Observer* (Seoul) (spring, 1973), p. 85.
41. Ibid.
42. "Hypotheses on Misperception," in *World Politics* (April, 1968), p. 455.
43. Roy Appleman, *South to the Naktong, North to the Yalu* (Washington: U.S. Government Printing Office, 1960), p. 10. Hanson Baldwin wrote in the *New York Times* of June 28, 1950, p. 12, that "Russian equipment is, of course, being used by the North Koreans, but there is probably more Japanese than Russian equipment in use, and the aggressors are also using some U.S. equipment."

    Another indication of the lack of Soviet equipment at the time of the invasion is furnished by Walter Sullivan in the *New York Times* of July 27, 1950: "The latest estimates are that neither the North Korean Army or Air Force has any post war weapons. . . . the latest date known to have been observed on the nameplates of captured equipment is 1945."

    An A.P. dispatch published in the *South China Morning Post* of July 13, 1950, p. 14, stated that "the North Korean equipment had been second line, but within the last two days there have been reports of the presence of Yak-12 jet fighters. These fighters are old by present standards, but are the first North Korean jets to appear over the front."

44. *New York Times*, Walter Sullivan dispatch from General MacArthur's Tokyo headquarters, July 31, 1950, p. 1.

45. Richard J. H. Johnston, in a Tokyo dispatch to the *New York Times* of October 11, 1950, p. 21. Emphasis added.

46. Dallin, op. cit., p. 61.

47. Whiting, op. cit., p. 44.

48. Rodger Swearingen and Paul Langer, *Red Flag in Japan* (Cambridge: Harvard University Press, 1957), p. 240.

49. *Khrushchev Remembers*, ed. Strobe Talbott (Boston: Little, Brown, and Co., 1970), p. 368.

50. Kim Ch'ang-sun, *A Fifteen Year History of North Korea*. Published in Seoul in 1961; translated by the Joint Publications Research Service, Washington, D.C. (1965), p. 79.

51. Yuri A. Rastvorov, "Red Fraud and Intrigue in the Far East," *Life*, December 6, 1954, p. 175.

52. Robert E. Ward, *Japan's Political System* (Englewood Cliffs, N.J.: Prentice-Hall, 1967), p. 83.

53. *North Korea: A Case Study in the Techniques of Takeover* (Washington, D.C.: U.S. Government Printing Office, 1961), p. 114.

54. Kyril Kalinov, "How Russia Built the North Korean People's Army," *The Reporter*, September 26, 1950, pp. 4–8.

55. *North Korea: A Case Study*, op. cit., p. 113.

56. Scalopino and Lee, op. cit., p. 396, recognize the possibility both that Kim Il-sŏng sought the approval of the Russians *and* that the key decision lay in Korean hands.

57. The symbolic significance of the fifth anniversary date is demonstrated by Kim Il-sŏng's Order for the Day of August 13, 1950, to the North Korean army. Despite the obvious reverses already being experienced, the Order read: "Kim Il-sŏng has directed that the war be carried out so that its final victory can be realized by 15 August, fifth anniversary of the liberation of Korea." The Soviet press gave great attention to the North Korean mid-June precipitous call for elections to be completed by August 8, with the all-Korean legislature meeting on August 15. Max Beloff has mused that these articles, "by the naming of the date for unification, could almost be described as an ultimatum." Beloff, op. cit., p. 182.

58. When the statement finally came, "it was obviously the result of considerable staff work and historical research." Adam Ulam,

Expansion and Coexistence: The History of Soviet Foreign Policy,
1917–67 (New York: Frederick A. Praeger, 1968), p. 523.

59. Ulam, op. cit., p. 521; Beloff, op. cit., p. 186.

60. Soviet propaganda and tactical behavior during the Berlin Blockade
of 1948 "can be studied as a classic exercise of strategic-military
pressure." Ulam, op. cit., p. 452.

61. Tang Tsou, *America's Failure in China*, 1941–1950 (Chicago: University of Chicago Press, 1963), p. 560.

62. *Hearings on the Military Situation in the Far East*, op. cit., p. 2621.

63. *South China Morning Post*, April 29, 1950, p. 14.

64. Ibid., May 25, 1950, p. 14.

65. Hanson Baldwin, in a Washington dispatch to the *New York Times* of
June 28, 1950, p. 12.

66. Cited in Committee on Foreign Relations, U.S. Senate, Staff Study,
*The United States and Communist China in 1949 and 1950: The Question
of Rapprochement and Recognition* (Washington: U.S. Government
Printing Office, 1973), p. 6.

67. Whiting, op. cit., p. 22.

68. The Chinese "had told Britain that they wanted British backing for
Red China's claim to a seat in the United Nations. . . . until Britain
makes up her mind on this question, British–Chinese efforts to
establish full diplomatic relations are likely to continue bogged
down." *South China Morning Post*, March 19, 1950, A.P. London
dispatch, p. 12. The same newspaper reported again in May that
China's price for recognizing Britain was the latter's support in the
United Nations (May 22, 1950, p. 12), A.P. dispatch from San
Francisco.

69. John Foster Dulles, *War or Peace* (New York: Macmillan Co., published April 18, 1950). On April 6 Dulles was appointed an adviser
to the State Department with great fanfare.

70. *South China Morning Post*, May 22, 1950, p. 12, A.P. dispatch from
Moscow.

71. Ibid., May 26, 1950, p. 14, A.P. dispatch from Lake Success.

72. Ibid., June 12, 1950, p. 12, U.P. dispatch from Lake Success.

73. Ibid., June 10, 1950, p. 14, A.P. dispatch from Lake Success.

74. Harrison E. Salisbury alludes to this hypothesis by arguing that
the basis of the Korean Civil War lay with the tensions between Mao
and Stalin; the latter began the war in order to have the potential to
"place Mao in a nutcracker." *The Coming War Between Russia and
China* (New York: Bantam, 1970), pp. 63–77.

75. *Nodong Sinmun* [Labor News] (P'yŏngyang), "Dulles Instigator of American Armed Intervention in Korea." Reprinted in *Pravda,* July 31, 1950, and *Izvestiya,* August 1, 1950. Cited in *Current Digest of the Soviet Press,* September 16, 1950, p. 15.
76. Ralph K. White, *Nobody Wanted War* (New York: Anchor Books, 1970), pp. 13–14. Prof. White presents a highly interesting survey of recent social-psychological literature to demonstrate that client states have a great deal of leverage over their mentors due to "cognitive dissonance." This volume is well complemented by a reading of Thomas Schelling's *The Strategy of Conflict* (London: Oxford University Press, 1963).

6

China's Crossing of the Yalu Reconsidered

In chapter 5 we presented an alternative hypothesis suggesting an intended date of about August 7 for the beginning of the Korean Civil War, and indicated the differences such a date would have meant for the parties involved: the end of the Chinese Civil War, with the PRC gaining control of Taiwan; the presence of the Soviet Union in the United Nations at the time of the attack; and a North Korea better prepared for the invasion. It should be stressed, however, that regardless of the accuracy of this hypothesis the strains described in the following pages were significant and dramatic.

This chapter is concerned with the political reactions of North Korea, China, and the Soviet Union to the early stages of the war. Although military considerations cannot be completely avoided, the focus is upon how each of these nations reacted to the outbreak of war and, in turn, to each other's actions and attitudes. The emphasis is upon the PRC and North Korean responses, with the Soviet Union being treated to some extent as an outside party because it did not become as intimately involved in the unfolding drama as did P'yŏngyang and Peking.

While the Soviet Union was responsible for North Korea's birth and early development, it was the intervention of the PRC's

Chinese People's Volunteers (CPV) during the Korean Civil War
which ensured the survival of the Democratic People's Republic
of Korea (DPRK). From this experience came lessons for all of the
parties involved. For China there was the reminder (if such were
needed) that Korea formed the natural invasion route into Manchuria, her industrial heartland. For North Korea there was the
feeling that the Russians (who had expended almost no blood in
the 1950–53 war) were undependable in the crunch, and contrariwise, a corresponding sense of gratitude toward China.
Perhaps most important, China also learned the bitter lesson that
when they were desperately needed, the Russians were not to be
relied upon. The Soviet Union, for its part, demonstrated that it
would not risk the possibility of a war with the United States.

China's Disappointment with the Soviet Union's U.N. Stance

The argument has been made in these pages that
the PRC was disappointed by the Soviet Union's absence from
the United Nations in the first half of 1950. Perhaps a good index
by which to measure this dissatisfaction is the manner in which
the PRC reacted to the Soviet Union's abstention when the
Korean Civil War began. One major work on this period concluded that "[our] research . . . has not disclosed likely sources
of tension in the [Sino–Soviet] alliance among the decisions
which led to intervention."[1] In fact, an analysis of the PRC's
attitude toward the Soviet Union's absence from the United
Nations Security Council before August 1 indicates the reverse.

Jen-min Jih-pao [People's Daily] of June 29 commented that
"anyone who is truthful to the United Nations should come
forward to restrain the violator of the United Nations—the
United States Government." The July 31 *Jen-min Jih-pao* announced in a headline (three days after Moscow's action, per-

haps indicating some concern among the Chinese leadership) that the "Soviet Union delegate Malik notifies the U.N. that he will preside over the Security Council in August. The U.S. and British clique, which has put the U.N. under its auspices in order to cover up its aggression, is in a panic." The authoritative *Shih-chieh Chih-shih* [World Culture] of August 5 followed up this idea sarcastically: "On the Korean battlefield the U.S. is already at a stalemate . . . just at this moment Russia comes back to the Security Council. This is a precisely brilliant employment of Russia's peaceful policy, and the manifestation of Russia's consistent spirit in her persistent fight for the unity of the United Nations."[2] The same article presented a sophisticated and accurate understanding of the leverage which the Soviet Union was now able to exercise:

> This change of the Soviet Union disturbed their [U.S.–U.K.] steps. They could not control the Security Council as easily as before. Their fears are not minor. According to the rules of the Security Council, the duties of the Representative of the Soviet Union, Malik, are to call all meetings besides the compulsory ones, permit the temporary agenda proposed by the Secretary-General, and decide the procedure suggested by the representatives, and he has the right to permit or deny the speech of the members.

Another article in the same issue of *Shih-chieh Chih-shih* declared that "the Security Council in August, presided over by the Soviet Union's delegate, *could in one way or another produce some profitable effect* in this tense international situation, no matter how hard the Anglo–American clique try to muddle things up."[3] A Shanghai newspaper said on August 8 that "we have the pleasure to tell the people of the world that with the Soviet delegation in the Security Council there is no more chance left for the adoption of resolutions subservient to the warmongers in violation of peace."[4] *Jen-min Jih-pao* of August 13 commented:

> Since June of this year, U.S. imperialism has been utilizing it, irrespective of the illegal state of the Security Council, to adopt illegal resolutions, which are used as a shame-concealing veil for the war of aggression which it has launched against Korea. . . . The original plan of the U.S. imperialists to expand their warlike activities by controlling the illegal Security Council is now greatly curtailed. . . .[5]

In an editorial of September 27, *Jen-min Jih-pao* continued this train of thought:

> The Soviet Union's veto power has always been a telling obstruction to the U.S. imperialist's exercising their aggressive policy. . . . It was encouraged by the experience it got from its aggression in Korea. During the Soviet delegate's absence from the Security Council . . . the U.N. Security Council was used by the U.S. aggressive clique as a tool to undertake an armed aggression in Korea.[6]

"It was under such circumstances," said the *Jen-min Jih-pao* of September 17, "that the Soviet Union returned to the Security Council." The Chinese media made almost every comment on the situation but the direct one: "Why wasn't the Soviet Union in the Security Council during June and July blocking the successful American pursuit of legitimacy?"

Was Washington Dismayed?

The generally accepted interpretation of the United States's reaction to the Korean Civil War has been that Washington's leaders were surprised, dismayed, and unprepared. The standard work on the subject, for example, explains:

> The Communist aggression took the American government by complete surprise. American policy-makers had believed that the Soviet leaders, like themselves, thought only

in terms of all-out war. It was precisely this single-minded preoccupation with total war that had accounted for Korea's being left outside the American defense perimeter.[7]

While Washington may have been surprised by the *location* of the war, however, the record unambiguously demonstrates that it saw the war as the serendipitous occasion needed to legitimize an international military posture that had already been decided upon at the highest levels of the American government.[8] While we are not arguing that Washington "staged" the war, it is clear that Korea provided the Administration with the justification needed to convince a weary public and a tax-conscious Congress of the necessity for Cold War expenditures.

Three months before the war began, the National Security Council, in a memorandum which is still classified (N.S.C. 68), called for a spectacular increase in the United States defense budget from $13.5 billion to $50 billion. In 1954 the chairman of the committee which wrote the memorandum explained that

> the dilemma involved in choosing between an unbalanced budget, higher taxes, and more stringent economic controls on the one hand, and a more adequate military posture on the other, was not *resolved* at the policy decision level until some three months prior to the outbreak of the North Korean aggression. These decisions were *translated into specific action* only after the aggression into South Korea had given concrete and bloody confirmation to the *conclusions already introduced by analysis.*[9]

It took a crisis to fully tap the financial and emotional resources already allocated on the drawing boards. Undoubtedly, the Truman administration sincerely believed in a Russian military threat and that in Korea it was witnessing only one example of the compulsive, monolithic, and expansive nature of communism.

Quite aside from those beliefs, it should be remembered that the administration was politically vulnerable about the recent "fall of China" and the charge that it was "weak on communism." The Korean Civil War offered the administration, at the start of a congressional election campaign, a chance to demonstrate its anticommunist zeal.

While much is made of the idea that the United States entered the war under the aegis of the United Nations, it would appear that this was not a necessity. Secretary of State Acheson, for instance, was later asked what the United States would have done if it had failed to receive the support of the U.N. in its military intervention. Acheson quickly responded: "We'd have gone in unilaterally. . . . We'd have gone in alone."[10]

If the hypothesis that the decision to resist communist expansion by conventional means was taken before June, 1950 is accurate, then President Truman's judgment to enter the war has a significance different from that generally attributed to it. Rather than being a decision of *strategic* proportions—i.e., should the United States engage in a limited war with communist troops—the decision was a *tactical* one: did this particular crisis warrant, in terms of anticipated costs and benefits, the use of American forces.

The question must then be asked: was the outbreak of *a* war really a total surprise, as is generally assumed? The truth appears to be the opposite, namely that the Truman administration expected a war *somewhere* along the rim of the communist states in 1950. Secretary of State Acheson later referred to this expectation circuitously:

> For some months, as tensions had mounted again after the Berlin Blockade, we had run exercises in danger spots for renewed Soviet probing of our determination. Korea was on the list but not among the favorites. Berlin, Turkey, Greece, Iran—all seemed spots where the balance of convenient operations dipped in favour of the Soviets.[11]

George Kennan, in his *Memoirs,* gives a more direct recounting of Washington's anticipation of a limited war in the summer of 1950:

> At some time in late May or early June, 1950, some of us who were particularly concerned with Russian affairs in the department were puzzled to note, among the vast "take" of information that flows daily into the ample maw of that institution, data suggesting that somewhere across the broad globe the armed forces of some communist power were expecting soon to go into action. An intensive scrutiny of the Soviet situation satisfied us that it was not Soviet forces to which these indications related. This left us with the forces of the various satellite regimes, but which?[12]

On the basis of intensive interviews with many of the participants in the Korean decision of June, 1950, Glenn Paige wrote about this expectation of crisis: "For the intelligence analysts there was a sense of growing tension in the international environment and even a 'hunch' that something important was about to happen somewhere along the Soviet periphery."[13] Consequently, Washington policymakers had been earnestly considering a reaction to aggression before the war began. One resulting action came in a likely area: Taiwan.

The Illusionary Taiwan Straits "Interdiction"

> The attack upon Korea makes it clear beyond all doubt that communism has passed beyond the use of subversion to conquer independent nations and will soon use armed invasion and war. . . . In these circumstances, the occupation of *Formosa* by communist forces would be a direct threat to the security of the Pacific area and to the United States forces performing their lawful and necessary functions in that area. Accordingly, I have ordered the Seventh

Fleet to prevent any attack upon *Formosa*. As a corollary of
this action I am calling upon the Chinese government of
Formosa to cease all air and sea operations against the mainland. (President Truman, quoted in the *New York Times*,
June 28, 1950, p. 1. Emphasis added).

In fact, the interdiction of the Taiwan Straits ordered by
President Truman on June 27, 1950, was little more than a show of
words. The U.S. Seventh Fleet was not in the Taiwan Straits in
the summer of 1950, nor would it have been able to defend the
island against a Chinese attack had one occurred.

As indicated previously, China had apparently completed
its invasion preparations of Taiwan before the beginning of the
Korean Civil War. The announced task of the U.S. Seventh Fleet
was now to prevent the anticipated Chinese attack. The military
editor of the *New York Times* indicated how difficult the Seventh
Fleet's job might be, because it "could not prevent some Communist infiltration, and if the navy's strength were split between
Korea and Formosa, a sizeable number of Communists might
reach Formosa." He then speculated that even a small number of
Chinese troops landing in Taiwan might well mean the end of
the KMT regime: "The goodwill the Nationalist Government had
last spring has been replaced among many by fear and some
hatred. . . . If this trend should continue, the landing of even a
few Communist soldiers on the island might set off a major
revolt." [14]

But the Seventh Fleet in the summer of 1950 was, thanks to
the prewar economy-minded Congress, seriously understrength: it possessed only one carrier, one heavy cruiser, eight
destroyers, and a supplement of one light cruiser and four more
destroyers stationed in Japan. Because the fleet's responsibilities
ranged over all of East Asia, its capabilities were stretched peril-
ously thin even before the war. [15] Once the war began, the full
strength of the fleet, such as it was, could not be assigned to

several places at once. The realities of war placed the fleet near Korea.

The official U.S. naval war history implicitly comments on the fact that the Seventh Fleet could not have operated in the Taiwan Straits in the summer of 1950:

> The first 82 days of the Korean War—from 25 June until the Inch'on Landing on 15 September 1950—were a retreat to a defensible perimeter and a desperate holding action. All military efforts—Army, Navy, Air Force—in these critical days were devoted to a single objective: Maintaining a Korean bridgehead around the port of Pusan and preventing South Korean and American soldiers from being overrun, outflanked, cut-off or eventually thrown into the sea. [16]

The first American ambassador to Taiwan, Karl Rankin, later stated that the Seventh Fleet was not sufficient to forestall Chinese landings on the island. [17] Finally, in the spring of 1951, the Secretary of State confirmed that the Seventh Fleet could not have prevented the Chinese invasion and capture of Taiwan in the previous summer. [18] Even if the Seventh Fleet had wished to protect Taiwan, its ships would not have been diverted from action in support of American forces in Korea. In short, the celebrated American "inderdiction" of the Taiwan Straits was not the defense of Taiwan that it is popularly supposed to have been.

The Seventh Fleet did not in fact enter the Taiwan Straits in any strength until October, 1950. Why did Truman, in reality, issue a bank draft predated by four months? Foster Rhea Dulles suggests that the gratuitous announcement of a U.S. action far from the Korean battlefield had a mainly domestic political purpose:

> President Truman's orders to the Seventh Fleet, which the Republicans lauded as finally drawing that defensive line in the western Pacific they had so long urged as vital to

American security, were a key factor in winning the bipartisan support necessary for our action on the Korean front. [19]

From this perspective, President Truman's verbal placement of the Seventh Fleet in the Taiwan Straits takes on a highly provocative aspect. Incapable of actually preventing a Chinese invasion at the moment when the Chinese were preparing to land, the American president had nevertheless visibly reversed himself on a specific assurance that he would not continue to interfere in the Chinese Civil War. The "interdiction" drove a wedge between Washington and Peking which was to persist for two decades, pushed China further toward the Soviet Union, and, ironically, encouraged China's entrance into the Korean Civil War four months later against a United States which had demonstrated its insensitivity to China's interests.

Of course, China did not know what the actual Washington response to such an invasion would be, particularly after the unpredictable Americans had already reversed their public stance towards intervention in both China and Korea. The devastation of U.S. bombings was always a possibility. Perhaps more to the point, however, it would appear that the most likely explanation of why China did not invade Taiwan after June 25 was not mostly the threat of American retaliation, but rather Peking's own prudence and the hope that the Korean Civil War might end soon enough to allow Washington to reverse itself once again.

Even after the Korean Civil War began, the PRC hoped that an early end to the conflict would be possible without its own involvement. Since June, 1950, Peking has seen not the onset of the war itself but rather the ostensible June 27 interdiction of the Taiwan Straits as the threshold event which prevented the ending of the Chinese Civil War. In commenting two years later on that event, for example, New China News Agency (NCNA) declared that: *"ever since then,* the U.S. Government has been actively aiding the KMT brigands and inciting them. . . ."[20] In declaring that the Seventh Fleet would be sent to the Taiwan Straits, President Truman stated on June 27 that the future status of Taiwan would have to await "the restoration of security in the Pacific, a peace settlement with Japan, or consideration by the United Nations." Truman continued to repeat his pre-June assurances to an increasingly skeptical Peking. For example, he said on July 10: "I wish to state that the United States has no territorial ambitions whatever concerning that Island." James Reston noted in the same issue of the *New York Times* that carried the President's statement that "Washington was not intending to remain in Formosa after the crisis had subsided."[21] This perceived tacit "understanding" with the United States may explain why People's Liberation Army (PLA) troops were not used on the Pusan perimeter in late July, even when that extra help might have ensured a North Korean victory.[22]

During the summer of 1950, the PRC put out feelers for an early end to the war.[23] Her overriding interest lay in Taiwan, as evidenced by her lack of diplomatic representation in P'yŏngyang and military assistance to North Korea. All signs pointed toward a Chinese attack upon Taiwan scheduled for late July or August. A *New York Times* dispatch from Taiwan on July 23 declared than an attack on Taiwan would have to come "by the end of August" at the latest because of the coming typhoon season. The KMT leadership was aware of this geographical constraint upon an invasion. The *South China Morning Post* of May 18 quoted Chiang K'ai-shek as follows: "If the Communists fail to launch an attack within three months, they will have no chance to take the island." The same newspaper on May 20 quoted Chiang Ching-kuo (Chiang K'ai-shek's son) as speaking of the coming "one hundred critical days," after which Taiwan would be safe.

If these appraisals were accurate, it then becomes more understandable that Peking would refrain from antagonizing the United States during July and even into August, hoping that the invasion might still be accomplished on schedule. The additional factor of weather would support this view. The *Times* reported:

> One week hence—July 28 and 29—there will be high tide at dawn along the Formosan coast. China's Red Armies will have better conditions for an invasion of Formosa than they are likely to see again for more than a month because typhoons will whip the shallow Formosa Strait through most of August.[24]

But the invasion did not take place, and from all available evidence it was from late August on that the PRC began to seriously consider intervening in the Korean Civil War.[25]

The usual interpretation of why the PRC did not invade Taiwan either just before or shortly after June 27, 1950, has been that a serious epidemic of Schistosomiasis among the sections of the PLA opposite Taiwan prevented the attack.[26] While it is true that *Jen-min Jih-pao* of March 3 and March 8, 1950, did report an 18-day conference of PLA medical personnel of the Third Field army (the army which was to invade Taiwan) for the purpose of preventing the spread of the disease, a threat to that army itself was not mentioned. More to the point, a PLA nonrepatriate of the Korean Civil War, Colonel Tun Ta-shih, later reported, in contrast to Robert Kierman's contention that the hardest-hit areas were the lower Yangtze Valley and Kwangtung and Fukien Provinces (the staging areas for China's invasion of Taiwan), that the worst areas were instead Southern Chekiang and Northern Fukien Provinces—and that only about 2 percent of PLA soldiers were affected. If Colonel Tung is correct, Taiwan was not invaded because of a *political* decision, and not on account of a lack of troops caused by an epidemic.[27]

In this light, we can understand the perspective in which MacArthur's dramatic trip to Taiwan in the last few days of July may have been viewed by the PRC. Rather than being seen as merely one of several consultations with Chiang K'ai-shek, or even as just a further proof of U.S.–KMT "collusion," it probably was taken by Peking as the signal that its policy of cautious bargaining with the United States over the "liberation" of Taiwan had failed. This definitive message by the United States ended most of the hope that China had held of gaining Taiwan by remaining aloof from the war. An indication that this was indeed how the PRC read MacArthur's trip was given in a *Jen-min Jih-pao* editorial of four months later:

> But America, while launching an aggression against Korea, has openly sent her naval and air forces to seize Taiwan. In particular, *since* the secret military meeting of MacArthur and Chiang Kai-shek toward the end of July, the American forces of aggression have not only directly occupied Taiwan, but have also, under the unified command of MacArthur, been combined with the forces of Chiang Kai-shek, in preparations for obstructing our legitimate liberation of Taiwan. [28]

The Valentine's Day Sino–Soviet Treaty

Allen S. Whiting's pioneering work has described in elegant detail China's cautious posture toward the Korean Civil War during the summer of 1950; his analysis need not be repeated here. Rather than replicating Whiting's valuable data, it might be more appropriate to reexamine some of it.

Professor Whiting, in an attempt to demonstrate that the beginning of the war caught the PRC by surprise, states that "no Peking newspaper reported the war for forty-eight hours following the North Korean attack" of June 25. [29] Actually, *Jen-min Jih-pao* devoted about 15 percent of its front page on June 26 to announcing the new hostilities to its readers. Summing up China's attitude toward the first month of the war, Professor Whiting states that "Peking appeared to avoid any specific and immediate commitment to assist North Korea." [30] Here he understates China's reluctance. In fact, the PRC was most emphatic about its desire for noninvolvement. *Shih-chieh Chih-shih* of July 14 phrased it in this manner: *Question:* China and the Soviet Union should be involved in this war, shouldn't they? *Answer:* We say, such an idea is wrong. . . . All peace lovers of the whole world sympathize with the liberation movement of the people of Korea, but this does not mean that we should enter the war with arms."[31] Canton's *Nan-fang Jih-pao* [Southern Daily] on August 1 stressed that "there is no need for our military aid, nor should we help them with our military forces."[32]

Whiting accurately points out (p. 56) that the American entrance into the war had foreclosed North Korea's hopes for a quick victory—and that the Chinese understood this fact. However, he erroneously dates the Chinese realization of this from the *Shih-chieh Chih-shih* issue of August 5, which, he says, introduced the significant term "prolonged war" (p. 56). In fact, China's appreciation of North Korea's dim prospects, as signaled by the phrase "prolonged war," came soon after the war began. For example, a *Jen-min Jih-pao* editorial of July 6 commented that American troops will

> of course make the Korean people's victory come a bit slower and the Korean people cannot but prepare to undertake prolonged and more arduous fighting. . . . Both China's war of resistance against the Japanese in the past and the present Vietnamese war of resistance against the French can be taken as evidence of a victorious future for the Korean people. . . . undoubtedly, the Korean people's forces . . . will speed up their political, military and economic preparations for a prolonged war.[33]

On pp. 84–85, Whiting quotes from two paragraphs of the August 26 issue of *Shih-chieh Chih-shih* which he considers to indicate a new posture of determination. His citation contains four errors; in fact, the PRC is, again, more restrained than Whiting indicates. First, the order of his two paragraphs is the reverse of the original, which changes the tone. Second, the correct translation of what Professor Whiting considers to be the key sentence (repeated twice on p. 85, and given again on p. 103), which is rendered by him as "North Korea's defense is our defense" should instead read the milder "The Korean people's sorrow and misfortune *(yu tsai nan)* is our people's sorrow and misfortune." Third, his version left out sentences which place the quotation in a more moderate context than is otherwise evident. *Shih-chieh Chih-shih* is here talking about China's admission to the United Nations in order that she might have a forum from which to denounce American actions. Fourth, the actual translation of what he has rendered as "cannot allow" is a more temperate "cannot watch and pretend not to have seen."

These and other instances indicate that Professor Whiting has understated his thesis: the Chinese in the summer of 1950 were even *more* cautious and *less* inclined to react to external events than his study concludes.

Mao Tse-tung and Stalin signed the Sino–Soviet Treaty of Friendship, Alliance, and Mutual Assistance on February 14, 1950. Professor Whiting has written of what he considers to be the extreme importance of this treaty for the PRC:

> Yet it must be noted at this point that the extended conditions of Soviet military support probably represented China's most important gain at the Moscow conference. Given the doctrinaire mistrust of imperialism and the association of the United States both with Chiang Kai-shek and more recently with a resurgent Japan, this reassurance of protection undoubtedly made the Soviet alliance seem worth whatever material or political costs it might entail. . . . Russia's modern military might offer protection against Japan, and perhaps the U.S. as well."[34]

This view represents what has, until recently, been the standard interpretation of the Sino–Soviet alliance, viz., China unhesitatingly turning toward her ideological mentor. Chapters 3 and 4 presented strong indications that this was in fact not the situation, and that furthermore the Moscow treaty was actually a victory for Russia's calculated policy of preventing the new PRC from forming alignments with other states. Moreover, the Whiting view does not square with Russia's nonsupport for her North Korean satellite. If the Soviet Union would not shed blood for its own client, what would be its behavior if American troops tried to topple the new government in Peking? Would Moscow defend it, use the attendant chaos as an opportunity to place someone like Kao Kang in power, or simply remain aloof from the crisis? In short, of what value to North Korea, or the PRC, was a partnership with the Soviet Union?

China's evaluation of the value of Soviet military protection was reflected in a later statement about its entrance into the war: "We ourselves preferred to shoulder the heavy sacrifices necessary and stood in the first line of defense of the Socialist camp so that the Soviet Union might stay in the second line."[35] The Sino–Soviet military alliance, conceived in Moscow on Valentine's Day of 1950, was to pass away on the Korean peninsula in the autumn of that same year.

Reactions to the War

The DPRK recognized the PRC on October 5, 1949; China reciprocated on October 6. The first North Korean ambassador arrived in Peking on January 28, 1950. (The Soviet Union had waited until October 2, 1948, to extend recognition, although North Korean autonomy had been proclaimed on September 9 of that year. The newly appointed Soviet ambassador was the same military proconsul who had helped to rule the country for the previous three years.) There apparently was no official Chinese diplomatic mission in P'yŏngyang until the summer of 1950. On July 10, 1950, Chih Keng-mao, described by P'yŏngyang Radio on that date as "Deputy Ambassador," and "First Consulor" Liu Yu-wan arrived in P'yŏngyang. Interestingly, Peking Radio of July 12 referred to the newly arrived legation of nine members as headed by "Chargé d'Affaires" Chai Chun-wu, perhaps indicating China's indecision over what status to grant its diplomatic representatives in P'yŏngyang. This apparent uncertainty may have been due to the fact that the problem of Taiwan still headed Peking's list of priorities.

P'yŏngyang Radio service was extended to Peking on July 13, suggesting warming relations between the two capitals accompanying the arrival of the new PRC diplomatic mission. The North Korean capital finally received the credentials of a Chinese ambassador on August 13, well after the beginning of the war. This new ambassador was greeted in P'yŏngyang by Wen Shih-cheng, identified by P'yŏngyang Radio as the Head of the "Northeast People's Government Commercial Delegation to Korea."[36] (This little-noted fact can only serve to fuel speculation about what plans Stalin had held for Korea, and where Kao Kang's Northeast [Manchurian] Government was to have figured in those schemes. Perhaps the pro-Soviet Kao Kang was to be granted an informal suzerainty over North Korea?)

Not until July 1 did North Korea issue a general mobilization order.[37] It became apparent to P'yŏngyang early on, however, that the American intervention in the war would doom its expectations of an early victory (if any). On July 16, 1950, Kim Il-sŏng, in a speech over P'yŏngyang Radio, declared: "Had not the American imperialists intervened in our internal affairs and begun armed invasion, our country would have been unified and the war terminated."

North Korean references to its allies at the beginning of the war were vaguely warm. Mention of the PRC was slight and usually grouped with expressions of thanks toward the European people's democracies for their help. Kim Il-sŏng's major speech of July 8 made no mention of the Soviet Union, while Moscow Radio, broadcasting to Korea in early July in Korean, expressed obscure signals of support for Korea. These broadcasts stressed the notion that the South Koreans had invaded the North only after "long preparations"; perhaps this often-repeated term was meant to convey a message to P'yŏngyang: "You will certainly win because *you* have long prepared." Throughout July Korean expressions of gratitude to the Soviet Union for assistance were mild, perhaps indicating P'yŏngyang's displeasure at Moscow's cautious reaction to the American intervention in the war. For example: "While the Americans have taken to direct aggression in Korea, the Soviet Union is morally supporting wars of righteousness, asserting that the Korean affair be left to the Koreans for settlement."[38]

On July 18, Moscow Radio broadcast to the PRC, in Chinese, the clear suggestion that the Soviet Union would not intervene militarily in the Korean Civil War, along with the implication that the war did present a direct security threat to China. (The commentary's title was "The American Imperialists Have Employed Armed Intervention in Korea so that They Could Carry Out Armed Aggression in China and Indochina.") On August 1 Peking Radio broadcast the following *only* to Tibet: "The People's Republic of China has offered military and naval assistance to the People's Republic of Korea. The People's Republic replied that assistance was unnecessary at this time." This could, of course, have been meant as a threat to Tibet, which was yet to be entered by PLA troops. Regardless of the immediate reason, the fact that Peking was not publicizing such messages directly to the DPRK does suggest that Peking was sensitive on the issue of aiding Korea.

In short, by the end of July, both the Soviet Union and the PRC had indicated that they were not anxious to become involved in the war. At this point, the North Koreans announced that their hopes for victory lay solely in the leadership of Kim Il-sŏng; significantly, this authoritative statement lacked any mention of either Communist neighbor.[39] On August 6, in an admission of the attrition which the North Korean army was suffering at the hands of vastly superior American air and naval power, Pak Hŏn-yŏng directed a message of protest to the

United Nations. This message was undoubtedly timed to coincide with a date which was sure to raise sympathetic responses in Peking and Moscow, namely, the date of the dropping of the atomic bomb on Hiroshima.

In addition to the awesome destruction which American bombs and missiles had caused, the unexpectedly rapid United States troop buildup inside Korea had stalled the North Korean offensive by early August. By August 4, American ground forces in Korea numbered 47,000, with more arriving daily; the South Korean combat troops totaled about 45,000. This meant that the two opposing sides were about equal in the size of their ground forces (the Americans, of course, held the great advantage in air and naval power). This was because the North Korean army had suffered about 58,000 casualities and by the beginning of August numbered no more than 70,000 men. [40]

On August 15, 1950—the fifth anniversary of Korea's liberation from Japanese imperialism and the date on which P'yŏngyang had apparently hoped to celebrate reunification—as it became obvious that North Korean arms were not to prevail against America's mobilization, the three allies marked the day in a common ceremony which clearly indicated the degree of commitment of each to the fighting. The North Koreans spoke of an all-out fight for an early victory. Russian Ambassador Shtykov spoke only of the "technical assistance" which had "played an important role in strengthening the defensive power of the Democratic People's Republic of Korea." [41] The Chinese ambassador did not speak. A PRC reporter wrote of the music show staged in P'yŏngyang in honor of the Korean People's Army on that August 15 that the music was either Korean or Russian (i.e., by omission, not Chinese). The report went on to further underline the Russians' responsibility for Korean security:

The stage was decorated with two large portraits of Kim Il-song and Stalin, for it was on this day that the mighty Soviet Army ended the predatory rule of the Japanese imperialists. The ambassador of the Soviet Union and the Peoples' Democracies brought warm words of their people's support for Korea's struggle for liberation."[42]

The writer stressed Russian accountability by almost completely omitting any mention of the PRC.

As the summer of 1950 progressed, the Soviet Union increasingly made clear to the PRC both its own intention of noninvolvement in the Korean Civil War and the probability of Chinese entanglement. On August 31, for example, Moscow broadcast to China a message which strongly implied that the fate of the PRC was tied to the successful military fortunes of Kim Il-sŏng:

> Northeast China, as well as Taiwan, are to be taken as military bases for the invasion of the People's Republic of China. This is the plan behind the American support of Syngman Rhee's puppet army of the "Republic of Korea."
> . . . No aggressor of Greater Asia could encroach upon the border of China without trespassing on Korea. *To date,* the valiant Korean People's Army forces have smashed and routed the puppet army troops of South Korea and beaten the American interventionist troops.[43]

The point of this sort of declaration to its ally by the Soviet Union—repeated frequently during the months of August through November of 1950, with a two-week aberration in early October—seemed to be that it was China which, in the crunch, must assume the burden of salvaging the North Korean regime. The Russians' logic was further explained in a Moscow Radio broadcast to Korea in early September speaking of China's resistance to the United States:

> If this is an example of American imperialism—to invade Korea with military forces after a long-range intervention—the Chinese reaction would be the same. The Chinese people have *finally* come to realize American tricks with indignation.[44]

Here, and in similar declarations, the Russians were telling their Korean allies, just as they had informed the PRC, that the ultimate defense of North Korea must depend upon the Chinese. Although "hard" data, such as documents from Moscow archives, are not available, open communications between the three communist capitals in the late summer and fall of 1950 clearly implied a possible Chinese intervention. For example, Pak Chung-ae, the Chairwoman of the North Korean Democratic Women's League, in a speech of September 9, 1950, dealing with American aggression, explained that "further, they are taking planned, intentional provocative actions against the People's Republic of China and the Soviet Union." Hereinafter, this theme of American territorial threat to the PRC, via the Korean Civil War, would accompany—and usually precede—similar mentions of threat to the Soviet Union in the DPRK's media.

After the September 15 disaster of the Inch'ŏn Invasion, the North Koreans stepped up the warnings to their allies that the war on the Korean peninsula was only a prelude to American invasions of their territories. The messages clearly read: the allies must help the now-routed DPRK. P'yŏngyang Radio stated on September 24, 1950, that the DPRK now held "secret correspondence of the Syngman Rhee gang on its plan for the invasion of Manchuria and the Soviet Far Eastern Territory."

At the end of September, while the North Korean army was being routed and MacArthur was poised to cross the 38th parallel, Moscow Radio's Home Service broadcast two significant indications of the Soviet Union's priorities. First, it reminded its listeners of the Soviet Union's vulnerability on the Western frontier. Interestingly, in this respect the Soviet Union and the United States saw the purpose of the Korean Civil War in "mirror image" fashion: each thought that the war was only a part of a large-scale plan, on the part of the other, either as a feint to throw defensive armed forces in Europe off guard, as a probe, or as a means of depleting the opponent's resources. For instance, Moscow Radio on September 29 warned its listeners that the Chief of the General Staff of the American Armed Forces, Bradley, has made his latest inflammatory speech, which has obviously provocative aims. Striving to intensify war hysteria in the country, Bradley calls upon the U.S. to locate in the near future, in the countries of Western Europe, Army, Navy, and Air Forces, and to keep them in a state of readiness for battle. . . . It is he who is one of the main organizers of the armed aggression in Korea.

The second indication of the Russian leadership's thinking was that, if necessary, the PRC would have to defend Korea, since the Soviet had other, more basic, commitments to China: "The constant selfless support of China by the USSR calls forth in the Chinese people a sentiment of gratitude toward their great neighbor."

In this context, it is perhaps significant that the instruments of ratification of the February 14 Sino–Soviet Treaty of Friendship, Alliance, and Mutual Benefit were not exchanged until September 30, 1950. One interpretation to account for this long delay is that neither side was willing to commit itself fully to the treaty until each understood what its responsibilities were to be in the Korean Civil War. (Interestingly, Peking Radio waited until October 18 to broadcast to Korea this development, which suggested China's willingness to help the DPRK with the assurance of Moscow's backing.) Perhaps as a reflection of China's unhappiness at Russian noninclination to become actively involved in the war, the portraits which dominated the PRC's October 1 National Day celebrations were those of Mao and Sun Yat-sen; the preceding year they had been of Mao and Stalin.[45]

That the DPRK was aware of the probable probing then going on between Peking and Moscow over who was to supply what aid to P'yŏngyang is indicated by the message which Kim Il-sŏng sent to Mao Tse-tung on the occasion of October 1: "We, the Korean people, have been carefully watching the fulfillment of the Chinese people's fighting with an increasing interest as well as admiration."[46] This, the first strong statement of concern about the new PRC, was to be followed by intensifying Korean expressions of interest in China, as opposed to mere declarations of hope for help from the Soviet Union.

The Deciding Factor in China's Entrance

Then came a major landmark date in the war. As already suggested, an agreement between Peking and Moscow about the possible entrance of the PRC, however unwillingly, into the war if necessary had previously been implied in the Soviet news media. The decisive incident that was, in effect, to put the signature irrevocably to this agreement was now to come. On October 8, the day after American troops crossed the 38th parallel, two American fighter planes of the Shooting Star F-80 type attacked a Soviet aerodrome sixty-two miles north of the Soviet's Korean border and eighteen miles southwest of Vladivostok. The attack took place at 4 P.M., in daylight, while the aerodrome building markings were clearly visible. The Russians claimed that the two fighters approached the aerodrome in a "hedge-hopping flight" and then "fired at the aerodrome from machine guns."[47] The United States staunchly denied this incident until October 19; on that day in the United Nations it apologized, and offered monetary restitution.

Regardless of the genesis of this provocative armed incursion into Russian territory, whether it occurred by design or by accident, it could have served only to solidify in the cautious mind of Stalin the firm resolve not to become involved in a shooting confrontation with the United States. Additional irritant incidents only confirmed this decision. Shortly before the jet fighters incident, "Far East Air Force planes 'bombed' eighteen principal North Korean cities with copies of General MacArthur's demand for surrender. . . . Planes equipped with loud speakers and recordings of these declarations soon will begin *to fly over the Soviet Union.*[48] On October 12, 1950, "the biggest Allied fleet ever assembled off the Korean east coast since the start of the war . . . blasted and burned a 105 mile stretch of the North Korean coast *just south of the Soviet border.* [49]

The PRC now becme the key member of the communist triangle. On October 9, the Korean Workers' Party daily organ, *Nodong Sinmum* [Labor News], published an article commemorating (three days late) the first anniversary of PRC–DPRK diplomatic relations. *For the first time,* in this article, the Korean media used the unequivocal term "aid" in reference to China; previously only the term "support" had figured in P'yŏngyang's statements on the PRC. [50] On October 11, P'yŏngyang Radio for the first time expressed its thanks to the PRC without, as had been the past practice, coupling it with gratitude to the Soviet Union, save for a slight acknowledgment. [51]

A further indication that the period of October 8–10 represented the threshold dates when Peking fully realized that its Soviet ally had unequivocally passed the torch is the October 10 statement by the Chinese Foreign Ministry, which "proceeded to alert the country for mobilization." [52] *Shih-chieh Chih-shih* [World Culture] and *Hsueh Hsi* [Study] then echoed this alert; their articles were probably written on October 9 and 10. [53]

The DPRK Asks for Help

On October 11 Premier Kim Il-sŏng appeared to come close to admitting the possibility that North Korean troops had initiated hostilities, though it was in response to South Korean-created tensions. Previous to this P'yŏngyang Radio statement, the DPRK had consistently maintained that South Korea had invaded the north without warning. The October 11 speech should be read as an extension of the earlier cited July 30 North Korean newspaper contention that the war might have started earlier than the Americans and South Koreans had originally planned. Now P'yŏngyang was implicitly acknowledging the possibility that the immediate outbreak of the war might have been due to a preventive North Korean strike against an expected South Korean attack:

> Having received reliable information early in May of 1950 that preparations were under way for the northern invasion, the government of the Democratic People's Republic of Korea was able to take measures at the proper time to repel it. At last, toward the end of June, the Syngman Rhee armed forces invaded areas north of the 38th parallel. Not only did the people's armed forces repel the invasion, but they also dealt annihilating blows to the Syngman Rhee armed forces, with the support of the partisans and all the Korean people.

Why would the north allow that it was the initiator of the large-scale fighting?[54] Essentially because at this point P'yŏngyang, on the verge of defeat and desperately in need of military assistance and troops from her allies, needed to offer up some explanation of why it had begun the war earlier than August. P'yŏngyang settled on this one need for a preemptive strike against an anticipated South Korean attack, based upon information gained in May. In particular, P'yŏngyang had learned that Seoul's army was reaching a military par with the DPRK; the northern attack appears to have been launched before the Chinese and Russians were expecting it in reaction to this. Of course, Peking and Moscow may well have asked why P'yŏngyang did not inform them of such sensitive information, acquired over a month before the war began—and the North Koreans probably had several coherent responses to that likely query.

When the ultimate moment in an alliance is reached—viz., the commitment of military force—an ally which is about to invest its human and material resources is anxious to believe that it is doing so for a worthy cause. Although its reason for fighting may, in the final analysis, involve its own self-interest, it wishes

to believe that the weaker ally to whose assistance it now comes
has heretofore followed a rational policy. Hence, the weaker
partner wants its ally to believe in the righteousness of the war.
Only then will the latter expend its resources freely and to its
utmost capability.

Accordingly, North Korea was asking its allies to accept
that, in beginning the war early, it had acted much as other states
would have behaved in a similar situation. Assuming that both
Peking and Moscow were aware of the actual situation on June
25—namely, that the South Korean Army did not begin a full-
scale invasion of the north on that day—it became mandatory for
P'yŏngyang to fit the facts that were known to her allies into a
believable, and strategically defensible, explanation.

The DPRK continued to solicit the support of its stronger
Russian ally. On October 12 Kim Il-sŏng wrote to Stalin that "the
Korean people are with ardent gratitude constantly feeling the
friendly support which is being given by the Soviet Union to our
people in the struggle for the independence of our Motherland."
Stalin responded with a brief note, wishing the Korean people a
"successful conclusion" to their struggle. [55] Russia's messages
had become unmistakably clear: she was principally worried
about the war being used as a springboard by the Americans for
an invasion of her own territory, and she was determined not to
commit her troops on the Korean peninsula.

In the first week of October, Moscow became so frenetically
worried about its own security that for a brief period of time its
media placed China—the country which increasingly was expected to defend both the DPRK *and* itself—as the *second* target of
a feared U.S. invasion. (Within two weeks, however, the countries were returned to their usual order, a diplomatic acknowledgment in the media that it was Chinese who were about to
die.) Moscow Radio of October 6, for example, declared that

in their aggressive plans, the transoceanic imperialists
have assigned an important place to Korea. Their policy

with respect to this country is subordinated to one purpose: to enslave the Korean people and turn Korea into . . . their military strategic base for an *invasion of the Soviet Union and China.* (Emphasis added.)

On October 12, Moscow Radio broadcast to P'yŏngyang, in Korean, a clear message that Korea might expect Chinese, but not Russian, military assistance: "The Americans will be ousted from Korea without fail in the same way as that in which they were kicked out of China." That is, without the aid of Russian troops. Shortly after this, the Soviet Union pulled most of its men and equipment out of the war. In a dispatch to the *New York Times* of October 22, 1950, Hanson Baldwin reported that

there are increasing evidences that the Russians have cut their losses in Korea and are moving out altogether. The flow of traffic down the east coast highway from Vladivostok apparently has been halted altogether and the Russian advisers and technicians apparently have fled over the border after attempts to destroy or conceal the supplies and material they could not evacuate.

The North Koreans were quick to realize that their only possible source of armed support was to be the PRC, and they were aware of which psychological buttons to press in order to raise China's interest in intervening in the Korean Civil War. On October 14, for example, Pak Hŏn-yŏng sent a letter (broadcast over P'yŏngyang on that date) to the United Nations, stating that "the United States is using Japanese troops in the war against the Korean people." These charges had started at the end of September, and were probably aimed specifically at the fear which the PRC understandably held of a resurgent Japanese militarism. Thus, P'yŏngyang was telling Peking that its entrance into the war would be in defense against renewed Japanese threats. Pak's charges received prominence in the October 16 *Jen-min Jih-pao.*

Intervention

It is interesting to speculate on what might have happened if the South Korean Army had marched into North Korea in October of 1950. It was then a far better army than that of the DPRK, and probably would have been able to reach the Yalu by itself. [56] On October 2, as South Korean troops were crossing the 38th parallel, Chou En-lai summoned the Indian ambassador in Peking to a midnight conference and told him that if American forces crossed into North Korea, China would enter the war. As Ambassador Panikkar later paraphrased the conversation: "He was emphatic, the South Koreans did not matter, but American intervention into North Korea would encounter Chinese resistance." [57] The PRC feared that the United States had the same predatory designs on China that Japan had practiced shortly before.

The PRC has generally cited two major reasons for intervening in Korea: its concern for its own defense against the United States, and the protection of North Korea. It seems clear, however, that the second reason ranked far behind the first in the PRC order of priorities. There were indications that the PRC would have been willing to accept a rump North Korean state as a buffer, with its southern boundary in the vicinity of the "neck" of the Korean peninsula, at about President Truman's October 17 announced boundary which had been ordered to halt U.N. forces fifty miles south of the Yalu. [58] The PRC had learned, however, to watch General MacArthur's actions in the field rather than listen to President Truman's more moderate words in Washington. On October 24, MacArthur abolished the last restraining line for American troops, and announced his intention of marching to the Yalu. Probably as an indication that this was the direct cause of the PRC's entrance into the war, October 24 has ever since then been given as the date of the official formation of the Chinese People's Volunteers (CPV). [59] (On this same date, October 24, the PLA was ordered to advance into Tibet, at the opposite end of China geographically. This probably was meant partly as a message to the outside world that Peking was more concerned with her internal affairs than with foreign adventures.)

Interestingly, Moscow Radio, also on October 24, broadcast to Mongolia the claim—never again repeated—that "on January 30 of this year, the Soviet Union recognized the Vietnamese People's Government and the Chinese People's Republic followed the USSR with the same recognition." This false assertion was perhaps meant to preserve the Russian role as leader of the communist camp—a role which was about to be challenged, at least in Asia, by China's action in contrast with the Soviet Union's unwillingness to defend a client state. In fact, as we have seen, China's entrance into the Korean Civil War, which stalled its economic reconstruction and brought the threat of an American invasion, was taken reluctantly. [60]

During September and October of 1950, Moscow Radio had been vague and cautious in its assurances of support to P'yŏngyang. The Russian statements of support became stronger, however, in direct correlation to the actions of the PRC. By late October, Moscow was convinced that the Chinese were definitely going to enter Korea. On November 1, for example, it said that "the Korean people, who have been emancipated by the mighty Soviet forces, will never throw themselves on their knees before the American capitalists." Moscow now felt calmer making such strong statements, as it had become apparent that "the mighty Soviet forces" were not going to be called upon once more to repeat their feat.

The CPV stationed itself in late October to guard the dams in northern Korea which helped to supply the PRC with hydroelectric power. [61] The North Koreans, along with the Russians, now stressed in their messages to Peking that the war was for the defense of China. For example, Sinŭiju (the temporary North Korean capital) Radio stated on November 5 that the Americans "exposed their ambition to invade China by infring-

ing on China's territory and bombing the Chinese population."
Moscow Radio, on the same day, echoed this line: "It is very
clear that the invader Americans have meddled in Korea and
Formosa for the purpose of invading the People's Republic of
China." Sinŭiju Radio stated on November 7 its new perception of North Korea's relationship with the Soviet Union: We
are fighting the American aggressors while striving to cement
our friendship with the Soviet people—realizing that this is a
guarantee of victory in our struggle for unification and independence." (Emphasis added.)

In other words, the Soviet Union could at best be relied
upon only for military hardware and some advisers. On the other
hand, P'yŏngyang well understood the fact that the CPV had
come to its aid largely in order to protect Chinese territory, rather
than as a spontaneous act to save the North Korean regime. For
example, the first North Korean announcement of the CPV's
fighting in Korea read:

> Participating in operations along with the People's armed
> forces, under the unified command of the general head-
> quarters of the People's armed forces, were volunteer units
> formed by the Chinese people who want to defend their
> homes and their fatherland, oppose the American aggres-
> sors and support the struggle of the Korean people. (Radio
> P'yŏngyang, November 5, 1950.)

Several interesting conclusions suggest themselves from
this brief quotation. Firstly, the mention of the "Chinese people." A sophisticated distinction, it begs the question: why
didn't similar "Russian people" volunteer? Undoubtedly, the
Koreans were aware of precisely what type of help they were
getting and from whom. Secondly, considering the decimation
which both the Korean army and the general population had
suffered, the mention of the "general headquarters of the
People's armed forces" under which the CPV was allegedly
operating can only draw attention to the logical surmise that the

North Korean regime was by now largely dependent upon the CPV for its viability. Thirdly, the order of priorities of the goals of the CPV as mentioned in the *North Korean* statement: obviously, P'yŏngyang itself was under no delusion as to why the PRC had intervened; not primarily to preserve North Korea, but rather in reaction to a perceived threat to it national security.

By November 19, as the war began to turn in China's favor, the tone of Moscow Radio's Home Service became increasingly self-confident: "The imperialist warmongers, rejecting all peace-loving Soviet proposals, are making threats toward the Soviet Union. These gentlemen should, however, know by now that the Soviet people have strong nerves and cannot be intimidated by threats."

In late November, Pak Hŏn-yŏng attended the Second World Peace Conference in Moscow. Realizing that no Soviet troops were to be forthcoming to Korea, he instead lobbied for arms and other material supplies.[62] During this month, the PRC press was full of stories telling of North Korea's help to the PLA during the Chinese Civil War. The Russians, in turn, made plain to the Koreans the reason for the PRC's aid, in order that Russian influence would not be completely negated. Moscow Radio of November 25 broadcast to Korea, in Korean, the information that "the participation by the Chinese volunteers in the Korean War is to maintain *their* country's independence and freedom."

Each of the three communist allies held different goals and each sustained different costs during the Korean Civil War. North Korea, subjected to merciless bombing and serving as the battlefield upon which the horror of the war was actually carried out, naturally now viewed the war as an unlimited one of survival. China saw the war as, for her, a defensive one, fought upon her neighbor's territory in order to forestall an American attack across the Yalu River.[63] For China therefore, the conflict was meant to be a limited one, ultimately aimed at convincing the United States that a land war with China would be one of attrition which Washington could not hope to win.

In a curious process of "mirror image," the Soviet Union perceived the war in much the same manner as did the United States: as part of a world chess game in which Europe, in the final analysis, was the crucial square. The most consistent component of the Soviet attitude toward the war was her desire not to use Russian troops on the Korean peninsula. This wish not to engage in an armed confrontation with the United States was the independent variable which governed her relations with China and North Korea in their common opposition to the presence of United Nations forces on the peninsula. [64]

The usual interpretation of China's entrance into the Korean Civil War has been that it was done cautiously, in an effort to protect the Manchurian frontier. While this is obviously correct, it is also an insufficient explanation of the circumstances and causes of China's crossing the Yalu. These can be fully found only in the interrelationship between the three communist allies. It was the Soviet Union's reticence which finally prompted China's intervention. The PRC entered the war not only when it seemed that the United States was actually threatening her territory, but also, and equally importantly, when it became obvious that Russia would steadfastly refuse to use her troops on the peninsula to protect China from an American incursion which was using the Korean peninsula as an invasion corridor. China's hopes for a successful military alliance with the Soviet Union were thus negated on the Korean peninsula in October. Moreover, Korea itself learned not to expect altruistic aid from either neighbor when her national survival was at stake.

Notes

1. Allen Whiting, *China Crosses the Yalu: The Decision to Enter the Korean War* (New York: Macmillan Co., 1960), p. 167.
2. The Observatory: "Su-lien ch'ung hui An-li-hui" [Russia Returns to the Security Council], p. 3. "The Observatory's," unsigned articles represent highly authoritative editorial comment.

In contrast, *Shih-chieh Chih-shih* devoted only two articles to the occasion of the Soviet Union's boycott of the U.N., on January 20 and January 27. Both were short and relatively mild. For example, that of January 27 said: "These actions and expressions of justice will definitely be supported by the democratic opinions of the whole world, including all the people of China."

3. Ibid., p. 2. Emphasis added.
4. *Shanghai Ta Kung Pao* [Impartial Newspaper], editorial: "Su-lien tsai An-li-hui shang-ti cheng-i li-ch'ang" [The Soviet Union's Just Stand in the Security Council], p. 2.
5. "One Week of the International Scene," subtitled "Kuo-chi i-chou An-li-hui ti tou-cheng [The Struggle Inside the Security Council], p. 1.
6. "Women chueh pu yun-hou pa Lien-ho-kuo tsu-chih pien-ch'eng Mei-kuo ch'in-lueh cheng-ts'e ti kung-chu" [We Will Never Allow the U.N. to Be Turned into a Tool of the U.S. Aggressive Policy], p. 4.
7. John Spanier, *American Foreign Policy Since World War Two*, 6th ed. rev. (New York: Frederick A. Praeger, 1973), p. 85.
8. See my article in *Without Parallel: Korean–American Relations Since 1945*, ed. Frank Baldwin (New York: Pantheon Books, 1974).
9. Paul H. Nitze, "The United States in the Face of the Communist Challenge." in C. Grove Haines, ed., *The Threat of Soviet Imperialism* (Baltimore: Johns Hopkins University Press, 1954), p. 374. Emphasis added. See also Paul Hammond, "NSC-68: Prologue to Rearmament," in Warner R. Shilling, Paul Y. Hammond, and Glenn H. Snyder, *Strategy, Politics, and Defense Budgets* (New York: Columbia University Press, 1962), pp. 271–378.
10. Robert Alan Arthur, "Harry Truman Chuckles Dryly," *Esquire*, September, 1971, p. 257.
11. Dean Acheson, *The Korean War* (New York: W.W. Norton, 1971), p. 19.
12. George Kennan, *Memoirs, 1925–1950* (Boston: Little, Brown, and Co., 1967), p. 511.
13. Glenn Paige, *The Korean Decision, June 24–30, 1950* (New York: The Free Press, 1968), p. 86.
14. *New York Times*, by Hanson Baldwin, September 11, 1950. Baldwin notes that his information about Taiwan's defenses was from mid-July 1950.
15. Paige, op.cit., p. 135.
16. Malcolm W. Cagle and Frank A. Manson, *The Sea War in Korea* (Annapolis: United States Naval Institute, 1957), p. 33.

17. Karl Rankin, *China Assignment* (Seattle: University of Washington Press, 1964), pp. 84–85.

18. *U. S. Senate, Hearings Before the Committee on Armed Services and the Committee on Foreign Relations, Military Situation in the Far East, 1951* (Washington: U.S. Government Printing Office, 1951), p. 1763.

19. Foster Rhea Dulles, *American Policy Toward Communist China, 1949–1969* (New York: Thomas Y. Crowell, 1972), p. 95.

20. NCNA, June 27, 1952. Emphasis added. See also Chou En-lai's 1960 comments about President Truman's action: "Beginning from that time the United States started new aggression against China." Cited in Edgar Snow, *Red China Today* (New York: Vintage Books, 1971), p. 116.

21. *New York Times*, July 11, 1956, pp. 1, 24.

22. By late August, American and South Korean troops in the Pusan perimeter outnumbered the North Korean forces two-to-one, and both their arms and morale were far superior. By late August it was only a matter of time before the North met defeat on the perimeter. See David Rees, *Korea: The Limited War* (Baltimore: Penguin Books, 1964), pp. 48–49.

23. "When, on July 9–10, the Chinese were reported to have accepted an Indian proposal that a solution be sought to the conflict along lines that involved, among other things, the restoration of the *status quo ante* in Korea, our government, as will be seen below, was quite unwilling to entertain this suggestion, considering that this would leave South Korea defenseless in the face of the possibility of a renewed North Korean attack." Kennan, op. cit., p. 515.

The *New York Times* of August 1, 1960, p. 5, reported that "the Communist government in China had proposed a settlement of the Korean conflict through mediation by Asian nations. He, 'an official British Commonwealth source,' said that Red China's position was presented recently by Prime Minister Chou En-lai and was conveyed a few days ago to the Indian Ambassador in Peking, K.M. Panikkar."

The difference in the dates of these two accounts suggests that China was involved in finding a peaceful solution to the conflict throughout the month of July. Another indication of the PRC's desire to not become involved in the war was given in a July 16 speech by Ch'en Yi, the commander of the East China Military Area, at the Second Session of the East China Military and Administrative Council, in which he spoke of the "*eventual* defeat of the American imperialists and Syngman Rhee's gang." Peking Radio, July 20, 1950. Emphasis added.

24. Burton Crane from Taiwan, in a dispatch to the *New York Times* of July 23, 1950, p. 1.

25. Whiting, op. cit., pp. 124–26. On p. 87 Prof. Whiting suggests that the PRC considered diplomatic and military intervention from early August.

26. Most of this speculation is based upon Robert Kierman, *The Fluke That Saved Formosa* (Center for International Studies, Cambridge: M.I.T. Press, 1954).

27. The information in this paragraph was obtained from Tai-hsun Tsuan, "An Explanation of the Change in U.S. Policy Toward China in 1950, unpublished Ph.D. dissertation, University of Pennsylvania, 1969, pp. 24–24.

28. "Check American Aggression in Taiwan," carried by NCNA, November 30, 1950. Ironically, the Truman administration had instructed General MacArthur *not* to visit Taiwan "since the State Department was still worried about the political repercussions of placing the Seventh Fleet in the Formosa Strait. The advice was ignored, and on 31 July the General flew to Taipeh. . . ." Denis Stairs, *The Diplomacy of Constraint: Canada, the Korean War, and the United States* (Toronto: University of Toronto Press, 1974), p. 96. Emphasis added.

29. Whiting, op. cit., p. 54.

30. Ibid., p. 53.

31. "Kuo-chi wen-t'i chieh-ta" [International Questions and Answers], p. 20.

32. "Ch'ao-hsien jen-min neng-kou tai-chi Mei-kuo ch'in-lueh chih ma?" [Are the Korean People Able to Repel the American Invaders?], p. 7.

33. "Ch'ao-hsien jen-min tui chieh-fang chan-cheng chih sheng-li ti chan wang" [The Victorious Prospect of the Korean People's Liberation War], p. 4.

34. Whiting, op. cit., pp. 28–29.

35. "Two Different Lines on the Question of Peace and War," *Peking Review*, no. 27, (1963). The "heavy sacrifices" included the death of one of Mao Tse-tung's sons in the war—a not inconsquential event in analyzing the consequences of China's involvement in the war for later Sino–Soviet relations. Furthermore, Peking borrowed at least $2 billion from Moscow in order to wage the war—money which it paid back fully. Allen Whiting, "Contradictions in the Moscow–Peking Axis," *Journal of Politics* (February 1958), p. 130.

36. P'yŏngyang Radio, August 12, 1950.

37. P'yŏngyang Radio, July 1, 1950. This order granted more authority to Kim Il-sŏng. The week's delay is interesting and peripherally adds to the hypothesis presented in chapter 5 that the timing of the war reflected a rather sudden decision.

38. *Nodong Sinmun* (Korean Workers' Party official daily newspaper) editorial of July 13, 1950: "Our Task is One of Righteousness, So We Are Destined To Win." Broadcast over P'yŏngyang Radio, July 14.

39. *Nodong Sinmun*, editorial of July 25: "The Korean People Will Not Tolerate the Barbaric Bombing of the American Imperialists." Broadcast over P'yŏngyang Radio, July 27.

40. Rees, op. cit., p. 43.

41. P'yŏngyang Radio, August 16, 1950.

42. *People's China*, "People's War in Korea," by Jack Chen, September 16, 1950, p. 14.

43. Moscow Radio, in Mandarin, "American Aggressors Are Planning to Invade Northeast China via Korea," August 31, 1950. Emphasis added.

44. Moscow Radio, in Korean, September 11, 1950. Emphasis added.

45. *South China Morning Post*, October 2, 1950. p. 14.

46. P'yŏngyang Radio, October 2, 1950.

47. *New York Times*, October 10, 1950, p. 11, quoting the Russian note of protest. Also see "Siberian Air Raid Admitted by U.S.," *New York Times*, October 20, 1950, p. 2.

48. *New York Times*, October 7, 1950, p. 1. Dispatch by Lindsay Parrott from Tokyo. Emphasis added.

49. *South China Morning Post*, October 14, 1950, p. 14. Emphasis added. Morton Halperin's belief that there were always tacit limits to the air war in Korea seems to be erroneous. The perceived threat of American air and naval involvement with the Soviet Union proved quite potent. See *Political Science Quarterly* (March 1963), p. 1339.

50. See "editor's note" in the *Foreign Broadcast Information Service Daily Reports*, no. 197, October 10, for an explanation of the Korean terms.

51. "The People of China under the People's Democracy are Enthusiastically Supporting the Patriotic Struggle of the Korean People."

52. Whiting, op. cit., p. 115.

53. Ibid., p. 192.

54. There is an unpersuasive literature which argues that South Korea launched the war. For a recent example, see Karunakar Gupta, "How Did the Korean War Begin?" in *China Quarterly* (October–December, 1972), pp. 699–716. Mr. Gupta based this argument upon confused press accounts of late June which momen-

tarily claimed that Seoul had attacked the North Korean border city of Haeju on June 25. First, however, it is doubtful that such an attack took place; secondly, and more importantly, the fact of an alleged attack upon Haeju is irrelevant to an understanding of the beginning of the war. Along an extended front line which had seen such attacks on both sides for a year, such an assault would not have "started" the war. See the rejoinders to Mr. Gupta's article by Chong-sik Lee, W. E. Skillend, and myself in *China Quarterly* (April–June, 1973), pp. 354–68.

55. Moscow Home Service, October 12, 1950.
56. "Only thirty per cent of the North Korean soldiers who had crossed the thirty-eighth parallel on June 25 remained in action by September 15." Robert Leckie, *Conflict: The History of the Korean War, 1950–1953* (New York: G. P. Putnam's Sons, 1962), p. 146.
57. K. M. Panikkar, *In Two Chinas* (London: Allen and Unwin, 1955), p. 110.
58. Harold Hinton, *Communist China in World Politics* (Boston: Houghton Mifflin Co., 1966), p. 213.
59. Ibid., p. 214. For an insightful account of China's reactions as American troops approached its border, see Edward Friedman, "Dealing with an Irrational Power," in *America's Asia,* ed. Mark Selden and Edward Friedman (New York: Pantheon Books, 1971).
60. See Edward E. Rice, *Mao's Way* (Berkeley and Los Angeles: University of California Press, 1972), pp. 123–26.
61. Here we differ in part with Whiting, op. cit., p. 159, who argues that neither the dams nor the heavy industry in Manchuria itself was vital to China's decision to intervene. Yet, if the war had been fought in Vietnam in 1950 it is quite conceivable that the Chinese would not have sent troops into the Indochinese peninsula in such numbers, or as "early" as they did in Korea. Tokyo Radio, for example, noted November 1, 1950, that "the Sinuiju Radio of the North Korean government, intercepted by the Korean Information Press [K.I.P.], said on October 31 that the North Korean People's Volunteer Corps Headquarters has organized and rushed especially trained volunteer corps to the Sup'ung–Pyoktong–Sambong area to guard the electric power generation zone along the Yalu River against the U.N. forces.

"The same broadcast as heard by the K.I.P. also said that the Chinese Communist Army in the same area on the Manchurian side is poised for action because of the great effect on industry in Manchuria of the electric power generation zone along the Yalu River."

It should be noted that the first CPV armed positions were indeed taken to defend these hydroelectric generators.

62. "A few days ago, when I left Korea, numerous people came to the People's Army General Headquarters from the area occupied by the enemy and asked for arms to fight against the enemy forces." Moscow Radio, in Korean, quoting Pak Hŏn-yŏng, November 22, 1950.

63. Thus, Wu Wei-chi, "one of the first volunteers to cross the Yalu River," is quoted as follows by New China News Agency (NCNA), December 20, 1950: "My unit asked three times in one day to be assigned to action against the Americans—not the puppets. We were scared that we might have been forgotten and there was no harm in asking. We volunteered to defend our country, not to sit around."

64. Adam Ulam, *Expansion and Coexistence: The History of Soviet Foreign Policy, 1917–1967* (New York: Frederick A Praeger, 1968), p. 525. "One thing remains clear, and that is the extreme reluctance of the Soviets to become involved militarily in any phase of the Korean conflict. The epithet 'peace-loving,' bestowed on herself by Stalin's Russia, was certainly well merited from that point of view."

7

War

The DPRK had fought for national reunification; an indication of this attitude is the fact that throughout 1950, and until the beginning of armistice talks in July of 1951, the North Korean media consistently referred to Seoul as "the capital of the Republic." As is often stated in western literature on the war, P'yŏngyang misjudged the American determination to defend South Korea. It should be noted, however, that American opinion at the time made the same mistake. The *New York Times* of June 27, for example, reported that the opinion in Washington "appeared to be to keep South Korea supplied with all the arms that General Douglas MacArthur could rush to the beleaguered country . . . but to avoid any semblance of direct military intervention by this country." Thomas J. Hamilton, the *Times's* chief correspondent at the United Nations, reported in the same issue that the United States had been "studying the possibility of asking the Security Council to authorize the use of United States troops . . . a usually well-informed source said tonight [June 26] that he did not believe it would go this far because of the increasing deterioration of the situation in southern Korea."

The North Korean judgment of America's reaction to the initiation of hostilities on the peninsula was thus a reasonable, if inaccurate, one. Moreover, DPRK documents captured by American forces in late July of 1950 indicate that P'yŏngyang had attempted to account for various contingencies before the June invasion. The North Korean timetable called for the conquest of

175

the south within ten days, but their plans, however, *did* consider
the possibility of the entrance of the United States into the war.
In that case, the expectation was of a two-month war, followed
by a North Korean victory.[1] Considering the undermanned
American occupation force in Japan, this was a reasonable contingency plan.

As noted earlier, North Korean hopes for a decisive victory
faded by mid-July 1950 with the stalemate on the Pusan perimeter. Apparently P'yŏngyang still felt at this time that some type of
success could be achieved, perhaps by keeping the United Nations forces bottled up at the southern tip of the peninsula. North
Korean internal propaganda stressed three points in mid-
September of 1950: 1) the USSR and China had offered military
assistance to North Korea, but Kim Il-sŏng had rejected this
offer; 2) the conflict was a civil war; 3) Japanese troops were
fighting with the United Nations forces. P'yŏngyang told its
people that they must fight without external military assistance
in order to prevent a third world war.[2]

Another Look at the U.S.–Soviet Nonconfrontation

At the beginning of the war, Washington had been
nervous about Russia's intentions. It dispatched a message to
Moscow on June 27 asking for the Soviet Union's "good offices"
in influencing the North Koreans to withdraw behind the 38th
parallel. On July 6, President Truman reversed an Air Force
directive that American planes would overfly Russian cities and
air bases on reconnaissance sorties. By mid-August, however, as
the Soviet leaders failed to respond militarily to the American
intervention in Korea, and as it became increasingly evident on
the battlefield that the North Koreans would not be victorious,
the United States began to think in less cautious terms, both in

relation to affronting the Russians and with respect to the goals of the war.

On August 10, American planes, for the first time, bombed Najin—the largest North Korean city nearest to the Soviet border (seventeen miles)—which was the major transmission belt for supplies coming across the frontier. Three weeks later, on September 4, a Soviet warplane was shot down over the Yellow Sea south of South Korea (lat. 38° 51'N, long. 123° 35'E). The pilot's body was recovered at the scene and identification was made, although no public announcement was made at the time.[3] Amazingly, at this juncture of America's accelerating interest in broadening the concept of "containment," and while provocative incidents were taking place which might have drawn the Russians into the war, Washington both chose to broadcast its goal of a reunified Korea and, from the available evidence, did not seek to mollify Russian fears about what this might mean in terms of United States troops stationed on the banks of the Tumen River (the border between the Soviet Union and North Korea), not far from Vladivostok.

At this point, in late August of 1950, important sections of the American intelligence community were pointing out the possibility of the USSR's returning to North Korea, by North Korean invitation, to reoccupy that country. In that case, they foresaw that: 1) world public opinion would favor a cessation of hostilities at the 38th parallel; 2) the United States, in that event, should not become militarily involved with Soviet forces in Korea; and 3) the de facto division of Korea at the 38th parallel would, therefore, continue.[4] In short, despite the fact that Washington had cause to worry about the Soviet Union's very real potential to steal its military triumph by the simple act of reintroducing Russian soldiers on the Korean peninsula, it continued its bellicose stance of "rollback."

As noted in the last chapter, these provocative incidents continued until the climactic American strafing of the Soviet aerodrome on October 8. At the end of September, 1950, as

American forces were poised on the 38th parallel preparing to strike into a communist country for the first time since 1919, the Soviet Union was dispatching open warning signals. For example, Moscow censorship allowed this A.P. dispatch through at the end of the month, which was printed in the *New York Times* of September 30: "Some diplomatic observers in this capital express their view that a United Nations move beyond the Parallel could bring about very serious consequences involving both the Soviet Union and China." In fact, however, the Russians did not reintroduce their troops onto the peninsula in an effort to bluff to a halt the advancing American forces, a gamble Moscow probably would have won.

As American troops prepared to enter North Korea—and approach the Russian border on the Tumen River—the Soviet delegate in the United Nations, Andrei Vishinsky, proposed a cease-fire along the lines of what the U.S. had wanted in the 1945–47 period, providing for all-Korean elections supervised by a United Nations commission. By this time, however, the United States and its allies were scenting victory, and Vishinsky's compromise proposal was defeated by a vote of 46 to 5 on October 3.

Mid-September of 1950 had seen the crucial moment for North Korean fortunes: General MacArthur's forces landed at Inch'ŏn on September 15 in conjunction with the United Nations military breakout from the Pusan perimeter. Within two weeks, the North Korean army, outnumbered and drained by its constant exposure to the technologically superior firepower of the American mechanized army and air force, was driven from South Korea. The DPRK, now defeated in the south and about to fight for its very existence in the north as the victorious U.N. forces moved across the 38th parallel after October 1, called upon its neighbors for aid and protection.

Before this reversal, Russian officers had been serving with the North Korean army. An American officer captured in mid-September of 1950, for example, was interrogated separately by a Russian captain, lieutenant colonel, and senior colonel.[5] In the first half of October, North Korean prisoners-of-war told their U.N. intelligence interrogators that the Soviet Union had promised to send an air force with Korean pilots to their aid. [6] This force, of course, did not appear. It was at this juncture that Kim Il-sŏng sent a five-paragraph sycophantic telegram, addressed to "Esteemed Generalissimo Stalin," to the Soviet ruler on the occasion of the second anniversary of the establishment of diplomatic relations between the Democratic People's Republic of Korea and the Soviet Union. Stalin sent back a very restrained two-paragraph telegram, the heart of which read, "I wish the Korean people, heroically defending the independence of their country, a successful conclusion to their struggle of many years' duration for the creation of a united, independent, and democratic Korea." [7]

That the Soviet Union was worried at this time that it might become involved in a military confrontation with the United States was indicated by the publication in mid-1951 of a novel, *Hwang Chen at His Post,* by Alexander Chakovsky. According to the plot, America envisaged only two alternatives in the summer of 1950. The first saw Soviet troops intervening in Korea, leading to a third world war. The second was that American troops would move to the rear of Vladivostok with the aim of starting a general war between the United States and the Soviet Union. [8] Kim Il-sŏng was aware of this Soviet fear and felt that North Korea was serving as a buffer for the Soviet Union against American aggression in Siberia, and therefore deserved Russian military aid.

As we can infer, however, from Stalin's restrained reply to Kim's telegram on October 12, Russian troops were not to be forthcoming. At this time, the North Korean armed forces had reached a nadir. For example, on September 15 the 35th brigade of the North Korean army was activated; it was composed of 8,000 troops, most of whom were South Korean conscripts. About 10 percent were pro-P'yŏngyang volunteers; all of the noncommissioned officers were North Korean. The other 90 percent were forced to join as a result of a house-to-house search.

Recruits ranged up to forty years in age. Anyone refusing induction was threatened with either the imprisonment of their parents, confiscation of their home and personal property, or the denial of their rice ration, U.S. intelligence reported.[9]

At the moment when Chinese troops were marching to the aid of the DPRK, the Russians were still quite concerned about the possibility of American involvement in Siberia. One suggestion of this is the fact that in mid-September the Soviet Union started broadcasting all weather reports in Russian code in the Far East.[10] Another is that martial law was reported to have gone into effect in the Soviet Maritime Province on October 28, after U.N. forces landed at the port of Wŏnsan on the east coast of Korea.[11]

The Soviet Union's Underwhelming Aid

The Chinese People's Volunteers (CPV) arrived as the DPRK was about to cease its existence as an independent state—cause enough for P'yŏngyang's gratitude to Peking. Reinforcing this appreciation was the realization that the CPV itself was not being supplied with sufficient Russian arms. By the same token, China's gratitude toward the Soviet Union must have been less than overwhelming. A breakdown of the sources of the arms captured from the CPV during the first half-year of Chinese involvement in the Korean Civil War suggests that Moscow had not been prompt in supplying badly needed modern weapons to the CPV.

Origin	November, 1950–January, 1951	February–March, 1951
	%	%
Chinese	4.78	6.70
Russian	20.12	6.85
Japanese	15.00	12.20
American	26.00	31.48

The remaining percentages in each time period were either mis-cellaneous or of unknown manufacture. The increase in Ameri-can weapons was due largely to battlefield gains by the com-munist forces. The respective percentages become even more dramatic, moreover, when the sources of the CPV's weapons are charted drawing only upon the two Chinese armies which were in constant contact with United States forces during the first half-year.

Origin	CPV 3rd Field Army	CPV 4th Field Army
	%	%
Chinese	7.10	6.70
Russian	4.30	6.84
Japanese	18.50	12.20
American	50.00	31.48

In sum, China's soldiers depended in large measure either upon pre–Korean Civil War weapons or upon American arms cap-tured on Asian battlefields, rather than upon an abundance of supplies from the Soviet Union.[12]

The potential for strain between the three allies becomes even more pronounced when the *type* of arms which the Soviet Union was supplying to North Korea and China is examined. Much of the heaviest Soviet military materiel, such as the 152mm M1943 howitzer, the 152mm M1937 gun-howitzer, the Joseph Stalin series of heavy tanks, and very heavy artillery, was not turned over to the communist forces fighting in Korea during the war. The North Korean army possessed no field artillery heavier than the 122mm M1931/37 corps gun, no mortar larger than the 120mm M1938, and no tank later than the T-34/85, dating from World War II. Most of these arms came from Soviet surplus stocks and were obsolescent. Interestingly, production was re-cent (1948–50), but the models were outmoded; i.e., the stock might cite a recent year of manufacture, but the quality in terms of fire power would be that of a decade-old weapon.

In sum, the conventional weapons supplied by the Soviet Union to its allies during the war were inferior to the American weapons which they faced. For example, the communist tanks were no match for American antiarmor weapons. Meanwhile, the Soviet heavier tanks were not used in Korea, while the best Soviet antitank weapons—e.g., the 85mm and the 100mm M1944—were also not used; what was supplied was generally incapable of stopping U.N. armored equipment.[13]

The awareness of weak Soviet support during the war deeply distressed China, and undoubtedly was a contributing factor to the Sino–Soviet split which was shortly to follow. A "senior Chinese official" told the editor of the authoritative Cairo newspaper, *Al-Ahram*, in the spring of 1973:

> In the Korean War, we interfered in the fighting. When we interfered, we found ourselves obliged to wait for help from the Soviet Union. The help was delayed at times. We felt torn apart and we suffered. Sometimes we were angry and we begged, but we had to tolerate it because we were on the battlefield and because the modern weapons came from the Soviet Union. The wise man also learns the lesson from the first experience. We have learned an important experience.[14]

CPV–Korean Relations

North Korea was thus faced with the dilemma of depending upon willing Chinese troops with inferior arms, while her more powerful neighbor supplied neither soldiers for the front nor sufficient first-rate military equipment to secure a communist victory in the war. It was under these conditions that the CPV entered Korea.

Following Chairman Mao's axiom that a successful people's army swims among the civilian population like fish, the CPV was anxious to increase its chances of success in the war by maintaining cordial relations with the Korean people. There were factors both helping and hindering this ambition. On the one hand, the Chinese were foreigners in a land of intense nationalism; on the other, in large sections of North Korea the U.N. forces were the hated enemy, against whom the Chinese had come as heroic defenders. The available "hard" evidence on the Chinese reception among the Korean population is scanty and somewhat contradictory, but its thrust seems to indicate that the Chinese were greeted kindly by a large segment of the North Korean population as a result of conscious effort on the part of the CPV.

The CPV soldiers who entered P'yŏngyang in early December of 1950 did not receive a particularly warm welcome, but instead suffered a largely indifferent reception. To overcome this apparent lack of enthusiasm, the CPV came supplied with "receipts" to pay for their food and lodging. The receipts read "Issued by the Supporters Society for Chinese Volunteers in Korea." The amount on the receipt would be deducted from the next food levy imposed by the North Korean authorities. [15] In this manner, the CPV sought to carry on the People's Liberation Army's (PLA) heritage from the Chinese Civil War: namely, that communist soldiers pay for what they take from the local people in order to win the sympathy of potential conscripts, informants, and suppliers. Chinese soldiers also worked in the Korean fields during the war, and by similar means cultivated good relations with the Korean civilian population.

On the other hand, however, CPV prisoners-of-war interviewed by U.N. intelligence interrogators in the fall of 1951 reported that the North Korean civilian attitudes toward the CPV had turned "generally cold." Middle-aged civilians were considered to be relatively cooperative, but the young and the old believed that the continued war and devastation were caused by the presence of the Chinese troops in Korea. Civilians in the rear areas were more kind and helpful toward the Chinese soldiers than those near the front line. By late 1951, according to these informants, the CPV troops did not pay for local food, and North Korean morale was low.

In contrast was a report at the same time that the DPRK Railway Ministry was run jointly with the CPV, and that there was no resentment on the part of the Korean railway workers; the Chinese behaved very well in this particular ministry. [16] It is thus not possible to make sweeping generalizations about the behavior of the CPV and their reception by the North Koreans, except to assert that the record was probably mixed and, considering the general devastation wreaked by American technology upon the DPRK, relations between the CPV and the Korean population were probably as good as an observer might expect in such a situation of attrition and prolonged suffering, with no victory in sight during most of the war.

A further source of Chinese–North Korean friction was the apparent inability of the two armies to work harmoniously with each other. In situations where fighting takes place upon the territory of a weaker ally, it understandably becomes a temptation for the stronger ally to attempt to impose its will upon the military organization of the weaker (consider, for example, American efforts to impose its will upon the South Vietnamese military during the Indochina War). In this context, it was reported in early 1952 that the CPV was refusing to return P'yŏngyang's recruits to the North Korean army according to previously reached agreements between the two allies. Apparently the Chinese were dissatisfied with the North Korean army's combat efficiency, and had therefore been recruiting Koreans directly into the CPV without authorization, using Chinese-speaking Koreans as interpreters. [17]

Although the DPRK army and government must have appreciated the arrival of the CPV as a *deus ex machina*, saving them from certain military defeat, there was hope that China would provide even more help than was actually offered. For example, on December 6, 1950, the South Korean Labor Party headquarters in southeastern Korea issued a directive—probably inspired by information from P'yŏngyang—which claimed that the CPV would be aided by additional forces from the PLA as soon as it reached the 38th parallel.[18]

In sum, however, considering the chaotic conditions under which both the Korean government and people labored during the war, the available evidence suggests that relations between the CPV and their hosts were only as troubled as would be expected in a not untroubled situation. On the other hand, Russian troops in the DPRK who served as advisers or backup forces for Soviet installations (who reentered Korea after the CPV) were often unwelcome among both CPV and North Korean units.[19]

Kim Il-sŏng's Survival

The political position of Kim Il-sŏng was probably tenuous in the late fall of 1950. He was now a defeated military leader and a disgraced one in the eyes of his neighbors, particularly if the hypothesis presented in chapter 6 of his "jumping the gun" is accurate. Because of his military weakness and imminently expected defeat, his survival depended upon the assistance and good will of China and the Soviet Union. This situation presents one of the great unsolved paradoxes of the Korean Civil War: why did China and the Soviet Union continue to support Kim after his defeat?

The question is especially puzzling in the case of China, which had supported the second strongest North Korean military leader, Mu Chŏng. With CPV troops entering Korea on the occasion of the defeat of the leader who had helped to keep Chinese influence out of the Korean peninsula, Peking must have been under strong temptation to support Mu Chŏng and oust Kim Il-sŏng. Kim, keenly aware of his political weakness and of the Chinese proclivity to supplant him with Mu Chŏng, moved quickly. At the third Plenum of the Korean Workers'

Party (KWP) which he chaired on December 21, 1950, he reprimanded Mu Chŏng for insufficient loyalty and failure to defend P'yŏngyang against U.N. forces.[20] (However, it is highly unlikely that P'yŏngyang could have been defended against the U.N. blitzkrieg.) Kim in this way successfully purged Mu Chŏng, and thereby removed his most dangerous rival for power. After Mu Chŏng's purge, Peking successfully asked Kim Il-sŏng for permission to move Mu Chŏng to China.

How was this extraordinary balancing act carried out? There are three possible answers. One is that the Russians and Chinese hesitated to remove Kim at what would be the embarrassing moment of the military defeat of the leader of the DPRK. This, at least on the surface, would appear to be the least satisfactory answer. The second and most persuasive explanation which has been advanced is that Kim's Soviet political adviser, who had lived with him since the retreat north, planned the Third Plenum and brought the Soviet Union's promises of rewards and sanctions to bear both upon China and upon Kim's internal opposition in order to maintain him in power.[21] Undoubtedly, the Soviet Union would not want to let the DPRK pass into China's hands. By the end of 1950 the Russian investment in Kim was too great to gamble on the possibility that the CPV might foreclose Korea from Russian influence.

A third explanation accounts for Kim's survival by the fact that he had been a member of the Chinese Communist Party in the 1930s, so that China now denied its support to Mu Chŏng because of comradely memories of Kim Il-sŏng during his Manchurian years. This last hypothesis suggests the practical manner in which Kim was able to exploit these past bonds: he enlisted the support both of the CPV and of many members of the Korean Yenan Faction through the good offices of a powerful member of the Korean Workers' Party, Ch'oe Ch'ang-ik, who was originally a member of the Yenan Faction before joining Kim's Kapsan group.[22]

Regardless of the means (or a mixture of these three reasons) by which Kim managed to maintain the support of his two communist neighbors, the fact remains that it was a political masterstroke. Kim somehow balanced off competing pressures upon his domestic control, a particularly arduous task considering the fact that each of the penetrating powers had intimate ties to important anti-Kim factions within the Korean Workers' Party. In this case, Kim Il-sŏng was a more successful nationalist leader than the rulers who had come before him.

The U.N. Brands China an "Aggressor"

By early December, 1950, the United Nations forces were retreating rapidly before the advancing Chinese People's Volunteers. On December 15 the United States told the United Nations Truce Commission that it would agree to a ceasefire based on the establishment of a demilitarized zone twenty miles deep, the southern boundary of which would be the 38th parallel. Peking rejected this proposal, which seemed to deny her victorious battlefield position, and repeated her demands for the withdrawal of all foreign troops, withdrawal of United States protection from Taiwan, and China's admission to the United Nations. [23]

In the United Nations, the Soviet delegate first declared that the Chinese People's Volunteers were not "foreign troops," and therefore could remain after other forces had left the peninsula. [24] A few days later, however, the Soviet Union stated in the U.N. that the withdrawal of foreign troops would "entirely dispose of the question of the Chinese People's Volunteers," indicating that a compromise had been struck. [25] Shortly thereafter, the Soviet Union gave qualified support and encouragement to the United Nations Truce Commission. Delegate Jacob A. Malik "spoke in unusually gentle terms about the work of the commission" and suggested that it work not only for a ceasefire, but for the termination of the conflict by linking a ceasefire with "existing issues" in the war. [26]

On January 11, 1951, the U.N. Truce Commission proposed a program which won U.S. support, consisting of: 1) a ceasefire; 2) withdrawal of all foreign troops from Korea "by appropriate stages"; 3) after a ceasefire, the U.S., the U.K., the Soviet Union, and China would hold a Far East Conference to deal with the problems of Taiwan and China's representation in the United Nations. Malik commented that the whole proposal was "foggy" and open to interpretation, except for the first item of a ceasefire; "everything is reduced to a question of ceasefire." [27] Considering the fact that the CPV was still advancing southwards on the peninsula, it is understandable that Peking would be hesitant to enter a ceasefire before some agreement had been reached relative to its political goals. (It should be remembered that the exact opposite of this situation took place in early October, as U.N. forces began their rapid drive into North Korea. The Soviet Union had called for an immediate ceasefire, withdrawal of all foreign troops, and an all-Korean election to be observed by the U.N., with the Soviet Union and China also observing. This proposal was spurned by the United Nations. [28])

China seemed to soften Malik's response on the following day by telling Indian authorities that it would be willing to accept the U.N. plan if all of the questions could be taken up "together." [29] This actually represented a compromise, in that China, for the first time, did not ask the United States to either immediately or unconditionally withdraw its forces from Taiwan. India, encouraged by this new Chinese position, queried Peking for an elaboration.

Meanwhile, the United States House of Representatives, on January 19, adopted a resolution urging the U.N. to declare China an "aggressor"; the Senate followed suit four days later. Because of domestic opinion, the United States government began to call in many of its political IOUs in order to push the "aggressor" label through the U.N., although "it soon became apparent that action similar to that taken by the Security Council in June in meeting the initial North Korean attack was unacceptable to most members of the United Nations as a way of dealing with the Chinese Communist military intervention in Korea".[30] Nevertheless, on January 20 the United States formally asked the United Nations General Assembly to find China guilty of "aggression."

On January 22, Chinese Foreign Minister Chou En-lai stated that "if the principle that all foreign troops should be withdrawn from Korea has been accepted and is being put into practice, the Central People's Government of the People's Republic of China will assume the responsibility to advise the Chinese volunteers to return to China."[31] Moreover, Chou declared, a ceasefire of a "limited time" would be acceptable if discussions were scheduled on the Korean Civil War and Taiwan. On the following day, through the Indian Ambassador to China, this new stance, which evidenced a willingness to compromise, was again presented: 1) if the withdrawal of foreign troops from Korea was "being put into effect," China would "advise the Chinese People's Volulteers to return to China"; 2) settlement of the war would be in two stages. The first would be an agreement at an international conference to "a ceasefire for a limited time period." The second step, after the ceasefire went into effect, would be the settlement of the war and other Far Eastern problems; 3) "The definitive affirmation of the legitimate status of the People's Republic of China in the United Nations must be assured."[32]

This counterproposal, actually not very different from the U.N. Truce Commission's of January 11—and certainly a basis for further negotiations—was immediately rebuffed by the United States, which continued to lobby for the "aggressor" label. On January 28, China told India that if the United States won the vote on accusing her of being an "aggressor" it would "close the door" on any possibility of peace in Korea.[33] On

January 30, by a vote of 44 to 7, the U.N. branded China as an "aggressor." However, as Thomas J. Hamilton noted in a dispatch from the U.N. to the *New York Times* of February 4, 1951, the vote did not allay doubts among third world states:

> Partly to keep the record clear and partly because the United States delegation would not take "no" for an answer, the United Nations General Assembly has now taken the plunge and condemned Communist China's aggression in Korea. The aggression was undeniable, but most of the Asian and Arab countries held back to the last, and the Western European nations accepted it only with the reservation that they would oppose almost any further action.

Probably to indicate that the member states did not agree with the quick and forceful manner in which the United States had pushed this resolution through, the U.N. then voted 42 to 7 to merely *study* the idea of sanctions against China, suggesting that the United Nations was not completely satisfied with a position which had decreased the possibilities of compromise.

The authoritative newspaper *People's Daily* of February 2, in an editorial entitled "The United States Is the Deadly Enemy of World Peace," commented that "the American resolution is a declaration to the people of the whole world that American imperialism does not want to solve the Korean problem through peaceful means and will continue to maintain its policy of war and aggression." In fact, with the passing of the U.N. resolution, the dust of battle settled on the Korean peninsula, not to begin to lift until the summer.

It would appear that the United States, in its anticommunist zeal, had missed an opportunity for negotiations—at the moment when the Chinese had indicated a desire to move toward a compromise position—half a year before they actually began. Furthermore, the barriers which subsequently arose to prevent the successful conclusion of the armistice negotiations until 1953 were not present in January of 1951. Finally, the longer that the war continued the more solid became the Sino–Soviet marriage of convenience.

A Common Cause?

Technically, the command of the North Korean and CPV forces was concentrated in a joint control, headed by Kim Il-sŏng and staffed by both North Korean and Chinese officers. Actually, however, operations were controlled directly, particularly in the latter two years of the war, by the headquarters of the CPV in Mukden.[34] Evidence about this command structure is scanty; it is noteworthy, however, that a joint headquarters of the communist command was reported in Chang Chun (Manchuria) in early December, 1950, headed by Russian Lt. General Kuzma Derevyanko, former chief of the Soviet mission in Japan.[35]

Although the USSR decided early on not to become involved militarily on the Korean peninsula, it did accept the role of supplier, however unsatisfactorily, to the communist forces in Korea. During late December and early January of 1950–51, it was reported that fourteen Soviet ships sailed through the Tsugaru Straits en route to Dairen from Vladivostok.[36] Also early in January the Russian Baltic fleet reportedly was ordered to transfer 3 destroyers, 15 submarines, one cruiser, and the battleship *October Revolution* to the Soviet Far East Fleet; this would increase that fleet by 20 percent.[37] In August, 1951, it was reported that the USSR and Eastern European ships using the Tsugaru Straits numbered 51, an increase of 33 percent over July.[38] Overall during 1950–51 the Soviet Union reportedly possessed approximately 526 commercial ships, and utilized 159 of them in the Far East. In the context of the importance of historical memories upon the exercise of a nation's foreign policy, an idea presented in chapters 1 and 2, it is interesting to note that the Russian fleet used only the Tsugaru Straits, rather than the shorter Tsushima Straits—where they had suffered a devastating naval defeat a half century before.

It was evident early in the war that relations between the Soviet Union and China were strained. The Sino–Soviet Agreement on the Frontier Waterways, ratified on January 2, 1951, may afford an indication of the state of relations between the two neighbors. While formal procedures for border crossings are common and useful, the tone of this document suggests mutual distrust. Article Fifteen, for example, stipulated that workers and technical personnel were permitted to cross the frontier only when they possessed the written approval of authorities in their own country, which was then to be acknowledged by the signature of the other contracting party. Personnel allowed to cross the border were permitted to do so only in daylight and had to be accompanied by a representative of the other side of the Joint Commission. Moreover, the defense organizations of both countries had to be notified in advance if such border crossings were intended. [39]

Another indication of the cautious manner in which these two fraternal states treated each other was the absence of Chinese consulates in the Soviet Union (the reverse was not true; the Russians maintained dispersed consulates in order to look after their many economic interests in the People's Republic). Again, data on this aspect of Sino–Soviet relations are scanty, but they do point to a surprising dearth of Chinese contacts within the Soviet Union. On September 6, 1951, New China News Agency reported that China's Consul-General in Vladivostok, Chou Tung, was recalled and appointed Chief of the Personnel Department in the Foreign Ministry; no replacement was recorded, nor were other Chinese consulates in the Soviet Union mentioned by NCNA in succeeding years. In China's 1958 *World Knowledge Almanac* there appeared no mention of Chinese consulates in the Soviet Union in a "list of nations exchanging consul generals and consuls with China."[40] Consequently, while Soviet potential for penetration of the Chinese political system by the use of diplomatic personnel was relatively high, no such ability apparently existed for China within the Soviet Union, perhaps reflecting Russian suspicion of any Chinese influence.

Throughout the war, Russian propaganda aimed at China constantly played upon a major Chinese fear (one which the Soviet Union shared): the threat of Japanese remilitarization under American auspices. In each instance in the past half-century, Japan's intrusions into Chinese territory had begun with the Korean peninsula. In this context, Russia could picture the Korean Civil War as an analogue of past Japanese aggression against China. Thus, Moscow Radio of January 17, 1951, broadcast to China, in Mandarin, the warning that "the American imperialists plan to use the human and material resources of Japan for their aggressive designs in Asia. Therefore, the American authorities in Japan are speeding up the remilitarization." Moscow usually stressed China's defensive self-interest in intervening in the war. But, as a March 7, 1951, Moscow Radio broadcast, in Mandarin, added:

> Everyone knows that the Japanese militarists have always been a threat to world peace, and *especially to the security of the USSR.* They were the ones who cooperated with the American interventionists in invading Siberia. They were forced to retreat, but since that time the Japanese militarists have always wanted to *invade the Soviet Far East.* (Emphasis added.)

By the spring of 1951, Peking could not have escaped the conclusion that she was fighting for Russian territorial integrity without an adequate supply of Soviet equipment. The North Koreans had already come to a similar realization. On February 4, 1951 (Soviet Army Day), Kim Il-sŏng sent a lengthy telegram to Stalin thanking him for Russia's help in the war; Stalin answered with one sentence, which expressed his "profound gratitude" for North Korea's struggle against American aggression. Radio

P'yŏngyang of February 4, reflecting its awareness that Soviet
help was not munificent, announced the slogans for North
Korean Army Day (February 8). The applicable ones, by number,
were:

4. "Reinforce the friendship between the Korean people's
   forces and the Chinese People's Volunteers."
30. "All people: Appreciate the Chinese people's earnest
    participation in the Fatherland Liberation War."
31. "Hurrah to the progressive good will between the
    Soviet people and the Korean People's Supreme Com-
    mittee."
32. "Hurrah to the Soviet military forces, which are the
    great strength for world peace as well as the Korean
    People's liberation, and the powerful military strength
    for the purpose."

The irony in such contrasting paeans of praise could not
have been lost on the careful observer. On the same day, Radio
P'yŏngyang broadcast a speech by a "high-ranking officer,"
Chon Yi-hwan, declaring that "owing to the Soviet assistance
during the past five years, we learned how to drive tanks and
how to fly airplanes. But for this assistance we could not have
achieved our victories." Conspicuous by its absence was any
"appreciation" for either Soviet troops or arms during the current hostilities.

By late January, 1951, the CPV southward thrust had been
blunted; as China suffered heavy casualties and outdistanced
her supply lines, her hopes for a decisive victory dimmed shortly
after her entrance into the war. In mid-February the United
Nations forces began counterattacking across the front and, in
most areas, began a slow, dogged advance back to the 38th
parallel. Seoul was recaptured by U.N. forces on March 14—the
fourth and last time that it was to change hands during the long
war. (Out of a prewar population of two million, Seoul's inhabi-
tants had now shrunk to 200,000, indicating the war's cost to
each side.) The following day Soviet Far Eastern Radio, based in

Khabarovsk, broadcast in Korean a message which appeared to indicate Russia's vital concern in keeping the U.N. forces away from Soviet territory. The broadcast cited a 1948 letter, allegedly written by Syngman Rhee's adviser, Chung Ku-yong, and addressed to Rhee, which it claimed was captured by North Korean forces when they took Seoul for the first time in June of 1950. Broadcast on Khabarovsk Radio on March 15, the letter described South Korea's prewar plans: "The Japanese army must maintain Japan's security from attack from Vladivostok; the South Korean and American armies must advance as far as Harbin; and the Chinese Nationalist army must retake China proper, starting from Kwantung Province." Indeed, everything was mentioned in this Soviet broadcast to Korea but Korea. P'yŏngyang could be forgiven if it felt that it was now playing the traditional geographical role of an invasion route, rather than that of a fraternal ally whose territorial integrity was the first priority of the war.

The Peace-Talk Proposal

With the data which we now possess about the inadequate equipment which the Soviet Union was supplying to the communist side, a rereading of some of the slogans of the period may afford added weight to the suspicion that not all was harmonious between the three states. A comparison of the 1950 and 1951 May Day slogans of China and the Soviet Union is a case in point.

In 1950, the PRC published its list of slogans one day after the Soviet Union issued theirs. China was probably suggesting respect—and perhaps wanted to synchronize slogans with its more powerful neighbor—by this short delay. In 1951, the PRC published its list of May Day slogans six days *before* the Soviet Union, perhaps as an indication of China's intention to act independently. In 1951 the PRC mentioned Korea six times directly and four times indirectly, while the Soviet Union spoke of Korea only once; the latter's May Day slogans made no mention of the CPV, while the PRC's list lacked any mention of Stalin. In the 1950 slogans, the PRC waxed eloquently about "Chinese–Soviet friendship, unity, and mutual assistance"; in 1951, the PRC waited until slogan number 27 to declare the relatively mild: "Long live the close unity between the two great Soviet and Chinese nations!" Of course, this type of Kremlinology is crude and its insight problematic; yet, given the known overall circumstances, the study of slogans may grant the observer an intuitive "feel" for the jargon within which the developing strains manifested themselves.

Communications between the three states may have been guised in esoteric garb, but a close reading of the exchange of radio broadcasts reveals certain developing patterns. For example, after Khabarovsk Radio broadcast its suggestion that Koreans must fight to safeguard their neighbors, P'yŏngyang Radio broadcast a message in Korean on March 20 which may well have been meant to underscore for the North Korean population the fact that the Soviet Union was not supplying the weapons and materiel needed to fight the invader. Although the statement comparing Moscow's 1940 and 1951 defense budgets was phrased in complimentary terms, the underlying message would seem to have been a complaint: "The Soviet Union's state budget for national defense for 1951 represents 2.2 percent of the total expenditure. Compare this with the 32.5 percent of the prewar national defense appropriation."

On the other hand, North Korea, enduring epidemic, ground fighting, and death from the sky, could not affort to alienate either of her benefactors, regardless of the degree of disappointment with the aid supplied. On a more personal level, Kim Il-sŏng, who apparently owed his survival from a Mu Chŏng–CPV threat to Moscow's support, continued to depend upon Russian assistance. Consequently, although dissatisfied with the type and amount of aid from Moscow, the DPRK often obscured this discontent.

An example of the manner in which the DPRK walked a fine line between her two suppliers was a P'yŏngyang Radio broadcast, in Korean, of April 15, 1951:

> The Korean people have been receiving tremendous material aid particularly from the Soviet Union. Even before the aggression by the American imperialists, the Soviet Union had been extending us tremendous moral and material support. Indeed, without Soviet aid, we could not hope to win ultimate victory.
>
> Meanwhile, also tremendous is the support of our neighbor, China. China has been extending material aid, and furthermore has sent volunteers to help us. China is also sending relief supplies as well as munitions.

Two weeks later, on April 30, P'yŏngyang Radio emphasized to its listeners that Koreans were fighting in the front line for the defense of their allies—the implication being that both of those beneficiaries should generously aid North Korea in the common fight: "The American imperialists are bent on making Korea a springboard for their aggression in Asia and eventually the whole world. Therefore, the war affects not only Korea but the *Soviet Union* and China as well." (Emphasis added.) The Soviet Union is now again placed first, probably to indicate dissatisfaction with the assistance being given to the DPRK for this common effort.

The Chinese and North Korean armies staged a massive attack in April and May of 1951 in an attempt to drive southward, but were driven back with tremendous losses. It is estimated that the Chinese and North Koreans lost over 90,000 men in the last week of their attack, May 17–23.[41] After this communist offensive, United Nations forces were never again to be driven south. As communist forces retreated toward the 38th parallel, the United States began to signal to the other side a willingness for negotiations. The communists, suffering severe losses of men and fighting with inadequate equipment, responded to these American overtures.[42]

Bernard Brodie notes that in the early spring of 1951:

the Chinese and their allies, terribly bloodied from the
events of the previous month, were in no position to withstand the powerful United Nations force that now began to
push northward, supported by a large and completely dominant airpower and by naval gunfire on both flanks of the
peninsula.

Professor Brodie argues that the PLA was "smashed" and was
then saved by the truce talks which began in June.[43]

The communist states reacted in different ways, with the
Russians stressing that they did not speak for the Chinese.[44]
Although there undoubtedly was communication between Moscow, Peking, and P'yŏngyang before Ambassador Malik made
his radio speech on June 23 in New York suggesting that the
Soviet Union was agreeable to Korean armistice negotiations,[45]
a rereading of the available data suggests that there was some
disagreement among the three states on the timing and flexible-
ness of that statement.

It should be kept in mind that throughout the Korean Civil
War the global center of gravity for Soviet foreign policy, just as
for Washington, was Europe. Korea was looked upon either as a
test or as a drain, but not as the focus of concern generally.
Perhaps the issue that worried the Soviet Union the most during
this period was the question of German rearmament.[46] A foreign
ministers' deputies conference convened in Paris on March 5,
1951, to discuss this sensitive topic. The Americans were pushing for German rearmament over the protests of their allies.
Because each of the states at the Paris meeting disagreed on the
major question before them, the conference collapsed on June
21.[47] It was most probably not a coincidence that Soviet Ambassador to the United Nations Malik issued his conciliatory statement on Korean negotiations immediately after the failure of this
conference. The Soviet Union had a vital interest in maintaining
communications with the West; the timing of Malik's speech
was apparently calculated to demonstrate the flexibility of the

Soviet Union, which might benefit its negotiating position in Europe as well as in Korea.[48]

Malik's speech of June 23 *omitted* the three political conditions on which the Chinese and North Koreans had previously laid much stress: 1) the withdrawal of foreign troops from Korea; 2) the return of Taiwan to China; and 3) the seating of China in the United Nations. Instead, Malik proposed a simple military armistice in the field. The reactions of the two affected states indicated their attitude toward this Russian initiative. *Jen-min Jih-pao* [People's Daily] published its first comment on Malik's proposals on June 25 in an article entitled "One Year of the Korean War." Although stating that China wholeheartedly supported Malik's proposal, the article complained about the American "seizure of China's territory, Taiwan."

Another indication of China's dissatisfaction with the Russian proposal is suggested by the contents of the June 29, 1951, Cominform publication *For a Lasting Peace, For a Lasting Democracy.* This issue was devoted to the thirtieth anniversary of the Chinese Communist Party; the main articles were written by Chu Teh, Teng Hsiao-p'ing, Liu Ting-yi, Ch'en Yun, and one anonymous Russian writer. The four Chinese writers totally ignored the role of Stalin in the development of Chinese communism, and attributed the CCP's success to the theories and leadership of Mao Tse-tung. They acknowledged the historical importance of the Russian revolution, but argued that it was valid only for some industrialized countries, though not for colonial systems.

The Russian author, on the other hand, credited Stalin with the "profound attention he paid to the struggle for freedom and independence and for the assistance to the Chinese Communist Party, past and present." Ch'en Yun, however, wrote not one undiluted word of praise about direct aid from the Soviet Union, although he did say that "we are not against receiving aid and the Chinese people realize that in the transformation of their economy they can expect help only from the Soviet Union and the other People's Democracies." Chu Teh, in his five-column article, left out all mention of Russian aid.

Similarly, the North Korean response to the Russian attitude toward armistice negotiations was one of elliptical hesitation and apparent disapproval.[49] The DPRK made no open comment on Malik's speech until the beginning of July, when it responded to the American proposal for specific negotiation meetings. However, its attitude was revealed by a roundabout means. The Soviet Union on June 10 had sent a memorandum to the United States on the problem of a Japanese peace treaty, and then had officially forwarded this memorandum to North Korea on June 11. The DPRK waited until June 27 to publicly respond to this Russian action. P'yŏngyang Radio on that date broadcast its response, addressed to the Soviet Minister of Foreign Affairs, Andrei Vishinsky. P'yŏngyang asserted that it "must be granted the right to participate in a peace treaty for Japan," and listed Korea's special interests in the Japanese treaty. This statement, directed to the Soviet Union rather than the United States, read very much like a message of protest at Moscow's handling of the armistice negotiations.

This impression takes on additional force when coupled with reports that there had been no discussion of an armistice within North Korea *until* shortly before Malik's June 23 speech. There then arose deep differences within the Korean leadership about the wisdom of engaging in the armistice talks. It was allegedly because of these internal disputes that the DPRK wanted to prolong the armistice discussions with the United States in the summer of 1951 in order to allow the leadership's opinions to coalesce.[50] Probably reflecting North Korea's desire to maintain some independence in the forthcoming negotiations, Kim Il-sŏng, in an unusually florid speech of June 30, sought to assure each of his neighbors, without mentioning the soon-to-commence talks, that he appreciated their assistance:

Our literary and artistic works have failed thus far to give full expression to the Soviet Union as the bastion of world

peace, and the Soviet Union as the liberator of our Fatherland, and the Soviet Union which will be our immortal
friend. Neither have they depicted ably our great comrades
in arms, the Chinese People's Volunteers, who are fighting
shoulder to shoulder with us in our sacred war against the
American imperialist savages. (P'yŏngyang Radio, in
Korean, June 30, 1951.)

Meanwhile, P'yŏngyang Radio, in Korean, continued to
report to its people that they were fighting to protect the Soviet
Union. Two examples of these broadcasts are one of July 29, 1951,
which commented that Japan was being remilitarized by the
United States "in order to carry on aggression against the
Korean, Chinese, Vietnamese, and other peace-loving Asiatic
peoples and then against the Soviet Union and other nations of
the people's democracies," and one of August 6, 1951, which
stated that the United States "insists that the proposed demarca-
tion line be drawn inside North Korea, which will give them
advantages in case of their attack on China and the Soviet
Union." Presumably, P'yŏngyang was repeating the same message in its conversations with Moscow.

The Chinese People's Volunteers, for their part, apparently
reassured the DPRK that they were sensitive to the fact that the
Soviet Union was not supplying arms *gratis,* and that therefore
there was a difference between the will of the Chinese and the
North Koreans, who were doing the actual fighting, and that of
the Russians, who were merely the suppliers. For example, the
head of the CPV, P'eng Teh-huai, stated at a North Korean
reception that "on our side, we had a few disadvantages which
prevented us from winning. We already have our planes. The
Chinese people are staging a drive to *buy* arms." (Emphasis
added.) This underlined the fact that the Russians in the past did
not supply enough arms, and that even now the Chinese were
forced to *buy* their weapons.

Friction between China and the Soviet Union over what
tactics to adopt in Korea was apparent as early as the summer of
1951. In July, a Chinese political mission reportedly arrived in

the DPRK. It became part of the Chinese military group resident in Korea, because the Russians would not allow a separate Chinese political mission in the DPRK. Later, under Soviet pressure, the political personnel became part of a combined Chinese–North Korean group. On September 2, 1951, the Russians allegedly abrogated the authority of the North Koreans to make decisions at the Kaesŏng Armistice Talks by encouraging the Chinese members to move to the joint military headquarters of the Chinese–Russian–North Korean commands at Chang Chun, Manchuria, thereby effectively dissolving the combined Chinese–DPRK mission. The North Koreans reportedly had only three liaison officers in Chang Chun, and therefore were essentially merely listening to Soviet and Chinese advice.[51]

By September, 1951, United States intelligence estimated that Soviet forces in Korea consisted of: three antiaircraft artillery divisions, 6,000 men; one security regiment, 1,500; military advisers, 2,000; engineers, 1,500; counterespionage guards, 1,500; miscellaneous antiaircraft artillery coast defense, 1,500; signal and radar, 1,000; civilian advisers, 400; one artillery division, 5,000; ground and air troops, 5,000; hospital and medical personnel, 500.[52] Rumors circulated within North Korea in the fall of 1951 that Russia would enter the war about June, 1952.[53] The Korean population's hope was understandable in light of the fact that Russian forces were present in numbers sufficient to gain attention and credence among North Koreans anxious for military support from their powerful neighbor.

On September 7, 1951, at the Chinese–DPRK border city of Antung, Chang Tsung-sun, a deputy commander of the CPV, and Ch'oe Yong-gŏn, North Korean minister of national defense, reportedly met with Gen. Malenchikoff, chief of the Soviet Military Advisory Group in Korea, and demanded that the Russians rush fresh supplies to Korea and that the Soviet navy be used to counter the U.S. navy.[54] Although the veracity of this report is, of course, not subject to empirical proof, what is known of the circumstances on the peninsula at the time lends it an air of credibility. The American navy had interdicted the Korean coast and was mercilessly bombarding North Korean cities, while the Soviet Union, which was publicly proclaiming itself the head of the socialist camp and the defender of Chinese and Korean interests, held back from active participation in the war.

Meanwhile, North Korea's bargaining leverage with her neighbors, because she was dependent upon them for men and equipment, was very weak. For example, a Korean–Chinese conference reportedly held in the DPRK on September 13, 1951, agreed that North Korean political commissars were to be subordinated to Chinese political commissars when on the same level.[55] Consequently, there were significant strains between the three states as the armistice talks began. Peking and P'yŏngyang were dissatisfied with the quality and quantity of the participation by Moscow; each appeared to be suspicious of the goals and commitments of its militarily stronger neighbor.

Notes

1. United Nations and United States Far East Command, Intelligence Summary (Tokyo), July 29, 1950.
2. Ibid., October 9, 1950.
3. United States Army, G-3 Memorandum (Tokyo), September, 1950.
4. Ibid.
5. Ibid.
6. *New York Times*, "Allies Tightening Arc on P'yongyang," by Lindsay Parrott, October 16, 1950, p. 3, Tokyo dispatch.
7. *Pravda*, October 12, 1950. Translated in the *Current Digest of the Soviet Press*, November 4, 1950, p. 37.
8. "Dulles in Korea," in *Literaturnaya Gazeta*, September 4, 1951. Translated in *Current Digest of the Soviet Press*, October 20, 1951, pp. 9–12.
9. United Nations and United States Far East Command, op. cit., October 15, 1950.
10. U.S. Air Force Plans, in United Nations and United States Far East Command, op. cit., September 28, 1950.

11. United Nations and United States Far East Command, op. cit., December 31, 1950.
12. United States Eighth Army Monograph (Tokyo), January 18, 1952.
13. Ibid. See also Department of the Army, pamphlet no. 30–51, *Handbook on the Chinese Communist Army*, (Washington, D.C., September, 1952), pp. 89–95.
14. *Foreign Broadcast Information Service, Supplement* (Washington, D.C.), March 7, 1973.
15. United Nations and United States Far East Command, op. cit., December 21, 1950.
16. Ibid., February 19, 1952.
17. Ibid., March 14, 1952.
18. Ibid., January 11, 1951.
19. Pavel Monat, "Russians in Korea," *Life*, June 27, 1969, p. 85.
20. Dae-sook Suh, "North Korea: Emergence of an Elite Group," in *Aspects of Modern Communism*, ed. Richard F. Staar (Columbia: University of South Carolina Press, 1968), p. 329.
21. Kim Chang-sun, *Puk-Han sip-o-nyŏn sa* [Fifteen Year History of North Korea] (Seoul: Shi-mun-kak, 1961). Translated by Joint Publications Research Service, Washington, D.C., 1965, pp. 124–125.
22. Rin Eiju et al., *Chōsen Sensoshi* [History of the Korean War] (Tokyo: Koria Hyoronsha, 1967), pp. 131–135, 182–184.
23. New China News Agency, December 22, 1950.
24. *New York Times*, "Vishinsky Demands Troops Quit Korea," by George Barret, December 10, 1950, p. 6.
25. *New York Times*, "Three Man Group is Aim," by Walter Sullivan, December 19, 1950, p. 1.
26. *New York Times*, "U.N. Truce Mission Would Go to China", by Walter Sullivan, December 19, 1950, p. 1.
27. *New York Times*, "U.N. Truce Project Backed by U.S.," by A. M. Rosenthal, January 12, 1951, p. 1.
28. *New York Times*, "Soviet Peace Plan Presented to U.N.," by A. M. Rosenthal, October 3, 1950, p. 1.
29. *New York Times*, "Peping Wants U.N.'s Talks To Sift All Issues Jointly," January 14, 1951, p. 1, "special dispatch" from New Delhi.
30. Leland M. Goodrich, *Korea: A Study of U.S. Policy in the United Nations* (New York: Council on Foreign Relations, 1956), p. 157.
31. New China News Agency, January 22, 1951.
32. *New York Times*, "New Stand is Cited," by Walter Sullivan, January 23, 1951, p. 1.
33. *New York Times*, "Mao Warns Censure by U.N. Would Bar Peace, India Says," by Walter Sullivan, January 30, 1951, p. 1. For a valu-

able discussion of this episode, see Denis Stairs, *The Diplomacy of Constraint: Canada, the Korean War, and the United States* (Toronto: University of Toronto Press, 1974), pp. 141–182.

34. Walter G. Hermes, *Truce Tent and Fighting Front* (Washington, D.C., Office of the Chief of Military History, United States Army, 1966), p. 76.

35. United Nations and United States Far East Command, op. cit., December 23, 1950.

36. Ibid., n. d.

37. Ibid.

38. Ibid., September 22, 1951.

39. Cited in Klaus Mehnert, *Peking and Moscow* (New York: Mentor Books, 1964), p. 255.

40. Cited in Chin Szu-k'ai, *Communist China's Relations with the Soviet Union, 1949–1957* (Hong Kong: Union Research Institute, 1961), p. 19.

41. David Rees, *Korea: The Limited War* (Baltimore: Penguin Books, 1964), p. 255.

42. In late May, 1951, the Swedish Foreign Ministry confirmed reports that the Soviet Union had offered to negotiate on a *status quo ante* basis, but stipulated that it would not take the initiative in starting negotiations. *New York Times*, "Soviet Denies Move for Peace in Korea," by Thomas J. Hamilton, May 29, 1951, p. 1. U.N. Secretary-General Trygve Lie, in a major speech in Ottawa on June 1, 1951, proposed a ceasefire and negotiations along the 38th parallel. *New York Times*, "Lie Makes New Bid for Truce in Korea," by P. J. Philip, June 2, 1951, p. 1.

43. Bernard Brodie, *War and Politics* (New York: Macmillan Co., 1973), p. 92.

44. After Malik's June 23 speech (see below), a U.S. "inquiry made through Ambassador Kirk in Moscow confirmed that the views expressed were those of the Soviet Government and that Gromyko was uninformed about those of the Chinese." Dean Acheson, *Present at the Creation: My Years in the State Department* (New York: W. W. Norton, 1969), p. 533.

45. Wilfred A. Bacchus, "The Relationship between Combat and Peace Negotiations: Fighting while Talking in Korea, 1951–1953," *Orbis* (summer, 1973), pp. 555–56.

46. In 1950–51, if the Russians had "tried to relieve the pressure on their allies and dissuade the Americans from a possible overcommitment in Asia, the most logical move would have been to increase pressure on Europe. In fact, as we have seen, they were doing the opposite.

In November 1950 the Soviet Foreign Ministry proposed a Four Power Conference to discuss the German problem and couched its proposals in what was for them and at the time fairly conciliatory terms. To the Chinese Communists was thus left the dangerous task of 'containing' the American imperialists." Ulam, op. cit., pp. 527–28.

47. Ibid., p. 513.
48. Ibid., pp. 5
49. Malik's speech gave all North Korean groups "an incentive and an opportunity to oppose the Soviet system of controls, for they tended to create widespread resentment among all of the northern leadership but the most "Sovietized" of the Soviet–Koreans." Joungwon Alexander Kim, "Soviet Policy in North Korea," *World Politics* (January, 1970), p. 243.
50. United Nations and United States Far East Command, op. cit., December 7, 1951. On June 27, four days after Malik's U.N. speech, Radio P'yŏngyang changed its major slogan from "drive the enemy into the sea" to "drive the enemy to the 38th parallel." The Communist reply to Ridgway was broadcast first in Chinese, then in English, and finally, two hours later, in Korean.
51. Ibid., September 28, 1951.
52. United States Army, G-2 memorandum (Tokyo), December 17, 1951. An American former POW later wrote that on the outskirts of the northern North Korean city of Sinŭiju "we walked by big ack-ack batteries manned by Russians" in the fall of 1951. Morris R. Wills, as told to J. Robert Moskin, *Turncoat* (Englewood Cliffs, N.J., Prentice-Hall, 1966), p. 46. See also Scalapino and Lee, op. cit., pp. 403–4.
53. United Nations and United States Far East Command, op. cit. October 7, 1951.
54. Ibid., September 12, 1951.
55. Ibid., September 28, 1951.

8

Attrition

As suggested in the last chapter, the initiation of the armistice talks, after Ambassador Malik's New York radio speech on June 23, 1951, was most probably a Soviet decision. In fact, there are grounds for believing that the North Koreans were even largely unaware of Moscow's thinking until shortly before June 23, while Peking was apparently unhappy with Malik's disinclination to include the Taiwan question as a topic intertwined with the Korean Civil War.

Coming just after the failure of the Paris negotiations on West German rearmament, the Korean talks, from Moscow's perspective, would serve to reassure the West that the USSR wished to keep communications (and the possibility of compromise) open, which, in turn, might serve to mute the United States' rapidly increasing military expenditures and possible mobilization. China's military, on the other hand, had waxed strong because of the war: the Soviet Union had supplied loans which were enabling the PLA to become a rapidly modernized force. Moscow, with its ambivalent and basically distrustful attitude toward Peking, may have wished that this modernization be reduced. In light of these factors, a Korean Civil War of attrition and stalemate was partially in Russia's interests: it continued China's dependence upon the Soviet Union and severely diminished Peking's options toward the West, while simultaneously tying down much of America's strength, which could otherwise have been allocated to NATO. Moreover, as the war wound its tortuous way through two additional years it contributed to some amount of disarray in the Western Alliance. [1]

The DPRK, of course, was committed to the war as a struggle of national survival. The P'anmunjŏm negotiations dragged on, while China seemed interested in withdrawing from the war if this could be done in such a manner as to be pictured as a victory. Peking continued to go to great lengths to explain that she wished an exit from the war and that, moreover, she had only entered it in the first place because she felt directly threatened by an American invasion. Mao Tse-tung, for example, explained on October 23, 1951 (commemorating the first anniversary of the CPV's entrance):

> So long as the U.S. Government is willing to settle the question on a just and reasonable basis and will stop using every shameless means to wreck and delay the progress of negotiations as it has done in the past, success in the Korean armistice negotiations is possible; otherwise it is impossible. . . . Everyone knows that *if* American forces had not occupied our Taiwan, had not invaded the Korean Democratic People's Republic and *pushed their attacks to our northern borders,* the Chinese people would not be fighting against American troops. [2]

Meanwhile, the feats of the CPV were downplayed in the Russian press; credit for the communist successes was given to the North Korean and Chinese armies—in that order. [3]

Peking and P'yŏngyang the Year After P'anmunjŏm

The Fourth Plenum of the Korean Workers' Party's (KWP) Central Committee of November, 1951, witnessed the purging of the foremost Soviet–Korean, Hŏ Ka-i. The prime

motive for his removal seems to have been domestic: Hŏ was
accused of admitting South Korean communists into the KWP
who had proved to be disloyal to the party during the early stages
of the war. He thereupon committed suicide.[4] Kim Il-sŏng's
authority within the party was consequently strengthened. It
has also been suggested that Hŏ was removed because Kim
Il-sŏng doubted that Hŏ could, or would, control Pak Hŏn-yŏng
and his still-numerous followers within the KWP.[5] A further
reason for Hŏ's purge, and perhaps the major reason why Kim
was able to carry out the removal of the prime instrument of
Russian influence within the KWP, was the growing realization
within North Korea that P'yŏngyang's interests were not identical with those of either Peking or Moscow. After Malik's June 23
speech, widespread resentment against the Soviet Union grew
within the KWP.[6]

Perhaps in an effort to reassure Moscow of Korea's appreciation for the (limited) support which the USSR was extending
—assistance which, however circumscribed, was crucial to her
survival—*Nodong Sinmun*, the official KWP daily newspaper,
published an editorial on November 11, 1951, entitled "The
Absorption of Soviet Culture on a Broad Scale Redoubles Our
Strength". The same organ on November 20, 1951, emphasized
the war's significance to Moscow: "In order to make our country
their springboard for the invasion of China and the *Soviet Union*,
the Americans provoked an internecine civil war, and then embarked upon naked aggression, dreaming of an easy conquest."[7]
Soon thereafter the Soviet Union acknowledged that P'yŏngyang
was indeed distracting the energies of the United States from an
invasion of Soviet territory. In a radio broadcast in Korean
beamed to North Korea, which played upon Korean memories of
the harsh Japanese occupation of 1910–45, Radio Moscow
prophesied that "the United States will send these [Japanese]
troops to occupy Russia and China, under the banner of the
U.N., of course."[8] This was followed on December 16, 1951, by a
Moscow broadcast in Korean which declared that North Korea

was "supported by their *powerful* friends, the Soviet people, the *friendly* Chinese people, and all the progressive people of the world." (Emphasis added.)

These assurances of Soviet support to North Korea, however, were counterbalanced by Moscow Radio's warnings to China, reminding Peking that although it certainly was true that the Soviet Union was an interested party to the war, it was China itself which had the most to fear from an invasion. Radio Moscow achieved a maximum impact in sending this message by concentrating on China's fear of Japan, at whose hands China had suffered less than a decade before. On December 17, 1951, Moscow Radio, in Mandarin, warned that the United States was rebuilding Japan's military bases; "such bases are to be used to invade Korea, China, and the USSR" (note that Moscow's broadcasts to China placed the Soviet Union third). Again in Mandarin on January 14, 1952, Radio Moscow broadcast a commentary entitled "The U.S. Is Establishing Japan as a Base from Which To Invade China."

The Soviet Union continued to use its multi-lingual broadcasts to convince both of its neighbors that it had the most to benefit from participating in the war, while assuring each that the Soviet Union was unselfishly aiding all. A more concrete indication of the nature of this Russian altruism arose when a Korean envoy extraordinary and ambassador plenipotentiary to the Soviet Union, Lim Hae, arrived in Moscow on January 31, 1952. He was met at the train only by the Russian Ministry of Foreign Affairs Protocol Deputy Head, Kulezhenkov—not an indication of Soviet enthusiastic support.[9]

The logical conclusion of the separate broadcasts to China and North Korea came on February 14, 1952 (the second anniversary of the Sino–Soviet Treaty), in a Moscow Radio broadcast in Korean which not so subtly reminded P'yŏngyang that although Chinese troops—rather than Russian—were fighting in the Democratic People's Republic of Korea, they were doing so for reasons important to *China*, rather than North Korea: "The

Chinese understand perfectly that in the course of this righteous war not only the fate of freedom-loving Korea but, furthermore, the future of their own fatherland will be settled."

P'yŏngyang reacted to Moscow's message by asserting its historic rights to seek help from China. On North Korean Army Day, February 8, 1952, the minister of national defense, Ch'oe Yong-gŏn, stated that "when the situation of the Korean people was most grave, the brotherly Chinese people threw the People's Volunteer force, which consisted of their excellent sons and daughters, into the Korean front." This statement, ignoring earlier expressions of gratitude which had explained that the CPV entered the war only when China itself was threatened, had been advanced in a P'yŏngyang broadcast, in Korean, of February 2, 1952, which seemed to suggest that China owed Korea active military support as the just due of previous Korean aid to the PLA:

> Countless numbers of patriotic Koreans participated in the war against Japan from 1937 to 1945 [in China], the People's Liberation War after 1945, and various other struggles which were carried out under the leadership of the Chinese Communist party, the glorious support of the Chinese people, and Chairman Mao Tse-tung, the great leader of the Chinese people.

This statement was perhaps in response to the cautious manner in which China had been treating P'yŏngyang. North Korea's first ambassador to Peking, Li Chu-yon, had been recalled on November 13, 1951, for unknown reasons. The new North Korean ambassador, Kwon O Chik (as spelled in radio translation by FBIS), did not arrive in Peking until March 7, 1952. His welcome in China was restrained. He did not meet with Chou En-lai until March 11, "to discuss the matter of presenting credentials"; the ambassador finally met with Mao Tse-tung on March 18 to present those credentials. This would seem to be a lengthy process by which to welcome the representative of the state for whom thousands of Chinese soldiers were then dying.

This apparent Chinese reticence may have reflected Peking's unhappiness with being involved in the war in the first place. The war represented a considerable drain on the new Chinese state's resources. It is unknown how many Chinese soldiers fought in the Korean Civil War; the United Nations has estimated, however, that at least 900,000 of their men were casualties in the conflict. [10] Recruitment for the CPV siphoned off a considerable number of trained personnel—doctors, engineers, students—who were urgently needed elsewhere in a China anxious to begin national reconstruction after the havoc of four decades of internal war. [11] The Soviet Union had only *lent* the funds for the modernization of the Chinese army and air force, so that finances which would otherwise have gone for domestic purposes now went to a war whose front lines were not to change appreciably after the beginning of armistice talks in July of 1951. Probably as a testimony of China's dissatisfaction with Russia's conditional terms of aid, there was no mention of the Soviet Union in the slogans of either May Day or PLA Day (August 1) in 1951. An indication of how the Chinese economy was suffering from the wartime expenditures is the fact that for the year 1951 revenue from taxes was 8.1 *yuan* per capita, while the defense budget itself ate up 5.06 *yuan* per capita. [12]

A further suggestion of China's difficulties with the Soviet Union is the fact that after early November, 1951, the Chinese media abruptly terminated its references to Mao Tse-tung's unique contributions to theory, and likewise ceased references to "Mao's Road" as a model for other developing countries. "There is reason to believe that the Chinese Communist elite accepted these conclusions grudgingly and only after a period of delay." Consequently, it seems that China reluctantly accepted Russian continuing leadership after November of 1951. [13]

Jumping ahead a bit, it is significant to note Peking's continuing displeasure with Moscow—as evidenced, for example, by the timing of the publication of Mao Tse-tung's "On Contradiction." Allegedly written in 1937, this article was issued in April of 1952, when Mao "must have known that it was out of harmony with the Soviet ideological line."[14] The article was published half a year after the corresponding volume of Mao's *Selected Works* appeared, and may well have been designed as a challenge to Stalin's supremacy in the communist ideological world and/or an indication of China's unhappiness with Russia's leadership during the Korean Civil War. Again, 1952 PLA Day slogans omitted mention of the Soviet Union.

In May of 1951 North Korea had initiated charges of germ warfare against the United States. Although soon picked up by China and the Soviet Union, these charges never reached the status of a concerted campaign by all three states.[15] In February, 1952, however, these claims were revived in a propaganda campaign coordinated by the Soviet Union. On February 18, 1952, Moscow Radio, in Korean, broadcast its first assertions of bacteriological warfare charges on the Korean peninsula. On February 19, NCNA domestic service relayed these charges. After this preliminary direction from Moscow, North Korean Foreign Minister Pak Hŏn-yŏng formally accused the United Nations forces of using bacteriological warfare.[16]

These events were followed by the only occasion during the war when the Soviet Union offered North Korea a sizeable gift—50,000 tons of flour. Neither before nor after this gesture was there anything in the public record to indicate that the Russians had been the least munificent in granting assistance to P'yŏngyang. According to Moscow Radio, in Korean, on April 20, 1952, Stalin telegraphed Kim Il-sŏng:

> I have become cognizant of the fact that provisions are needed by the Korean people. We have 50,000 tons of flour stacked in Siberia. We can send the flour to the Korean people as a present. Let me know your answer by telegram. If you desire it we can forward the flour immediately. My congratulations to you.

The outpouring of gratitude on the part of P'yŏngyang for this gift suggests that the offer was indeed unique; moreover, this implicitly says a great deal about the general lack of Soviet economic assistance to the decimated North Korean population. P'yŏngyang's ambivalent feelings toward its rich and powerful neighbor were reflected in two government publications of May Day, 1952. The official slogans listed "Long Live the Soviet Union!" in third place; yet Kim Il-sŏng's official proclamation of that day, full of praise of the CPV and China, left out any mention of the Soviet Union. A further, subtler, indication of the strains between the small state which was fighting its own total war and the cautious Soviet Union would appear to be present in the message which Kim Il-sŏng sent to the Soviet Union in honor of Liberation Day, August 15, 1952. Kim declared that "our people proudly call Comrade Stalin 'our father and savior.'" This seemingly straightforward statement takes on an artfully ironic implication, however, when a *Pravda* dispatch, broadcast over Moscow Radio domestic service on January 5, 1951, is recalled: "In Korea they have a saying that 'a good friend is better than a relative.' The truth of this ancient proverb can be seen with special clarity today, the time of the severe joint struggle of the Korean and Chinese peoples against the foreigners." Taken in conjunction with the constant declarations of P'yŏngyang Radio that the Soviet Union was also threatened by the United Nations forces—and that, therefore, Korean and Chinese soldiers were also defending the national territorial interests of the Soviet Union—along with the lack of Russian aid extended to the DPRK during the war, Kim Il-sŏng's message of August, 1952, may well have been meant as an indirect rebuke to the Soviet Union.

Up until this moment, the DPRK had been on the edge of starvation. It was only the intervention of emergency food shipments from other communist countries which forestalled widespread starvation. In severe circumstances such as this, it is most probable that P'yŏngyang would not have harbored totally favorable feelings toward the Soviet Union.[17]

Meanwhile, there were further grounds for North Korean dissatisfaction with the direction and support supplied by the Soviet Union. It was reported in early May of 1952 that P'yŏngyang wanted to launch an offensive prior to the South Korean election; the Soviet Union and China vetoed this proposal.[18] This had allegedly been preceded on April 3, 1952, by a confidential statement made by the DPRK's minister of national defense, Cho'oe Yong-gŏn, at a meeting of the North Korean military staff. While perhaps not an exact quotation (because of its source), the statement does seem to reflect accurately the feelings of the leaders of the DPRK government:

> The Soviets are now attempting to start a general war in which all Asiatics will eventually engage the U.S. alone. The Chinese Communists are unable to understand why the Soviets do not support more strongly the North Korean and Chinese settlement at P'anmunjom. True Korean and Chinese nationalists are becoming suspicious of the Soviet's real intentions, for the Soviets have openly shown that they are more interested in seducing Japan than in peaceful reconstruction of territories which have been liberated by the People's Republics. Unless the USSR makes a definite promise to intervene in the Korean War, the only alternative is for North Koreans and Chinese to come to terms with the U.N. An armistice will permit the communization of South Korea from within; however, the recently revealed Soviet policy clearly shows the Soviet desire to provoke the Chinese into making rash decisions designed to widen the war in Asia. The Soviets plan to keep Asians fighting Americans while the Soviets sit back and talk about Soviet peace. They do not care about the unification of Korea; they merely invested material and professional aid in order to pin down U.N. forces and weaken U.S. strength.[19]

A Thwarted Peace

It appeared in the early summer of 1952 that both the North Koreans and the Chinese were eager to break the impasse at the P'anmunjŏm negotiations over the question of the return of POWs. A *New York Times* dispatch from New Delhi reported that China had presented a proposal through the Indian Embassy in Peking that: 1) the 70,000 or so U.N. prisoners who had already expressed the desire to return to communist territory would be repatriated immediately; 2) the 100,000 others, whose attitude toward repatriation was in dispute, should be removed to a neutral zone, possibly an island off the Korean coast; 3) a neutral agency, to be agreed upon, should then screen the disputed prisoners and its findings would be accepted by China as final. The *Times* reporter noted that there were "high hopes among informed circles in New Delhi and London" over this proposal. [20]

This plan, however, which was probably known in Washington and was highly similar to the final P'anmunjŏm solution one year later, was aborted by the U.S. bombing of hydroelectric plants along the Yalu River for the first time. These devastating attacks began on June 23, 1952, and lasted for three days. The American armada was made up of more than 500 airplanes. North Korea had a complete power blackout of fifteen days, while it was estimated that Manchuria lost 23 percent of its power requirements for the entire year of 1952 as a result of the raids. [21] The *New York Times* military editor noted at the time that "these raids are definitely a first step of a program to bring greater military pressure upon the enemy to force a cease-fire. The second step in this program may be attacks upon Najin [seventeen miles from the Russian border] and the vital rail link that connects this port to the Soviet Union." [22] The *Times* reporter in New Delhi concluded in mid-July that these air attacks had brought an abrupt end to the earlier Chinese proposal to India. [23] This was because China did not wish to appear to be giving in under this new American pressure. Moreover, it is not unlikely that this pressure was counterproductive in the sense that the Soviets could now warn the Chinese and North Koreans that peace was not as easily obtained as they had hoped.

The Chinese and North Koreans, dismayed by the Yalu bombings, waited four days before making a (relatively mild) protest. On July 1, 1952, the Soviet Ambassador to China, Roschchin, left for Moscow, probably spurred home by Chinese insistence upon additional Soviet support and the need for further consultations between the two communist powers over the now aborted Chinese peace proposal. The Chinese sent a further signal about their keen desire to end the war shortly thereafter; Chou En-lai agreed to the Geneva Convention on POWs on July 13, 1952. An indication of the Chinese foreign minister's eagerness to resolve the repatriation morass was his statement that the neutral agency protecting the POWs must be agreeable to the POWs' own nation; this seemed to echo the proposal of India.

Chou En-lai visited Moscow from August 17 to September 22, 1952. During this visit, Washington, apparently unaware of the fact that increased pressure was hindering the truce negotia-tions in that it gave Moscow leverage to tell the Chinese and North Koreans that peace with the aggressors was demonstrably impossible at the moment, continued to increase the bombing terror on the Korean peninsula. P'yŏngyang suffered its heaviest bombing of the entire war on August 29, while Aoji, eight miles from the Russian border, was bombed on September 1 for the first time. Chou En-lai's arrival speech in Moscow was a clear request for additional Russian aid:

> The Chinese people understand full well that these vic-tories [building communism] are the property not only of the Soviet people, but also of all peace-loving peoples of the world, for these victories multiply many times the forces standing for peace in the whole world. [24]

Chou was accompanied by a high-powered delegation of economic and military experts who would have had authority to negotiate further assistance and defensive assurances from the Russians: Ch'en Yun, vice-premier and economic expert, Li Fu-ch'un, vice-chairman of the Committee of Financial and Economic Affairs, Chang Wen-t'ien, Chinese ambassador to the Soviet Union, Su Yu, deputy chief of general staff of the People's Revolutionary Military Council, Chen Yü, minister of fuel industry, Wang Ho-shou, minister of heavy industry, Sung Shao-wen, chief of the Secretariat of Financial and Economic Affairs, and Liu Ya-lou, commander of the air force of the PLA. When Chou left Moscow, Li Fu-ch'un, Ch'en Yun, Liu Ya-lou, Sung Shao-wen, and Wang Ho-shou—although they were unheralded in both the Russian and the Chinese press—stayed behind to continue negotiations.

Premier Tzedenbal of the People's Republic of Mongolia arrived in Moscow on August 28 to take part in the Soviet–Chinese talks, and was met at the airport upon his arrival by Chou En-lai and Soviet Politburo member Anastas Mikoyan. Tzedenbal's presence testified to China's continuing interest in maintaining some of her traditional influence in Mongolia, a concern from which she had been thwarted by the Russians in 1949, as noted previously. As a recognition of this continued Chinese interest in Mongolia, Premier Tzedenbal visited Peking on September 28 to initiate a ten-day "Friendship Period" (October 1–10) declared for Mongolia and China. On October 5, China and Mongolia signed a ten-year economic and cultural agreement—a tangible benefit which Peking derived from her participation in the Korea Civil War, as this agreement must first have earned the blessings of a Moscow whose influence was predominant in Mongolia.

During Chou En-lai's visit, *Pravda* devoted two pages to a review of the first volume of Mao Tse-tung's *Selected Works* by a leading Soviet theoretician, Pavel Yudin. This volume had appeared in Russian several months previously, but *Pravda* now chose the occasion of Chou's visit in the Russian capital to comment on the value of Mao as a Marxist philosopher. Yudin found that there were no major theoretical propositions in Mao's works, and moreover stressed that Mao owed an intellectual debt to Stalin. [25]

An examination of an article in the September 27, 1952, issue of *Shih-chieh Chih-shih* by a Russian China specialist, Ye Zhukov, printed at the request of the journal, demonstrates that Moscow continued to reject Peking's claims to ideological originality. As we have seen, Moscow's diminution of Peking's theoretical contributions was not new. The significance of this article is that it was printed in China's leading foreign affairs journal. "For the first time, the Chinese people received an explanation—from an authorative Soviet spokesman—of why it was that 'Mao's Road' was no longer applicable to other Asian revolutionary movements." [26] *Shih-chieh Chih-shih's* implicit acknowledgment of Soviet ideological hegemony now opened the way for improved Russian aid on the Korean front. And, in fact, it was in mid-September of 1952 that the communists "for the first time were able to use a large amount of Russian-made artillery." [27]

On September 16 a joint Sino–Soviet communiqué announced that the Soviet military presence in Port Arthur would be prolonged beyond the end of 1952, which had been the cutoff date in the original agreement. The *Jen-min Jih-pao* editorial of that date, which celebrated this new pact, injected a new note of Chinese militancy into their relationship with the heretofore reticent Russians. This editorial is an indication of China's impatience with the Soviet's cautious help, and suggests China's eagerness to pursue its own national interests under a more active Russian umbrella of protection—particularly from renewed Japanese–American aggression, which Port Arthur, a symbol of earlier Japanese imperialism, represented. The communique, wrote *Jen-min Jih-pao*,

is based on the fundamental interests of the people of both countries and *particularly as regards the practical interest of*

China. The acceptance and endorsement of the Chinese proposal [on Port Arthur] by the government of the Soviet Union indicates that the Soviet Union is faithfully abiding by the obligations of the Sino–Soviet Treaty of Friendship, Alliance, and Mutual Assistance, and that the Soviet Union *is prepared to shoulder all responsibilities* beneficial to peace in the East and the whole world.[28]

This editorial, entitled "Develop the Mighty Strength of the Sino–Soviet Alliance," then goes on to make the point that it is China herself who is actually shouldering the responsibility of safeguarding the interests of communism in the East:

In the East, the danger of war *directly* threatens the security of China; there is the danger that the U.S. will continue to prolong and extend its aggressive war against *China's* neighbor, Korea [i.e., it is China which is doing the fighting!]. The American air force invading Korea is continuing to intrude over northeast China and is carrying out inhuman bacteriological warfare against the Chinese and Korean people. U.S. forces are still continuing to occupy the Chinese territory of Taiwan, and are blockading China's coast. . . . In particular, the U.S. is speeding up its revival of Japanese militarism, which creates an increasingly grave war menace. . . . Japan's militarists all along have been working hand in hand with the U.S. and are relying on the U.S. in an attempt to unleash new aggression. (Emphasis added.)

On August 9, 1952, a statement on government policy was issued by Mao Tse-tung providing for autonomous regional governments for minority groups, authorizing them to administer their own finances and to organize their own security and militia units. On September 9, (DPRK National Day), NCNA announced that the first such autonomous region had been organized in Kirin Province (in Manchuria) for the Korean minority population on September 3, V-J Day. Named the "Yenpien People's Government," it claimed a population of half a million

Koreans, a "Yenpien University," thirty secondary schools, and 2.8 million books published in the Korean language in 1951, along with Korean newspapers, cultural clubs, and movie theaters. (The establishment of the next similar autonomous minority government, that of the Thai Nationalist Autonomous Area in Southern Yunan Province was announced on January 23, 1953.) Interestingly, P'yŏngyang Radio waited until September 16 to note the establishment of this Korean region in China, with a commentary entitled "All the Korean People are Hailing the Establishment of the Autonomous Government for the Korean Residents in China."

Regardless of the relationship between China and the Soviet Union, the DPRK continued to suffer in the role of minor partner, despite the fact that the war was being fought on its territory. On October 12, 1952, Kim Il-sŏng sent another fervent telegram to Stalin, which began: "Dear Joseph Vessarionovich, the Korean people's liberator and best friend." The six paragraphs in Kim's message were answered by a two-sentence telegram from Stalin, the heart of which read: "Comrade Chairman, I wish the Korean people, who are courageously defending their national rights, successes in their heroic fight for the freedom and independence of their motherland." The reaction of the North Korean press to this lukewarm Russian support was shown in their contrasting expressions of gratitude to China upon the occasion of the second anniversary of the entrance of the CPV into the war. Kim Il-sŏng, in a major speech on October 24, keynoted the increasingly circumspect North Korean policy toward the war. While recalling old victories, he acknowledged that the opportunities for a repetition of such triumphs were slight:

> The Korean People's army and the Chinese People's Volunteers have many times seen only the backs of retreating Yankees. It was so in October and November, 1950, it was so again in January and February, 1951, it will be so in the future, too, if the Americans break off the armistice talks.

Nodong Sinmun [Labor News] of October 25, 1952, repeated its claim that North Koreans were bearing the brunt of an invasion which was really meant for China and the Soviet Union: "The enemy embarked on their armed aggression against Korea with the idea of conquering Korea and invading China, and eventually the Soviet Union."[29]

By this time, North Korea's media had reversed its previous claims: instead of calling for driving the American invaders from Korea, or even declaring that the U.N. forces had been defeated, P'yŏngyang now stated that the war had been won:

> The enemy is stubbornly trying to take the offensive, but we are defending our positions and our defensive lines are strong. If the enemy launches any offensive we can foil his attempt and smash him. *We have won,* but we cannot boast of our exploits and we must improve our war tactics.[30]

Interestingly, about this time the Russians also changed their stand on the origins, and therefore the purpose, of the war. Previously, they had maintained that the war had been initiated by the Americans as a prelude to invading China, and then the Soviet Union itself. For this reason, ran their argument, it was the duty of the communist world to support the DPRK.

On November 24, 1952, however, Moscow Radio declared in Korean that the United States "started the criminal war in Korea in order to maintain their highest profits and head off hard times and the economic depression America is facing." The implications of this new Soviet position would appear to have been two: 1) that the Korean Civil War was not as intimately tied up with the territorial defense of the Soviet Union as had been previously stated in Russian propaganda; 2) that if the war helped the American economy, perhaps it would be in Russia's interests to bring the war to an end.

Meanwhile, China also appeared anxious to reach some sort of accord in Korea. The Peace Conference of the Asian and Pacific Region, held in Peking from October 2 to 12, 1952, was attended by delegates and observers from thirty-seven countries. As compared with the Trade Union Conference held in the same city in 1949, the rhetoric was markedly less that of militant revolution; rather, the stress was now on "peaceful coexistence." The speeches contained more mentions of a fear of Japanese resurgence than of the Korean Civil War itself.[31]

Stalin Moves to Leave the War

Significantly, Liu Shao-ch'i, the number-two man in the Chinese Communist party arrived in Moscow (shortly after Chou En-lai had left) on the same day that the Peking Conference opened. Liu was ostensibly in Moscow to attend the 19th Congress of the Communist Party of the Soviet Union; however, he stayed for more than three months in the Soviet Union, returning by air to Peking on January 11, 1953. Liu made several speeches full of praise for the Soviet Union during his stay in that country; these talks, however, lacked any details on the nature of the negotiations which were certainly proceeding between the Chinese and Soviet leaders at this time. The nature of the 19th Congress, though, gives some clues as to what policies were evolving. The main speech was given by Georgii Malenkov on October 5, 1952; it was a partial departure from previous statements, which had been more bellicose. Malenkov now declared that "the Soviet Union has always stood for and now stands for the development of trade and cooperation with other countries irrespective of differences in social systems. The party will continue to pursue this policy on the basis of mutual advantage."[32]

China was caught in a paradox: she wished to end her involvement in a war that had become stalemated militarily and was a tremendous drain on her economy; yet, to exit from that war, she had to win the assent of her powerful neighbor, who was the only country equipped to help her in the about-to-be announced first Five Year Plan. Chou En-lai's and Liu Shao-ch'i's visits to Moscow may well have been negotiating missions meant to gain Moscow's agreement to end the war. If so, Chou En-lai's speech to the Fourth Session of the Chinese People's Political Consultative Conference in Peking on February 4, 1953, can be taken as an indication that the Russians had agreed to an early end to the war:

> We are not discriminating against any capitalist country which desires to develop trade relations with us on the basis of equality and mutual advantage. We feel that countries with different systems can coexist peacefully. . . . We are ready *to resume* and to establish trade relations, to develop a peaceful economy with *all* countries which desire to maintain peaceful relations with us.[33] (Emphasis added.)

A further indication that important decisions had been reached on the ending of the Korean Civil War is contained in the year-end review of world events published in *Pravda* on December 31, 1952. This editorial contained only one reference to the war, and even this was coupled to developments in Europe:

> The aggressive, adventurous policy is manifested in all the activities of the aggressive North Atlantic bloc. The intervention against the Korean people, the splitting of Germany, and the militarization of West Germany and Japan were the results of this policy, which is aimed at the suppression of the last vestige of bourgeois democratic freedom, the liquidation of the national sovereignty of nations, and the unleasing of a third world war.

Clearly, the war now seemed less important to Soviet policy makers.

The 19th Congress of the Soviet Communist Party also provided indications that Moscow had decided to cut its losses in the Korean Civil War. Stalin, with his instinct for the dramatic, published his last work, *Economic Problems of Socialism in the*

Soviet Union, a few days before the opening of the congress, thus assuring its central place in the congress's discussions. Stalin noted that some comrades believe that "wars among capitalist countries have ceased to be inevitable." He then explained why this position was incorrect:

> Let us first take Britain and France. There is no doubt that these countries are imperialist. Undoubtedly cheap raw materials and guaranteed markets for their goods are of primary importance to them. Is it to be assumed that they will endlessly tolerate the present state of affairs, in which the Americans, using the stratagem of Marshall Plan aid, are penetrating the economies of Britain and France, seeking to turn them into appendages of the U.S. economy, in which American capital is seizing the raw material sources and export markets in the Anglo-French colonies and thereby preparing a catastrophe for the high profits of Anglo-French capitalists? Would it not be more correct to say that first capitalist Britain and then capitalist France will ultimately be forced to wrest themselves from the embraces of the U.S.A. and enter into conflict with the U.S.A. in order to assure themselves an independent position and of course high profits? Let us now proceed to the chief vanquished countries, Germany (Western) and Japan. These countries are now leading a sorry existence under the heel of American imperialism. Their industry and agriculture, their trade, their domestic and foreign policies, all their way of life, are shackled by the American occupation "regime." But it was only yesterday that these countries were still great imperialist powers which shook the foundations of British, U.S., and French domination in Europe and Asia. To think that these countries will not attempt to rise to their feet again [an interesting parallel to Mao Tse-tung's famous phrase of October 1, 1949, that "China has stood up!"], smash the U.S. "regime," and break away on a path of independent development is to believe in miracles. It is said that the contradictions between capitalism and socialism are greater than the contradictions

between the capitalist countries. Theoretically this is of course true. It is true not only now, at the present time, but it was also true before the second world war. And this the leaders of the capitalist countries did, more or less, understand. Yet the second world war began not with a war against the USSR, but with a war among the capitalist countries. Why? First, because war with the USSR, as a socialist country, is more dangerous to capitalism than a war between capitalist countries, for if a war between capitalist countries raises only the question of supremacy of certain capitalist countries over other capitalist countries, war with the USSR must necessarily raise the question of the existence of capitalism itself. Second, because the capitalists, although for propaganda purposes they raise a hubbub about the aggressive nature of the Soviet Union, do not themselves believe in its aggressive nature, since they take into consideration the peaceful policy of the Soviet Union and know that the Soviet Union will not itself attack the capitalist countries. . . . Consequently, the capitalist countries' struggle for markets and the desire to drown their competitors turned out in actuality to be *stronger* than the contradictions between the camp of capitalism and the camp of socialism. The question is, what guarantee is there that Germany and Japan will not again rise to their feet, and that they will not try to wrest themselves from American bondage and to live their own independent lives? I think there are no such guarantees. But it follows from this that the *inevitability of wars among the capitalist countries remains.*

It is said that Lenin's thesis that imperialism inevitably gives birth to wars should be considered obsolete, since powerful peoples' forces have now grown up which are taking a stand in defense of peace, against a new world war. This is not correct. The aim of the present movement for peace is to arouse the masses of people for the struggle to preserve peace and to avert a new world war. *Consequently, it does not pursue the aim of overthrowing capitalism and establishing socialism. It limits itself to the democratic aims of*

> *the struggle to preserve peace. In this respect the present*
> *movement for the preservation of peace differs from the move-*
> *ment during the first world war to turn the imperialist war into a*
> *civil war, since this latter movement went further and pursued*
> *socialist ends.*
>
> Under a certain confluence of circumstances, the
> struggle for peace may possibly develop in one place or
> another into a struggle for socialism. This, however, will no
> longer be the present peace movement but a movement for
> the overthrow of capitalism. [34]

This passage deserves notice because it would appear to
have been a clear signal from Stalin that he wished to concentrate
on Russia's internal problems, rather than flirt with war with the
West. As part of this strategy, it is highly probable that Stalin
wished to disengage from the Korean Civil War, a conflict which
was a constant drain on Soviet economic resources, helped to
build up the Chinese military for a future which Stalin felt he
could not completely manipulate, provoked continual increases
in the belligerency of the American military forces in Europe,
and was itself in constant danger of reescalation.

A further indication that the above quotation was meant to
convey to a multifaceted audience the idea that the Soviet Union
was preparing to leave the war was the fact that Stalin was in the
midst of preparing the most intensive purge of the Soviet leadership since the late 1930s (the so-called "Doctors' Plot"). A pattern
of Stalin's politics had been that increased domestic tensions led
to a lower-profile foreign policy. If Stalin were indeed planning a
system-wide purge which would severely dislocate much of
Russia's bureaucracy, then it would have been probable that he
would move to disengage the Soviet Union from foreign entanglements.

Stalin's concluding remarks to the 19th Congress on October 15, 1952, underlined this cautious attitude toward foreign
adventures. His speech contained only one, rather vague, reference to the Korean Civil War: "Now, when new 'shock brigades'

have appeared in the vanguard of people's democracies from China and Korea to Czechoslovakia and Hungary. . . ."

In December of 1952, Stalin offered to meet with President-elect Eisenhower.[35] Perhaps to indicate the fact that he was concerned with the static and harsh nature of Russia's relations with the United States, and with being able to explain the importance of improving those relations, Stalin appointed a new ambassador to Peking, A. S. Panyushkin, who arrived in China on December 9 (the post had been vacant since the past July). Significantly, Panyushkin had previously been the Russian ambassador to Washington.

On January 16, 1953, NCNA published an interesting attack on the United States that had not been made before. It claimed that Eisenhower now wished "Asians to fight Asians." This, NCNA claimed, "is a white supremacist tactic to reduce the 'human cost' of the war of aggression in Korea." Considering what we know about the tensions between Moscow and Peking and the underlying racial hostility between the two peoples, this first use of the term "white supremacist," in reference to the enemy, perhaps symbolized the reaching of an agreement between China and the Soviet Union. Peking no longer was hesitant about using an epithet which might previously have been misconstrued by Moscow as a veiled criticism of Soviet chauvinism.

At about this time, perhaps aware that her two supporters were now in earnest about withdrawing from the war, and uncertain about what her fate might be, P'yŏngyang Radio began to broadcast ever more intense praises of her two neighbors, particularly of the Soviet Union. An example was this rewriting of history: "The establishment of diplomatic relations between Korea and Vietnam was possible only because of the fact that *both* countries were liberated from the Japanese imperialists by the Soviet Union." (February 4, 1953, emphasis added.) Kim Il-sŏng's message to the Korean People's Army on February 7 again acknowledged the division of labor between his two neighbors:

> In the course of the Fatherland Liberation War, the Korean
> People's armed forces have developed greatly as regards
> quality and quantity, supported by advanced Soviet mili-
> tary science and the noble fighting experiences of the
> heroic Soviet armed forces. . . . The valiant Chinese
> People's Volunteers, inspired by a new spirit of interna-
> tional aid, are supporting our righteous struggle *with their
> own blood*. . . . (Emphasis added.)

On the same day (February 7), Moscow Radio's Home Service
broadcast a commentary on the fifth anniversary of the Korean
People's Army which summarized Russia's attitude toward disengagement:

> When in the autumn of 1950 the hordes of the interven-
> tionists approached the Chinese frontier en masse in their
> endeavor to enslave the Korean people, and *when they
> threatened the security of China*, thousands of Chinese pa-
> triots hurried to the assistance of the fraternal Korean peo-
> ple. The fraternal, selfless support on the part of the great
> Chinese people strengthens the faith of the Korean people
> in their victory over the interventionists and plays an
> enormous part in the preservation of peace in Asia and
> throughout the world. . . .
>   The Soviet people, who themselves have suffered the
> bloody hardships of the bloody war against the Hitlerite
> robbers, well understand the sufferings of the Korean peo-
> ple and *express their warm, fraternal sympathy and
> enthusiasm* for their heroic steadfastness and valor. (Em-
> phasis added.)

The message seemed to be that if *China* considered her territorial
integrity to have been safeguarded by her participation in the
Korean Civil War, she was now free to leave the war. Russia, for
her part, was willing only to extend "sympathy."

Mao Tse-tung made a speech on February 7, 1953, at the
fourth session of the first national committee of the Chinese
People's Political Consultative Conference. Prof. Harold Hinton
refers to this speech as "defiant,"[36] and parts of it were. Perhaps

more important, however, were the passages which referred to the need for China's economic rehabilitation. For example: "We are going to carry out great national construction. The work facing us is hard and our experience is not enough. So we must take pains to study the advanced experience of the Soviet Union . . . in order to build up our country."

On February 22 and 23 Chou En-lai visited Port Arthur. On February 23, the NCNA quoted Chou as noting that "the power and might of the Soviet army is for the benefit not only of the Soviet Union, but also of the whole of mankind. . . . " On the same day (Soviet Army Day), the chief of the general staff of the Korean People's Army, General Nam Il, underlined the fact that the Soviet Union was concerned mostly with its own interests: "The Soviet armed forces have been, are, and will be the invincible bastion and staunch vanguard for the national interests of the Soviet Union, the fatherland of all the working peoples of the world."[37] It appeared that Stalin had promised his protection to Peking as the war came to an end, and P'yŏngyang was expressing its concern over its own fate at war's end. If this were the case, Moscow's assurances to P'yŏngyang continued to be less than substantial. As a small, but typical, example, Moscow Radio on February 25, in a program, in Korean, which concerned the defense of Korea, began with some Russian music, but the remainder of the broadcast contained only Chinese music and reports of China's efforts to defend Korea; there was no mention of the Soviet Union.

On the other hand, by the fall of 1952 the DPRK was also eager to leave the war if this could be done on terms favorable to the regime.

> A careful survey of North Korean domestic propaganda would indicate that, at the time of the 1953 armistice, the morale of the North Korean people was dangerously close to the breaking point. It must have constituted an enormous pressure upon the regime to reach some agreement with the U.N. Forces. Editorials and news columns were

filled with what amounted to pleas to "hold on," retain the ties of solidarity with the Party, and obey the government's orders. An almost equal number of stories and comments, however, dealt with problems of corruption, poor work habits and low production. . . .

In North Korea, a substantial breakdown of discipline throughout this period was frankly admitted. State property was being stolen, waste was taking place on a large scale, and in general there was far too little concern for the effective utilization of scarce materials. The majority of the people, to be sure, were "sacrificing themselves willingly for the nation," but "anti-state and anti-people" behavior was serious, and had to be challenged.[38]

End of the Beginning

It was at this point, on March 5, 1953, that Stalin died; the process of Soviet disengagement from the Korean Civil War, which had begun half a year before, now accelerated drastically as Stalin's successors concentrated on factional infighting at home. None of the *Pravda* editorials on the death of the leader, for example, mentioned the Korean Civil War. At the Peking memorial meeting for Stalin on March 9, Russian Ambassador Panyushkin hardly mentioned the war that had held the world's attention for the previous two and three-quarter years. His sole inference read: "As a result [of Stalin's genius], the laboring people of Poland, Hungary, Rumania, Czechoslovakia, Korea, Bulgaria, and Albania have established people's democratic rule in their own countries and carried out social reforms. . . . "[39]

On March 10, a new Soviet ambassador, V. Kuznetsov, was appointed to China; on the same day *Pravda* published the famous cropped photograph showing Malenkov, Stalin, and Mao alone in a warm pose. (This photo obliterated four other men in the original, taken February 14, 1950, on the occasion of the signing of the Sino–Soviet Treaty.[40]) The *Pravda* editorial of

the following day continued the deemphasis of the Korean Civil
War; its only mention being teamed with reference to the Vietnamese war: "In a stubborn struggle against the American aggressors, the heroic people of Korea are fighting for the indepen-
denče of their country. The people of Vietnam are fighting
courageously against their imperialist enslavers, for freedom
and national independence."[41]

Both Peking and P'yŏngyang quickly extended their congratulations to the new leadership in Moscow, particularly to
Malenkov, who, in the first week, seemed to be the "first among
equals." P'yŏngyang probably had been told that the Soviet
Union was withdrawing much of its active support from the
DPRK. The decision having already been made, Stalin's death
would have been only one major event regardless of whether or
not the Kremlin had already decided upon this course in the
latter half of 1952. Kim Il-sŏng, in an article published in *Pravda*
on March 11, 1953, seems to have fully realized that his only hope
for continuing the war in Korea rested upon China's sustained
support. In the middle of the essay, entitled "Stalin's Ideas
Inspire the Peoples' Fighting for Their Freedom and Independence," which was devoted almost entirely to praising the Soviet
army for the "liberation and regeneration of our country," a
paragraph appears completely out of context with the rest of the
article:

> Our people are not alone in their selfless and valiant fight.
> Mighty People's China has sent its volunteers to our assis-
> tance. This aid is *a good example of Stalin's friendship for the
> peoples of the mighty socialist camp.* The heroic resistance of
> the Korean people is a worthy example and inspiration for
> other peoples in their selfless struggle for their freedom and
> independence. [42]

This was a clear (if bitterly ironic) reminder to both Peking
and Moscow that Stalin had offered military protection to neither
Peking nor P'yŏngyang during the fall of 1950 and, moreover,
that the rest of the socialist camp considered China to have taken

the honorable path in coming to North Korea's aid. Another indication that the DPRK appreciated the fact that the war was scheduled for an early end was the statement on March 16, 1953, by Pak Ch'ong-ok, the secretary of the Central Committee of the KWP, that "at the U.N., Soviet delegates are fighting valiantly to win peace in Korea." This was the first statement in this vein in over a year, and it suggested that the resolution of the conflict was about to revert to the diplomatic arena. The Russians, at this same moment, signaled their intention to reduce tensions with the West. Malenkov, in a speech at the fourth session of the Supreme Soviet on March 15, 1953, declared that

> at present there is no disputed or unsettled question that could not be settled peacefully on the basis of mutual-agreement between the countries concerned. This applies to our relations with all countries, including our relations with the United States. States that are interested in preserving peace can be assured both now and in the future of the Soviet Union's firm policy of peace. [43]

Chou En-lai and the Chinese delegation which had represented Mao Tse-tung at Stalin's funeral returned to Peking on March 26; two days later the Chinese and North Korean commands accepted the United Nations suggestion of February 22 for a discussion of the exchange of sick and wounded prisoners. On March 30, Chou En-lai issued a conciliatory statement which opened the way to a rapid solution to the up-to-then insoluble problem of the repatriation of POWs. He proposed that

> both parties to the negotiations should undertake to repatriate immediately after the cessation of hostilities all those prisoners of war in their custody who insist upon repatriation, and to hand over the remaining POWs to a neutral state so as to ensure a just solution to the question of their repatriation.

Chou then continued, in a face-saving statement which reiterated China's position: "Nor do we acknowledge the assertion of the U.N. command that there are among the POWs individuals who allegedly refuse repatriation."[44] The way had now been cleared for an armistice. Significantly, the Soviet Union, which had previously always been the state to announce important decisions from the communist side, now *followed* Chou's declaration with an endorsement. On April 1, Soviet Foreign Minister Molotov gave an indication that it was now Peking which was taking the lead in determining communist policy on the war:

> I am authorized to state that the Soviet government expresses its full solidarity with this noble act of the government of the People's Republic of China and the government of the Korean People's Democratic Republic. . . . the Soviet government also expresses confidence that this proposal will be correctly understood by the government of the United States.[45]

Pak Hŏn-yŏng, DPRK foreign minister and one of Kim Il-sŏng's major rivals for power within the KWP during the period after World War II, had been arrested in late December of 1952; Pak was determined "to fight to the death rather than accept the armistice."[46] Perhaps as a result of this, and as an attempt to reassure the Soviet Union of its fidelity to the agreements that were actually being worked out regardless of its own wishes, P'yŏngyang's media abruptly shifted its emphasis of favoritism from Peking to Moscow in April and May. Before, as noted, P'yŏngyang stressed its reliance upon the CPV and indirectly criticized the Soviet Union for its lack of active military support. But now the North Koreans overdid themselves in expressing their loyalty and gratitude to Moscow. Kim would understandably have been more anxious to placate Moscow, since the likely source of economic aid needed by the decimated postwar DPRK economy would be Moscow, rather than the much poorer China.

This development was reflected in the relative prominence with which some of North Korea's May Day slogans for 1953 (announced April 20) mentioned the Soviet Union and China:

2. Long live the ironlike strength of the international friendship and solidarity among the communist parties and labor parties of the whole world, headed by the great Soviet Communist party.
4. Long live the great Soviet Union, the invincible bulwark of peace, democracy, and socialism of the world.
5. Enthusiastic congratulations to the great Soviet people, who are successfully carrying out the great work of communist construction under the ever-winning Lenin–Stalin banner and are encouraging and inspiring the Korean people in our Fatherland Liberation War for the freedom and independence of the fatherland.
6. Enthusiastic congratulations to the fraternal Chinese people, who are achieving brilliant victories in the construction of people's democracy. New China is helping with blood our Fatherland Liberation War under the just banner of the resist-America aid-Korea movement.

On April 16, *Minju Chosŏn* [Democratic Korea], the organ of the Central Committee of the KWP, published its May Day editorial, "Let Us Arm Ourselves with Proletarian Internationalism More Firmly Than Ever." It rang with passages more adulatory of the Soviet Union than in the previous year: "Particularly, to become a proletarian internationalist, one must unconditionally support the Soviet Union, the fatherland of socialism and democracy. Support for the Soviet Union is the touchstone for testing internationalists."[47]

On May 13, 1953, P'yŏngyang Radio broadcast an undated *Minju Chosŏn* editorial entitled "Let Us More Extensively Study and Absorb Advanced Soviet Culture." Before this time, P'yŏngyang had often made mention of the need to learn from its neighbors, but it had always been sure to mention both China *and* the Soviet Union in such homilies. Now however, Russia alone was mentioned: "For the sake of the blossoming of our national culture, our cultural workers must constantly study the advanced Soviet culture."

The War's End

In early June of 1953, as the armistice negotiations approached a successful conclusion, the South Korean government of Syngman Rhee began to threaten to unilaterally release the communist POWs who were held in the camps guarded by South Korean soldiers. Indeed, the actual release of these prisoners on June 18 did not come as a surprise.[48] Peking was aware that the truce negotiations were endangered by Rhee, and called for an early agreement before Seoul could abort an armistice:

> The Syngman Rhee clique evidently intends to detain POWs by force. It must, therefore, be recognized that true settlement of the POW repatriation question now still depends on whether the American side is able to carry out swiftly the provisions of the agreement and avert the danger of possible detention of the POWs.[49]

Peking was charging that Rhee, by releasing the POWs would actually be "detaining" them away from the U.N. camps as a means of stalemating the Armistice negotiations. The actual release of the POWs by Rhee caused different reactions in the three communist countries. Peking understood that the action was probably taken independently by South Korea. NCNA on June 19 quoted approvingly from a U.P. dispatch from Tokyo which said: "The U.N. command and the U.S. Government are powerless to prevent Rhee from taking any of these [provocative] courses. . . . The immediate vital question of whether Rhee's action today would destroy chances of a truce could not be answered in Tokyo." On June 26, General Teng Hua, deputy commander of the CPV, was quoted by NCNA as saying that "the only way of settling international disputes, *as shown by the development of the armistice talks,* is by peaceful negotiation." On June 28, NCNA commented that "the Syngman Rhee 'tail' has been wagging furiously, and has pushed the armistice to the edge of the precipice. Whether it is the 'head' that commands the 'tail,' or vice versa, is up to Washington to decide and answer." Clearly, Peking was willing to ignore Rhee's sensational action and get on with the signing of the armistice. Implicitly, this meant that she was willing as well to entrust the restraining of Rhee's aggressive impulses to the Americans (emphasis added).

P'yŏngyang, sensitive to the fact that any future South Korean aggression would be aimed at her, reacted furiously to Rhee's precipitous action. On June 27, for example, P'yŏngyang Radio noted that "all provocative acts and all illegal actions by the traitor Syngman Rhee are scheduled with the connivance and guidance of his master, which is admitted by the world." On July 2 P'yŏngyang Radio broadcast another comment, which contrasted with the earlier Chinese questioning of which was the "tail": "America can take Syngman Rhee any place and fasten him by the collar; you cannot look upon America as a master incapable of controlling the dog he has raised." *Minju Chosŏn,* in an editorial published on July 1 in honor of the thirty-second anniversary of the CCP, observed that China had now "*completely* mopped up and driven out the forces of foreign imperialists and their lackeys from the soil of their country. . . ."[50] In neglecting to mention the problem of Taiwan, P'yŏngyang might have been alluding to the possibility of adhering at least in the short run, to the forthcoming Korean armistice. Alternatively, their remark could have been meant as a pointed reminder to China that it had an interest in opposing American imperialism, which was occupying Taiwan. In fact, both messages could well have been directed from a nervous P'yŏngyang toward its past—and hopefully future—protector.

Moscow, at this moment when the armistice negotiations were endangered by Syngman Rhee's release of the POWs, was more worried about the Berlin riots of June 16 and 17. Most of Moscow Radio's commentaries on foreign affairs were concerned with this European crisis rather than with Korea. *Pravda's* main editorial of June 23, for example, entitled: "The Failure of the Foreign Hireling's Adventure in Berlin," con-

238 THE STRAINED ALLIANCE

trasted the two situations in a manner which clearly indicated Russia's priorities:

> There is no doubt that these two events, which took place on different continents of the globe, are closely connected. The question here is of the criminal intrigues of the enemies of peace, the intrigue of those reactionary circles who are afraid of peace, who do not want it, and who are doing everything to prevent the easing of international tensions.

The editorial, blaming problems on the vague "enemies of peace," then went on to say that the POWs were released "on Syngman Rhee's orders," while in Berlin "provocations took place under the direct leadership of the U.S. military authorities." Apparently, Moscow considered Rhee the villain in Korea, while the U.S. played this role in Germany. America, therefore, was not to blame for Rhee's actions.[51]

P'yŏngyang, meanwhile, was not as tranquil about the release of the POWs, nor as charitable about the role of the U.S., as either of its two allies. On June 22, for example, P'yŏngyang Radio charged that "the vicious American imperialist aggressors and the Syngman Rhee traitor gang are carrying out the outrageous act of driving the POWs out of their camps by using tank guns against empty-handed POWs." Unlike Peking and Moscow, which were willing to affix the blame for endangering a Korean armistice upon Seoul, P'yŏngyang suspected Washington machinations in purposefully prolonging the war.

On July 8, NCNA declared that the U.S. was obliged to agree that "your side must shoulder the absolute responsibility for ensuring that no such incidents occur *again*." In short, Peking would not allow Rhee's action to hinder the concluding of an agreement on Korea if Washington would bind Seoul to that agreement.

On July 9, P'yŏngyang Radio, in a sudden and dramatic softening of its position on the United States, began to state that it was indeed Syngman Rhee who was the bad guy in the scenario, rather than Washington:

> If President Eisenhower had not encouraged Syngman Rhee, the vicious disturber of peace, with a Republic of Korea–United States defense pact, if Clark's headquarters had been more active and decisive in retrieving the situation caused by the provocations of Syngman Rhee, and if Robertson, the U.S. envoy to Rhee, had avoided the dirty show of trying to find a way of compromising with Syngman Rhee, the open enemy of peace, the situation would not have developed the way it has, and would not be that way in the future. If Clark's headquarters really want an early armistice in Korea and the realization of peace, the bestial, indiscriminate bombing of inhabited areas in the rear, which has been intensified viciously since the provocative act of Syngman Rhee, would have been unnecessary. The American government and military authorities, however, have not acted that way. Instead, they have become an *unintentional* inspiration for Syngman Rhee. (Emphasis added.)

The reason for this new North Korean expression of conciliation became evident on the night of July 13–14, when the CPV attacked and heavily damaged the South Korean elite Capital Division, while largely avoiding contact with nearby American forces in this last offensive of the war. NCNA of July 20, 1953, referred to this attack as a lesson "against the Syngman Rhee puppet army, which has been obstructing the Korean armistice and provoking the People's forces." China had apparently offered North Korea assurances that she would guarantee P'yŏngyang's interests; the attack upon the Capital Division was meant as a demonstration of her intention to make good on these assurances.

The war ended only a few miles north of where it began, while the 1949 population of North Korea, nine million, had been reduced by one-ninth. The end of the war found the three (unequal) communist partners eagerly expressing their desire for peace. This was perhaps best suggested by the pacific telegram which Kim Il-song sent to Malenkov on July 29, thanking the Soviet Union for its aid during the war:

> It is believed to be a trustworthy assurance of successful fulfillment of such an important task raised before the Korean people after the armistice as an attainment of unification of the Fatherland and quick rehabilitation of the people's economy, which has been destroyed by the war. [52]

In its home service of July 30, Moscow Radio broadcast the telegram with but one addition: Kim's "unification" had now become the more quiescent "peaceful unification."

Unlearned Lessons from the U.S. Side

To a jaded North American public, to whom fragmentation bombs and televised napalm attacks have been everyday sights, the parallels between the Korean Civil War and the Indochinese War are numerous. In both cases the United States backed corrupt and unpopular governments, preferring to believe that "international order" was more important than the legitimate nationalism of the peoples involved.

The reader is urged to consult Washington's official histories of the Korean Civil War, which, in stark, bureaucratic language, detail the fruitless attempts made by the United States to cut off enemy supplies—all the while, of course, inevitably striking also at civilian targets. Later air generals apparently had not learned a lesson from their attempt to interdict enemy supplies in Korea. One official narrative, for example, after detailing the massive destruction to rails, roads, bridges, and cities from bombing, concludes that "despite the air force's efforts, the Communists were able to stockpile supplies to sustain themselves from thirty to forty-five days in the forward areas." [53]

Another tactic that will be familiar to the Indochina genera-tion was the bombing of North Korean dikes. The use of dike bombing was buried within a twelve-paragraph daily communiqué about United States air action on May 15, 1953: "F-84s also struck an earthen dam at Tokchon, 10 miles north of Sukchon, with unobserved results."[54] The official military his-tory of the war has a dryly interesting description of what hap-pened:

> About twenty miles north of P'yŏngyang lay the big Toksan irrigation dam with a 3 square-mile lake behind it. Air Force planners had long realized that destruction of irriga-tion dams would have a serious effect upon the rice crop of North Korea, but humanitarian considerations had argued against the bombing of such targets. As the war pro-gressed, however, more and more of the rice crop found its way into military and international barter channels and this knowledge overcame the objections against destroy-ing the dams.[55]

After detailing the military tactics used, the history continues: "Floodwaters poured forth and left a trail of havoc. . . . Build-ings, crops, and irrigation canals were all swept away in the devastating torrent."

The air force, "elated by the success of the Toksan Mis-sion," struck against other dikes; however, "the Communists had learned their lesson by this time and efforts in June to repeat the earlier success at Toksan found the enemy quickly draining the reservoirs under attack. The water was lost, but flood damage was averted."[56] A widely read history of the war notes regret-fully that "the fifteen remaining irrigation dams could have been destroyed in as many days. Much too late, the USAF had at last found a possibly decisive target system."[57]

The intervention of the United States in the Korean Civil War had disastrous consequences both for America and for the Korean peninsula. A potentially swift and relatively bloodless reunification was converted into a carnage. For Korea, both north and south, the devastation was awesome. By the end of September, 1950, for example, the U.S Air Force had dropped 97,000 tons of bombs and 7.8 million gallons of napalm.[58] The results of the bombings rivaled Dante's *Inferno*. P'yŏngyang's population, for instance, was 400,000 when the war started, 80,000 when the war ended. Only two public buildings in the capital remained intact by 1953.[59] In 1949 the North Korean population was 9,622,000; by 1953 it had declined to 8,491,000. Incredibly, the peninsula's total population in 1950 had been 30 million.

The United States suffered 142,091 casualties in the war, including 33,629 killed. The DPRK's military casualties have been estimated at 500,000, with 1 million civilians missing.[60] The ROK's situation was similar; their military casualty list officially reads 300,000, with 1 million dead civilians. At the end of the war, 2½ million refugees roamed the south, and another 5 million people were living on some form of relief.[61] It may be assumed that the bulk of North Korea's population was living at a subsistence level in 1953. In short, the 1950–53 war was one of the most destructive conflicts in history.

❙From an American perspective, nonintervention would have brought welcome consequences. First, the Chinese civil war would have ended with the liberation of Taiwan. Thereupon, in all probability, Washington and Peking would have reached a working relationship, averting China's forced alliance with the Soviet Union. Secondly, without the continuing identification of nationalism and communism that America's entrance into the Korean Civil War reinforced, it is possible that the Indochina adventure might have been forestalled.❙

In the first three months of the war, the entire peninsula was largely devastated. General Emmett (Rosie) O'Donnell, head of the Bomber Command in the Far East, put it succinctly:

> I would say that the entire, almost the entire Korean peninsula, is just a terrible mess. Everything is destroyed. There

is nothing standing worthy of the name. . . . Just before the Chinese came in we were grounded. There were no more targets in Korea.[62]

Considering the next civil war in which the United States was to intervene, Indochina, perhaps the most unsettling legacy of the war for North Americans is that many of the shibboleths about the conflict are still accepted, while its lessons have often been only partially learned.

Notes

1. Adam B. Ulam, *Expansion and Coexistence: The History of Soviet Foreign Policy, 1917—1967* (New York: Frederick A. Praeger, 1968), p. 533.
2. New China News Agency (NCNA), October 23, 1951. Emphasis added.
3. Ulam, op. cit., p. 532.
4. Byung Chul Koh, *The Foreign Policy of North Korea* (New York: Frederick A. Praeger, 1969), p. 14.
5. Robert A. Scalapino and Chong-sik Lee, *Communism in Korea* (Berkeley and Los Angeles: University of California Press, 1972, p. 409.
6. Joungwon Alexander Kim, "Soviet Policy in North Korea," *World Politics* (January, 1970), pp. 241–43.
7. P'yŏngyang Radio, November 11 and 20, 1951. Emphasis added.
8. Moscow Radio, December 1, 1951.
9. P'yŏngyang Radio, February 5, 1952.
10. David Rees, *Korea: The Limited War* (Baltimore: Penguin Books, 1964), p. 461.
11. John Gittings, *The Role of the Chinese Army* (London: Oxford University Press, 1967), pp. 77–83.
12. Ibid., p. 89.
13. Philip Bridgham, Arthur Cohen, and Leonard Jaffe, "Mao's Road and Sino–Soviet Relations: A View from Washington, 1953," in *China Quarterly* (October–December, 1972), p. 682.
14. Stuart Schram, *The Political Thought of Mao Tse-tung* (Baltimore: Penguin Books, 1969), p. 89.
15. Guy Wint, *What Happened in Korea: A Study in Collective Security* (London: Batchworth Press, 1954), p. 84.

16. John C. Clews *Communist Propaganda Techniques* (London: Methuen, 1964), pp. 189–90.
17. Scalapino and Lee, op. cit., pp. 421–22.
18. General Headquarters, United Nations and United States Far East Command, Tokyo, May 8, 1952.
19. Ibid., April 23, 1952.
20. *New York Times*, "Yalu Raids Ended Red Truce Plan; New Delhi Hears of Peiping Offer," by Robert Trumball, July 19, 1952, p. 2, dispatch from New Delhi.
21. *United States Air Force Operations in the Korean Conflict, 1 July 1952–27 July 1953* (Washington, D.C.: Department of the Air Force, historical study no. 71, 1956), p. 33.
22. *New York Times*, "New Phase in Korea," by Hanson Baldwin, June 26, 1952, p. 2.
23. *New York Times*, Robert Trumball, op. cit., p. 2.
24. Moscow Radio, August 17, 1952.
25. Yudin cited Stalin writing in 1927 that the Chinese revolution had "entered into a higher stage of its development, into the phase on an agrarian movement." *Pravda*, August 24, 1952; translated in the *Current Digest of the Soviet Press*, September 20, 1952, p. 15.
26. Bridgham, Cohen, and Jaffe, op. cit., pp. 691–92.
27. Bernard Brodie, *War and Politics* (New York: Macmillan Co., 1973), p. 102.
28. Peking Radio, September 16, 1952. Emphasis added.
29. P'yŏngyang Radio, October 25, 1952.
30. P'yŏngyang Radio, October 26, 1952. Emphasis added. The speech, moreover, was given by a "deputy commander" (no name) of the CPV. This suggests that both China and North Korea were indicating their strong desire to end the war.
31. E.g. NCNA, October 12, 1952.
32. Translated in *Current Digest of the Soviet Press*, November 1, 1952, p. 34.
33. Peking Radio, February 4, 1953.
34. Stalin's essay appeared in *Pravda* on October 3 and 4, 1952, and was translated in the *Current Digest of the Soviet Press*, October 18, 1952. Emphasis added. A further reason why Stalin's emphasis upon war among capitalist states rather than between capitalist and socialist states, is significant is the fact that he preferred to concentrate on one problem at a time. The removal of foreign entanglements would allow him to deal with his prime priority of the moment: domestic factionalism in the USSR.

Robert C. Tucker has put forward a somewhat different emphasis in *The Soviet Political Mind: Studies in Stalinism and Post-Stalin Change*, rev. ed. (New York: W.W. Norton, 1971), p.99. "Contrary to some Western interpretations, which have seen in it [*Economic Problems of Socialism in the Soviet Union*] a signal of an impending Soviet switch to a "softer" line in foreign policy, this part of Stalin's final work carried as its implicit theme and message the need for the Communist world to wage *political* war against the West without letup" (emphasis added). Prof. Tucker's acknowledgment of Stalin's wish to wage political war, however, would appear to substantiate the thesis that the Soviet dictator now was turning away from military confrontations (e.g., the Korean Civil War) with the West.

35. Ulam, op. cit., p. 538.
36. Harold Hinton, *Communist China in World Politics* (Boston: Houghton Mifflin Co., 1966), p. 22.
37. P'yŏngyang Radio, February 23, 1953.
38. Scalapino and Lee, op. cit., pp. 422–23.
39. Peking Radio, March 9, 1953.
40. Hinton, op. cit., p. 228.
41. Moscow Radio, March 11, 1953.
42. Moscow Radio, March 11, 1953. Emphasis added. Although Kim wanted an early conclusion to the war, he needed continued CPV support for satisfactory peace terms.
43. Moscow Radio, March 15, 1953.
44. NCNA, March 30, 1953.
45. Moscow Radio, April 1, 1953.
46. Kim Sam-kyu, *Konnichi no Chōsen* [Korea Today] (Tokyo: Kawade Shobo, 1956), pp. 91–103.
47. P'yŏngyang Radio, April 26, 1953.
48. Rhee had been threatening such a step for several months. Reporters on the scene commented on the likelihood of such an event. For example, Robert Alden, in a dispatch from Seoul to the *New York Times* of June 19, 1953, p. 2, commented that "a release was imminent and had been clear for some time. Several newspaper reports even had been published that South Korean guards at the camps were encouraging prisoners to break out of the stockades. Yet despite this advance information and despite the fact that there were sufficient American troops available for guard duty, in reserve areas of Korea and Japan, there had been only a token change in the procedure for handling prisoners in the camps."

In a dispatch of the following day, Alden noted that "officers in Tokyo had been warned that such a measure might be taken by the Government of the Republic of Korea. However, the POW command was assured by higher headquarters that Dr. Rhee was 'bluffing.'"

Regardless of the cause of the POWs' release, China and North Korea, based upon accounts published in newspapers of the period, had reason to suspect American connivance in Rhee's action. In 1951, this might well have been cause for the communist side to break off the negotiations. But in their eagerness for an armistice in the summer of 1953, Peking and P'yŏngyang reacted prudently.

49. Peking Radio, June 9, 1953.
50. Moscow Radio, June 23, 1953. Emphasis added.
51. Moscow Radio, June 23, 1953.
52. P'yŏngyang Radio, July 29, 1953.
53. Walter G. Hermes, *Truce Tent and Fighting Front* (Washington, D.C., Office of the Chief of Military History, 1966), p. 400.
54. *New York Times,* May 15, 1953.
55. Hermes, op. cit., p. 461.
56. Ibid.
57. Rees, op. cit., p. 382.
58. Joyce and Gabriel Kolko, *The Limits of Power: The World and United States Foreign Policy, 1945–1954* (New York: Harper and Row, 1972), p. 615.
59. Wilfred Burchett, *Again Korea* (New York: International Publishers, 1968), p. 65.
60. Rees, op. cit., p. 461.
61. Kolko and Kolko, op. cit., p. 615.
62. *Military Situation in the Far East, Hearings Before the Committee on Armed Services and the Committee on Foreign Relations,* United States Senate, 82nd Congress, 1st Session (Washington, D.C.,: U.S. Government Printing Office, 1951), p. 3075.

9

The Strained Alliance

In its attempt to "get a handle" on reality, any social science model inevitably distorts the world which it is viewing. This occurs because the model's manipulator has already decided what perspective will be used in simplifying the available data, and the model incorporates that decision. Utilizing a model consequently entails both costs and benefits. A model allows important questions to be asked in a replicable fashion. It also permits the ordering of a large, often unclassified, body of information which is of interest beyond the specific case under study at the moment. On the minus side, the use of a model often persuades the investigator to ignore some information while stressing other, sometimes less significant, data. In short, the use of a given model and its perspective will offer insights into particular problems (if the investigator first poses theoretically interesting questions), but it also runs the risk of ignoring or slighting other information or problems. This is the price that the observer must pay for the fact that any given model can afford only one perspective on a multifaceted reality.

This being said, the "alliance model" nonetheless offers a worthwhile perspective on comparative foreign policy. Although this book deals with one particular alliance during the Korean Civil War, this chapter draws upon several other examples. This is because the value of the model lies in its cross-national character. Other examples, and aberrations from them, may be used as the basis for "if-then" statements which are necessary both to a fuller understanding of each case and as an attempt at primitive prediction.

Until recently, the study of alliances has dwelled upon the reasons why a coalition would first combine and then continue united. In fact, it would seem that something of an opposite starting point is more fruitful for the study of alliances: viz., the assumption that these fragile joinings are brief. The preceding pages have pointed out some of the causes for mutual dissatisfaction between Peking, P'yŏngyang, and Moscow, both before and during the war. Enough space has been spent on narrating the reasons for *that* alliance's causes and demise; it is now time to devote a briefer space to extrapolating from these experiences to more generalized lessons.

The reader of this volume will have noticed that attention has been paid to the historical precedents of the 1950–53 alliance. This is because alliances do not spring up suddenly; rather, they must be seen in context, as the result of historical circumstances. The careful reader will also have noticed that I have attempted to distinguish between types of coalitions, between "alignments" and "alliances." These distinctions are vital if one wishes to see beyond the mass of available data in order to draw meaningful generalizations.

It is important to formulate theoretical propositions about the communist alliance during the Korean Civil War in an effort to comprehend why China was dissatisfied with the Soviet Union, and why she remained allied with the Soviet Union after this dissatisfaction began to surface. If this is done in an analytical, rather than merely descriptive, manner, it will provide a basis for comparisons between that alliance and others.

Such hypotheses should also assist in predicting the outcome of present alliances. In this context, for example, it is valuable to seek similarities between the Korean Civil War alliances and the more recent Chinese–North Vietnamese and United States–South Vietnamese coalitions. This chapter will first survey the literature on alliance and then present its own definition, which may serve as a tool in analyzing events that are usually only chronicled.

Previous Definitions of an Alliance

The mechanism and nature of the bonding relationships between states in international relations are as various as are the connections themselves. Today, states which have mutual bonds are described as being either "aligned" or "allied." In fact, one of the most important works on the subject of international coalitions, *Nations in Alliance,* by George Liska, uses these two terms interchangeably. [1] Perhaps because of the different functions of international coalitions before World War I—both offensive and defensive, aggregating and fragmenting, short- and long-term—the concept of "alliance" has become both ambiguous and ubiquitous.

Bandied about as it is in both popular and specialized parlance, the term "alliance" currently lacks precision; the expression has become an elusive one, permitting widely divergent definitions. It is variously used to refer to a technique, to various degrees of international cooperation, to the operations of commercial corporations at the international level, to an international organization, or even to some type of economic or sociopolitical federation. This vague use of the term "alliance" means that it is almost impossible not to find it describing quite different types of interstate relationships.

In his *Nations in Alliance,* Professor Liska carefully and lucidly explains the nature of an alliance:

> When they are sufficiently intense, and security is the chief concern, conflicts are the primary determinants of alignments. Alliances are against, and only derivatively for, someone or something. The sense of community may consolidate alliances; it rarely brings them about. When com-

munity feeling is sufficiently strong, it commonly seeks other institutional forms of expression. Cooperation in alliances is in large part the consequence of conflicts with adversaries and may submerge only temporarily the conflicts among allies. [2]

In a subsequent section of his book, however, Liska violates his own definition and its implications. For example, he cites the North Atlantic Treaty Organization, NATO (from 1949 to 1962), the Southeast Asia Treaty Organization, SEATO, the Organization of American States, OAS, and the "Sino–Soviet Bloc" as major instances of mid-twentieth-century alliances. However, the definitional question then must be asked: Is NATO of 1949 the same as a decade later—or beyond? Indeed, is NATO of any of those years the equivalent of either the OAS or the "Sino-Soviet Bloc"? Is security the chief concern of the OAS? Has "community feeling" been strong enough to transform NATO into more than an alliance?

Most works which deal with alliances spend a great deal of space on NATO. As Liska explains, however, alliances are neither politically integrated nor do they have the goal of integration. In fact, the evidence indicates that where there is an alliance more durable forms of political community already exist. [3] For the sake of analytical precision alone, therefore, the concept of "alliance" must be kept separate from the more vague forms of international coalition such as NATO, which, in fact, has become in a significant sense the military arm of an embryonic political community. [4] NATO's intrarelationships and functions have become broad and multifarious.

A more recent instance of an overbroad but otherwise excellent analysis of alliance is presented by Astri Suhrke. In his categorization, such linkages as those between the U.S. and South Korea from 1945 to 1973 are seen as "alliances." Similarly, New Zealand is seen as forming an "alliance" with the United States. [5]

Another example of the loose use of the term "alliance" is evidenced by the title which Francis A. Beer chose for his recent book of readings: *Alliances: Latent War Communities in the Contemporary World.* [6] The phrase is taken from Robert Osgood's concept of alliances as "latent war communities." [7] Beer approvingly notes:

> Osgood's definition appropriately includes organizations with core security activities, such as the North Atlantic Treaty Organization, the Southeast Asia Treaty Organization, the Western European Union, the Central Treaty Organization, the Australia–New Zealand–United States Alliance, the Warsaw Treaty Organization. It also has room for such other organizations with important, though less central, security concerns, as the Organization of American States, the League of Arab States, and the Organization of African Unity. In addition, it encompasses less structured security arrangements, such as the Brussels Treaty, the series of agreements between France and the former French Territories, analogous British agreements, the Balkan Pact, and a host of other bilateral agreements. [8]

It would appear, however, that by including almost any international linkage which includes some provision for contemplated military action, Osgood and Beer have vastly diluted the theoretical efficiency of the concept of "alliance." How, except in a very loose manner, can one compare the functions of NATO in 1949 with those of the Organization of African Unity in 1974?

Of course, if a former alliance partner becomes feared, the alliance has by then long since collapsed. Examples of this are the relations between China and the Soviet Union starting in the latter 1950s and the strains between China and the DPRK in the latter 1960s for a short while.

Raymond Aron has recognized the necessity for distinguishing between different types of alliances. He draws a distinction between "permanent" and "occasional" allies. The former are those states which, "whatever the conflict of some of their interests, do not conceive, in the foreseeable future, that they can be in the opposite camps, while

> occasional allies, in fact, have no bond other than a common hostility toward an enemy, a hostility capable of inspiring sufficient fear to overcome the rivalries that yesterday opposed and tomorrow will again oppose the temporarily allied states. Moreover, occasional allies, on a deeper level, may be permanent enemies: by this we mean states that are committed to conflict because of their ideology or their position on the diplomatic chessboard. [9]

Although this definition has the advantage of separating types of alliances, it also suffers from the attempt to include too many interstate relationships under one conceptual umbrella. Aron's "permanent allies," for example, may well be states involved in an ongoing integrative process, with close socioeconomic underpinnings, such as Australia and New Zealand. Such a situation is not an alliance. A caution must also be entered about Aron's idea of "occasional allies." His emphasis on the normal rivalry between these states is perhaps misleading. It is, in fact, by no means unusual for states which previously had some bonds of commonality to form an alliance.

It is the purpose of the following pages, for reasons of both analytical rigor and empirical application, to delineate clearly the concept of an "alliance." In order to be more precise about the phenomena that are being described, it is necessary to first formulate separate categories of international bonding relationships. It is important to note, however, that these categories are "ideal types." In the empirical world there is apt to be some overlapping, particularly because the crucial variable in determining the applicable category—viz., the perception of the participants—is partially subjective.

The first category advanced shall be termed "association." This term refers to the fact that many states share multifaceted connections which are not considered vital to their existence. For example, Liberia trades with Ecuador, and may vote with Burma on certain issues in the United Nations. However, neither of these acts is considered by Liberia to be crucial to its national security or survival; each is carried out as a specific deed meant to enhance Liberia's welfare.

The second category is that of "alignment." The states in this relationship collaborate on a particular problem of *core* interest to each, with the expectation of some form of mutual assistance; each perceives that cooperation will be helpful in achieving its necessary interests. Such relationships as international cooperation, economic partnership, and political integration fall within this category.[10] Interstate relations in an alignment have become predictable and stable enough as to be considered continuously structured toward the vital interests of the involved states.

In this category, states may be aligned with different countries at the same time over different issues. For example, in the winter of 1971–72 the United States was "aligned" with Pakistan on the war with Bangladesh, while it was also "aligned" with India by virtue of its interest in India's continued economic and political survival. (Within this perspective, Henry Kissinger's phrase that the United States had "tilted" toward Pakistan during the crisis was accurately descriptive.)

There is obviously a great deal of variation of interstate contacts and interests within this broad second category, which needs a case-by-case analysis in order to achieve some empirical utility. The category was created in order to set off the contemporary idea of "alliance"—the category which comprises the most intense (although not the most durable) form of interstate bonding.

An operational definition of this last category must be broad enough to identify the specific phenomena which one wishes to consider "alliances," yet narrow enough to distinguish it from other aspects of international bonding. This will provide a common vocabulary for disparate observers analyzing different categories of international cooperation. For a relationship to constitute a successful alliance, one must have:

1. Existence of a common enemy or enemies, either real or anticipated.
2. Shared expectation of imminent war; or the states must be engaged in a common war effort at the moment, with a mutuality of interest in the outcome. (It should be emphasized that neither "associated" nor "aligned" states expect an early common military action.)
3. Perception on the part of each ally that the other is committing a significant percentage of its resources to the common effort.

There are two subdivisions within the category of "alliance": "partnership–alliance" and "protectorate–alliance."[11] Only by analyzing the individual perceptions of the participating states can we determine into which subdivision a relationship falls. A "partnership–alliance" exists when each ally feels that the other is willing to spend or risk an equivalent amount in material, territorial, or human costs: i.e., when there is a symmetry in the expenditure by each of similarly treasured core values. During the Korean Civil War, for example, China and the Democratic People's Republic of Korea were partner–allies because each was willing for a time to expend equivalent core values: the North Koreans suffed loss of lives and territory, while China both expended lives and suffered a delay in its national economic reconstruction.

The second subdivision is that of a "protectorate–alliance." In this case, the (usually) stronger state is unwilling to share costs and take on risks equally with its ally, although it does expend a significant amount of its core values. Within this context, the Soviet Union was a protectorate–ally of both the DPRK and China throughout the Korean Civil War. That is, the Russians expended a relatively small amount of their assets in support of their allies and were not ready to commit an equivalent measure of their resources—nor were they agreeable to running the same risk of war with the United States as their two allies had undertaken.

As has been noted in chapter 7, the weapons that the Soviet Union supplied to its allies during the war were inferior and vulnerable to the American technology that they faced. Both allies realized early on that they were defending themselves with inadequate Russian weapons. Peking's and P'yŏngyang's dismay at Russia's aloofness from the war increased as the battlefield stalemate continued. [12]

The cutting edge of an alliance is the immediate fear of war. Grounded in Thucydides, all modern commentators on alliance agree on this cardinal point. [13] The corollary of this statement is that alliances are of relatively short duration, on account of the limited length of the war threats themselves, and because of the judgment of each partner that the other is not likely to remain deeply committed to risking its own resources in a prolonged conflict. Unfortunately, current alliance theory often does not pursue this implication.

As we remarked earlier, states may *align* with different countries over different issues. State A may align with state B about issue X, and state A may also align with state C at the same time over issue Y. But state A and B don't have to be in agreement about issue Y. Alliances, on the other hand, are highly restrictive as to prospective partners. Because the issue of national survival is at stake, alliances are composed of partners who are willing to expend significant portions of their resources in pursuit of a common war effort and thus are likely to be in agreement over a wider range of issues. Hence, a state will have fewer alliance partners than alignment partners.

A state may enter into an alliance in order to reinforce the regime's stability and legitimacy if it feels imminently threatened by an opponent (either foreign or domestic). While this function of an alliance was occasionally served prior to World War I, it has now become so prevalent that it deserves

specific mention. This type of alliance may prop up a government by the importation of aid or ideology. An example of this
supportive function of an alliance would be Cuba, in the early
years of the Castro regime. The feeling that Cuba was not alone
in its contest with the United States, but was instead a part of the
Soviet bloc, probably helped to maintain the Havana
government's stability, particularly during the Bay of Pigs and
Cuban Missile crises. Our definition of an "alliance," however,
requires that for such a linkage to remain an alliance, it must be
of a relatively short duration, within the context of a specific
threat from a particular enemy. Over a longer period, the relationship ceases to be an alliance and begins to resemble an
"alignment."

It should be noted that these types of alliances are always
protectorate–alliances. In such cases, the stronger is willing to
expend only a limited amount of its core resources, a fact to
which its ally is sensitive. The Russian–Chinese–Korean
1950–53 alliance, as well as the later Soviet Union–Cuba and
United States–South Vietnam alliances, fall within this category.
Because the weaker partner tends to be dissatisfied with the
amount of support supplied by its ally, it is to be expected that it
will seek some ties beyond the existing bond.

Some Further Alliance Variables

The weaker and more vulnerable a state is, the
more it will wish to transform an alliance from protectorate to
partnership status. Of course, a stronger state may no longer
desire an alliance relationship with a state under the latter circumstances. The existing disparity in power means that the
weaker state is (at least initially) militarily dependent upon the
stronger; in such cases, an alliance relationship may be entered
into by the weaker state with the expectation of imminent war,
while the stronger may not consider such a prospect to be so

immediate. On the other hand, this power disparity can also mean that stronger states will seek to impose their conflicts upon weaker partners at the same time that the latter are trying to form a partner–alliance in order to bring the stronger ally into its own local conflicts. Such a situation obviously has the makings of asymmetrical perceptions, different goals on the part of each partner, and potential broken commitments.

During the Korean Civil War, the Democratic People's Republic of Korea sought to form and maintain partnership–alliances with both China and the Soviet Union. China sought only a protectorate–alliance with North Korea during the summer and early fall of 1950, while the Soviet Union systematically avoided a parnership–alliance with both China and the DPRK throughout the war. P'yŏngyang's appeals during the war clearly indicated its desire that the Soviet Union dispatch either Russian troops or sufficient material aid to help drive U.N. forces from the Korean peninsula. Moscow, for its part, supplied inadequate economic and military aid to achieve North Korean goals. The strains born of this wartime alliance go a long way to explaining both China's and the DPRK's "sudden" independence of a few years later.

Some Conditions for Alliance Transformation

Of course, an alliance may, as a war crisis develops, transform itself in either direction: protectorate–alliances may change into partnership–alliances, or vice versa. The United States' involvement in South Vietnam may illustrate this two-way effect. Before 1961, the United States–South Vietnamese relationship from a Washington perspective was one of limited aid, concern, and commitment—i.e., an alignment. After 1961, the United States increased all of these factors and the relationship evolved into a protectorate–alliance. The South Vietnamese, on the other hand, were eager to transform this into a partnership–alliance. The United States, however, never perceived its linkage with South Vietnam in this light; Washington's cost tolerance and willingness to expend resources was not equivalent to Saigon's.

Because imminent war is expected by alliance members, each must perceive that the other is willing to share equally the risks involved; each may need constant reassurance of the other's ability and will to come to its aid. In a partnership–alliance each ally must feel that the other is willing to expend the functional equivalent of what it is sacrificing. This is difficult to quantify: i.e., how many dollars, pounds, *roubles, yuan,* or *won* equal the death of one soldier? Nonetheless, each partner–ally must perceive that the other is suffering more-or-less equally in the common cause.

If one ally is dissatisfied, it may opt out of the alliance in search of an ally which it perceives will provide an anticipated higher satisfaction quotient (or it may simply want to leave the war). An example of this is the action of Finland during World War II. Finland sided with Germany in order to regain territories which had been previously lost to the Soviet Union. As the war progressed and the lost territory remained unobtainable—and as Germany began to lose—Finland switched to the side of the Soviet Union. A similar situation was developing, as we saw in the last chapter, between China and the DPRK, on the one hand, and the Soviet Union on the other.

Some Consequences of Different Perceptions of Demands and Commitments

As was suggested before, one state may view a bonding relationship as being one type of alliance, while another will perceive the linkage in a different light. This asymmetry of expectations by alliance partners will lead to unbalanced demands and commitments. A weaker ally can draw larger powers into an essentially local conflict by making it a "test" of the larger power's belief system. This is particularly so in a loose, bipolar world, where the international system is permeated with ideological perceptions and jargon. In this situation, the weaker state can often take the large-scale patterns of the international system for granted and use the stronger power's own ideology as a bargaining counter in seeking aid (as did the DPRK).

Because alliances are creatures of their time and purpose and hence necessarily short-lived, the formal signing of an agreement is usually the high point of the linkage. What follows is often an anticlimax and, if the perceived common threat diminishes, inevitably a transformation, such as happened to NATO shortly after its founding. Moreover, the heavier the price a member has to pay for the continuing viability of an alliance (particularly that member whose territorial integrity is more secure), the quicker it will be to question the alliance's value—as Moscow did in its relationship with the DPRK.

The less-threatened member is hesitant to pay continued high costs. It is, therefore, in the interest of the weaker ally to underline the menace which the crisis holds for the stronger ally. Consequently, Raymond Aron's observation that "the leader of the coalition is the only one inclined to identify the coalition's interest with his own"[14] is inaccurate. In a protectorate–alliance the stronger state is less eager to expand a significant percentage of its resources in support of its allies, while the weaker, under more pressure, is apt to solicit support by identifying the interests of the alliance states as common, if not congruent. Thus, during the Korean Civil War the Soviet Union was anxious to minimize its costs and risks in support of China and the DPRK, while the latter two were eager to impress upon the Russians that Soviet national and ideological interests were inextricably involved in the war.

By the very nature of the international system, alliances are not made between exact equals. However, an alliance implies little loss of identity (as opposed to autonomy). Of course, there are all sorts of equalities, and it is therefore true that states are usually in some type of an imbalance of power. On this basis, Julian R. Friedman draws the conclusion that "alliances cannot create equals out of non-equals."[15] Although this might be correct in the narrowest of senses, history amply demonstrates that an alliance may make an originally feeble ally more of an equal, by the weaker state being willing to endure a higher cost tolerance than the stronger ally (e.g.the Soviet Union during World War II, or China and the DPRK during the Korean Civil War).

Perhaps the traditional view of alliances, which emphasizes the function of aggregation, overlooks a major cause for their later fragmentation: viz., the fact that most allies, particularly the weaker ones, bring as many problems and deficits as they do benefits to the coalition. Consequently, alliances are under constant centrifugal force as each ally weighs both the pluses and the minuses of linkage. In particular, the credibility of the stronger member is inevitably diminished if it knows (not to mention if the weaker ally believes) that it must itself be largely destroyed in order to save its ally. A corollary is that alliances between nuclear and nonnuclear powers involve an extra measure of tension. The nuclear power is unwilling to afford nuclear protection to its allies, while the nonnuclear countries, which are called upon to endure the bulk of the suffering, may pressure the stronger state for (at least verbal) nuclear support. This is one additional incentive for the nuclear power to consider its relationship as something less than a partnership–alliance, since it does not wish to risk a nuclear exchange involving its own territory. In this respect, it is noteworthy that NATO has become less of a partnership–alliance as the Russian capability to deliver nuclear weapons onto the American continent has improved. Similarly, the Soviet Union has been unwilling to enter into a partnership–alliance, characterized by a nuclear guarantee, with either China or North Korea.

Alliance Partners Have Different Goals

Because alliances are relatively short-term agreements concluded in tense circumstances which often threaten the very existence of their members, each partner has a dominant reason for joining. The resulting asymmetry of motivation, combined with the fluidity of situation, leads to many possibilities for feelings of dissatisfaction on the part of each member of the alliance.

Further definitional delineations may be made beyond the protectorate-partner distinction. There are, for example, two major, although not pure, additional types of alliances: distributive (status quo) and redistributive (significant revisions of territorial boundaries).[16]

On a general level, it is possible to describe an alliance as tending toward one or the other of these types (e.g., the axis powers during World War II were primarily redistributive while the allies were generally distributive). A more significant point, however, is that the different members of an alliance frequently see the same alliance differently or hold different goals for it. For example, one way in which to view both the Chinese–DPRK alliance of 1950–53 and the Chinese–North Vietnamese alliance of 1965–73 is that Peking wished to see each as both protectorate and distributive alliances, while in both cases China's ally desired the alliance to be of a different type. A further ambiguity often arises once a war has commenced. A state may then change its perceived goals from distributive to redistributive, as for example, was true of the United States on the Korean peninsula in the fall of 1950. The reverse may, of course, also take place. For example, a problem arises when each decides what type of alliance, distributive or redistributive, it desires. At this point, the perceptions and intentions of each may well differ; what is distributive for one may be redistributive for the other. It would appear, for instance, that Hanoi viewed her efforts in Indochina

in the redistributive light of extending North Vietnamese influence throughout the peninsula; Peking, on the other hand, did
not seem to hold such redistributive goals on Hanoi's behalf.[17]
In other words, if the objectives of allies are noncongruent, if
purposes and needs are perceived differently, stress in inevitable. And just as the lessening of the common threat can put
severe strains on the maintenance of an alliance, so the very
attainment of the objectives of the alliance can lead to its
dissolution—as, for example, the Western–Soviet alliance in
World War II.

How Big an Alliance?

Most contemporary thinking on alliances envis-
ages an optimum number of members. The assumption is that
there is a size beyond which additions would reduce the net
advantage of the alliance for its members. William H. Riker, the
preeminent exponent of this idea, argues that "in social situations similar to n-person, zero-sum games with side payments,
participants create coalitions just as large as they believe will
ensure winning and no larger".[18] (Actual situations such as this,
of course, seldom occur in international politics.) George Liska,
writing at the same time as Riker, noted that

> in order to act "economically," alliance builders must not
> collect haphazardly all available allies and seek the most
> demanding commitments; they must consider the mar-
> ginal utility of the last unit of commitment to a particular
> ally and the last unit of cost in implementing
> commitments.[19]

An objection to these hypotheses might be that there is no
margin given for the very human urge to "hedge" against uncertainty by the addition of extra allies. Moreover, alliances may
seek additional members not merely to win, but to win sooner,
which is often considered a value in itself. For example, the

United States sought the Soviet Union's entry into World War II (in the Pacific in 1945 against Japan) because it was felt that this would end the war more quickly. In fact, the Riker–Liska formulation seems to be geared solely toward offensive alliances; a distributive alliance may seek additional members in order to impress others with the credibility of its defensive stance.

Riker's theories, in particular, draw upon gamelike contexts, wherein allies must split a single reward; hence their goals are necessarily competitive. In the real world of international relations, however, different allies may actually seek separate rewards from the common enemy. Thus, a largely distributive alliance (mostly interested, for example, in the territorial *status quo*) would yield noncompetitive benefits to its members, all of whom could gain essentially equal benefits. In these circumstances, each member's goal (preservation of boundaries) is achieved in this instance, but not necessarily at the other allies' expense. In such a case, even the nonmembers could conceivably share in the distribution of the noncompetitive "spoils."

Redistributive alliances may also be at least partially noncompetitive if each ally seeks a different goal from the common enemy. For example, if the World War II allies Germany and Japan had each sought individual rewards only in their respective world regions, their individual "spoils" would not have reduced the potential mutual benefit to the alliance. Similarly, China and the DPRK sought somewhat separate goals during the 1950–53 war.

The current literature on alliances has borrowed heavily from the field of economics, as evidenced by its use of the theory of public goods. One article, in particular, has exercised great influence: "An Economic Theory of Alliance," by Mancur Olson, Jr., and Richard Zeckhauser. The core of the Olson–Zeckhauser argument is expressed in their tautological assertion that "in equilibrium, the defense expenditures of the two nations are such that the 'larger' nation—the one that places the higher absolute value on the alliance good—will bear a *dis-*

proportionately large share of the common burden." They do, however, note one exception to this otherwise universal rule: "During periods of all-out war or exceptional insecurity, it is likely that defense is (or is nearly) a superior good, and in such circumstances alliances will not have any tendency toward disproportionate burden sharing."[20] (As we have seen, however, during the Korean Civil War both China and North Korea were engaged in disproportionate burden sharing relative to the Soviet Union—a reality which led to severe strains within the tripartite alliance.) Having grudgingly allowed this point, the writers then return to their central theme: "There is no equivalent exception to the rule that alliances provide suboptimal amounts of the common good. The alliance output will always be suboptimal so long as the members of the alliance place a positive value on additional units of defense."[21]

Although the Olson–Zeckhauser formulation holds for many interstate coalitions, particularly protectorate–alliances, it would appear to be misleading when applied to partner–alliances. How, for instance, does one weight a "share of the common burden"? How much technology supplied by a stronger state equals one life given up by the weaker state? Were China and the Soviet Union providing more of the cost of the Indochinese War than North Vietnam? Did jeeps, tanks, and planes weigh more in either Russian, Chinese, or North Vietnamese eyes than the destruction absorbed by the Indochinese? (The same problem applies to the United States–South Vietnamese relationship.) In short, how does one compare provision of material with loss of life?

A corollary to this point is the concept of "will." The crucial factor about an ally's credibility is his will, not necessarily his arms inventory. Consequently, an analysis of an alliance must assess, over time, the changing perceptions and attitudes of each member of the alliance in order to calculate the impulse of each to pursue the goals of the alliance. If the will is lacking, an alliance will diminish in status, at least on the part of one member.

In addition, one can take issue with the Olson–Zeckhauser notion that alliances always provide suboptimal amounts of the collective good. The point may be convincing in the sense that states can never reach 90% (and most probably not even 80%) efficiency during a wartime mobilization of resources. However, its emphasis blunts a most important, if banal, fact: for the country whose territory has become a battleground, the war is total; for the intruding power, the war is far from so. In fact, if one of the external power's main purposes is to avoid being drawn into a larger war itself, then it is inevitable that that state will see the coalition as less than a partnership–alliance.

Of course, it is possible for a weaker state to evolve from being largely a power consumer to being both a consumer and a producer, with the emphasis on the latter. This is preeminently evident in so-called "wars of national liberation," where the international system realizes that, although much of the modern war technology used is being imported, it is the battleground state itself—by its willingness to absorb a high level of cost tolerance—which has, in reality, become the major power producer. The result of this is that the weaker states emerge from the war prepared to challenge claims which the stronger ally may wish to make. This happened to the Chinese–Soviet Union–DPRK relationship in the 1950s and 1960s, and it is likely to occur in the North Vietnamese–Chinese and North Vietnamese–Russian relationships.

Interestingly, Riker and Olson–Zeckhauser disagree about what game theory indicates concerning the numbers in an alliance. Riker's "size principle" states that alliances will only be large enough to win, allowing each state to maximize its share of spoils.[22] Olson and Zeckhauser believe the opposite, namely that alliances "provide collective goods the supply of which should increase as the membership increases".[23]

It is clear, however, that much of the cement of a successful alliance rests upon the reciprocal credibility and will of each of the members. The analysis of a specific international coalition must carefully examine each member's expectations, while the observer must keep in mind that an alliance is a dynamic international event, with variables of cost tolerance, will, expectations, and perceived national interest constantly changing. And, finally, each "alliance" must be sharply defined for comparative analytical purposes.

Last Thoughts

Both the United States and China tend to speak of international ties as "alliances." Each international coalition is claimed to have the full support of Washington or Peking. This rhetoric complicates the task of the observer, who must first analyze which type of alliance is involved (if it is, in fact, an alliance) before comparisons and primitive predictions can be made. In sum, at this stage of conceptualizing perhaps the major value of the alliance model is its ability to arm the observer with such questions as: "Is this an alliance?" "Of what type?" "What are its chances of durability and mutual satisfaction?" and "What are the perceptions of the subnational bureaucracies which filter the process of "stimulus-response" toward the alliance?"[24]

The model stresses the strains and dissatisfactions which are built into alliances because of the disequilibrium in terms of both power and goals. The "weaker" ally actually holds a considerable amount of leverage over the "stronger" by reason of its ability to manipulate the ideological proclivities of the latter, and also because of its capacity to become a power producer and more of an equal in the alliance by dint of its higher cost tolerance.

The model reminds us that, because there are different types of alliances, an understanding of which type we are analyzing at a particular moment will help to explain the nature of the linkage. Also explicit in the model is the necessity to analyze the perceptions, capabilities, and goals not only of one country, but of all the actors involved in the alliance. For instance, with regard to the evolving Sino–Soviet coalition of 1950 it is important to understand not only China's position, but also the attitudes of the Soviet Union. One value of the alliance model, then, is its underscoring of the observer's need to ask questions about what *each* of the allies is seeking. This perspective differs from the usual case-study approach, wherein the focus of the observer is primarily on only one of the involved states.

Another advantage of the model in the study of authoritarian foreign policies is its deemphasis of such microfeatures as personalities: e.g., the cult of Mao Tse-tung. Although individual leaders play an undeniable role in the formulation of policy outputs, it is necessary first to evolve a general framework in which to pose important comparative questions. Otherwise, we are left with a great many (otherwise interesting) case studies which will provide little foundation for even the most primitive types of prediction.

The alliance model also deemphasizes the previous stress in the literature on the domestic-ideological determinants of Chinese foreign policy. This is because the alliance model, as a field, attempts to picture *two* levels of the process: the internal decision making, which includes the perceptions of the various identifiable interest groups, *and* the external constraints. For instance, to return to the 1950 Sino–Soviet example, the available information suggests that the threat which Peking perceived from the United States along with the Soviet Union's walkout from the United Nations were the prime determinants of China's relationship with the Soviet Union. Clearly, action from the environment must be taken into account when studying the output of a state's foreign policy.

The cases briefly touched upon in this chapter can, of course, be described without reference to the alliance model. However, explicit models allow us to order our data in a meaningful and replicable fashion. The simple process of carefully defining what is meant by an alliance permits a common vocabulary and locus point for disparate observers of diverse coalitions. Hopefully, an unambiguous examination of what alliances are will lead to a clearer understanding of what binds nations together in certain circumstances, and of the strains which are inherently present in such situations.

Without doubt, the Peking–P'yöngyang–Moscow coalition during the Korean Civil War was an alliance. Just as clear, however, is the fact that this alliance carried within itself the severe strains which were soon to lead to its disintegration.

Notes

1. Baltimore: The John Hopkins University Press, 1962, p. 30.
2. Ibid.
3. "In sum, the *alliance* had already emerged when the *treaty* was signed. Like most treaties, the North Atlantic Pact publicized and made official the pre-existing relationship." Edgar S. Furniss, Jr., "A Personal Evaluation of the Western Alliance," in *The Western Alliance,* ed. Edgar S. Furniss, Jr. (Columbus, O.: Ohio State University Press, 1965), pp. 161–62.
4. "Yet no other alliance approaches the working collaboration which NATO exhibits, since none rests on anything so solid as a political capacity for effective cooperation." Robert E. Osgood, *Alliances in American Foreign Policy* (Baltimore: The Johns Hopkins University Press, 1968), pp. 3–4.
5. "Gratuity or Tyranny: The Korean Alliances," in *World Politics* (July, 1973), p. 510.
6. New York: Holt, Rinehart and Winston, 1970.
7. Osgood, op. cit.
8. Beer, op cit, p. 5.
9. *Peace and War, A Theory of International Relations* (New York: Frederick A. Praeger, 1968), p. 28.
10. These forms of collaboration are also present in the so-called "special relationships" (e.g., Australia–New Zealand). However, since our definition of "alliance" contends that the immediate threat of war is absent, these special relationships, while obviously some-

thing more than an "alignment," would cause a loss of theoretical efficacy if termed an "alliance." See, for example, Raymond Dawson and Richard Rosecrance, "Theory and Reality in the Anglo–American Alliance," *World Politics* (January, 1966). They purport to show that the ties of sentiment between the United Kingdom and the United States have maintained an alliance within which other interests were working in the opposite direction. However, I would argue that they are, in fact, involved in an ongoing integrative process with vital socioeconomic underpinnings. Such a situation does not fulfill a narrow definition of an alliance, while it weakens the usual, broader one.

11. These terms are used by Steven L. Spiegel in his *Dominance and Diversity: The International Hierarchy* (Boston: Little, Brown and Co., 1972) p. 27. Professor Spiegel also supplies cogent examples of "power-producers" and "power-consumers."
12. Allen S. Whiting in *China Crosses the Yalu: The Decision to Enter the Korean War* (New York: Macmillan Co., 1960), p. 167, presents a somewhat different perspective: "Soviet military assistance to China after the latter's entry into the war completely re-equipped the PLA and provided Peking with a first-line jet air force second to none in Asia, except that of the United States."
13. "A mutual fear is the only solid basis on which to organize an alliance." *A History of the Peloponesian War*, book 3, paragraph 2.
14. Aron, op. cit., p. 45.
15. "Alliance in International Politics," in *Alliances in International Politics*, ed. Julian Friedman, Christopher Bladen, and Steven Rosen (Boston: Allyn and Bacon, 1970), p. 5.
16. Steven Rosen, "A Model of War and Alliance," in Friedman, Bladen, and Rosen, op. cit., p. 218.
17. Robert R. Simmons, "China's Cautious Relations with North Korea and Indochina," *Asian Survey* (July, 1971).
18. *The Theory of Political Coalitions* (New Haven: Yale University Press, 1962), p. 32.
19. Liska, op. cit., p. 27.
20. In Friedman, Bladen, and Rosen, op. cit., p. 181, emphasis in original. It is noteworthy that only two are reprinted in both of the two major anthologies on alliances published in the past five years, the Beer and Friedman–Bladen–Rosen books—viz.,the Riker and Olson–Zeckhauser pieces. Economic analysis has indeed had a marked influence upon the hitherto political-science preserve of the study of alliances.

21. Ibid., p. 183.
22. Riker, op. cit., pp. 35–42.
23. Olson and Zeckhauser, in Friedman, Bladen, and Rosen, op. cit., p. 189.
24. This last question implies a vital caveat to the alliance model: the recognition that the "black box" of a state is not monolithic. I have dealt with this analytical problem by content-factor analyzing the journals of the Chinese Foreign Ministry and the Central Committee of the CCP for the years 1950–53. An extrapolation from their vocabularies strongly suggests that these two ministries in fact had differing perceptions of China's role in the world. See "The Concept of Alliance in the Study of Chinese Foreign Policy," in *Advancing and Contending Theories of Chinese Foreign Policy,* ed. Roger Dial (Halifax: Dalhousie University Press, 1974).

A Selected Bibliography

Books

Acheson, Dean. *Present at the Creation: My Years in the State Department.* New York: W. W. Norton, 1969.

Appleman, Roy. *South to the Naktang, North to the Yalu.* Washington, D.C.: Office of the Chief of Military History, 1961.

Aron, Raymond. *Peace and War: A Theory of International Relations.* New York: Frederick A. Praeger, 1968.

Beer, Francis A., ed. *Alliances: Latent War Communities in the Contemporary World.* New York: Holt, Rinehart and Winston, 1970.

Beloff, Max. *Soviet Foreign Policy in the Far East, 1944–1951.* London: Oxford University Press, 1953.

Brodie, Bernard. *War and Politics.* New York: Macmillan Co., 1973.

Brook, David. *The United Nations and the China Dilemma.* New York: Vintage Press, 1956.

Bueschel, Richard M. *Chinese Communist Air Power.* New York: Frederick A. Praeger, 1968.

Cheng, Yu-kwei. *Foreign Trade and the Industrial Development of China.* New York: Frederick A. Praeger, 1956.

Chin, Szu-k'ai. *Communist China's Relations with the Soviet Union, 1949–1957.* Hong Kong: Union Research Institute, 1961.

Choi, Woonsang. *The Fall of the Hermit Kingdom.* Dobbs Ferry,

271

N.Y.: Oceana Publications, 1967.

Chun, Hae-jong. "Sino–Korean Tributary Relations in the Chi'ing Period," in *The Chinese World Order*, ed. John K. Fairbank. Cambridge: Harvard University Press, 1968.

Clark, Charles Allen. *Religions of Old Korea*. New York: Fleming H. Revell Co., 1932.

Clews, John C. *Communist Propaganda Techniques*. London: Methuen, 1964.

Clubb, Edmund O. *China and Russia: The Great Game*. New York: Columbia University Press, 1971.

Cohen, Warren J. *America's Response to China*. New York: John Wiley and Sons, 1971.

Connroy, Hilary. *The Japanese Seizure of Korea, 1868–1910*. Philadelphia: University of Pennsylvania Press, 1960.

Dallin, Alexander. *The Soviet Union and the United Nations*. New York: Frederick A. Praeger, 1961.

Dallin, David J. *The Rise of Russia in Asia*. New Haven: Yale University Press, 1949.

Dallin, David J. *Soviet Foreign Policy after Stalin*. Philadelphia: J. B. Lippincott, 1961.

Dennett, Tyler. *Roosevelt and the Russo–Japanese War*. New York: Doubleday and Co., 1925.

Djilas, Milovan. *Conversations with Stalin*. New York: Harcourt, Brace and World, 1962.

Dulles, John Foster. *War or Peace*. New York: Macmillan Co., 1950.

Eden, Anthony. *Full Circle*. Boston: Houghton Mifflin Co., 1960.

Fitzgerald, C. P. *Revolution in China*. London: Cresset Press, 1952.

Floyd, David. *Mao Against Khrushchev*. New York: Frederick A. Praeger, 1964.

Friedman, Edward. "Problems in Dealing with an Irrational Power," in *America's Asia*, ed. Edward Friedman and Mark Seldon. New York: Random House, 1971.

Friedman, Julian. *Alliances in International Politics*, ed. Julian Friedman, Christopher Bladen, and Steven Rosen. Boston: Allyn and Bacon, 1970.

Friters, G. M. *Outer Mongolia and Its International Position*. Baltimore: John Hopkins University Press, 1951.

Furniss, Edgar S., Jr. "A Personal Evaluation of the Western Alliance," in *The Western Alliance*, ed. Edgar S. Furniss. Columbus: Ohio State University Press, 1965.

Gittings, John. "The Origins of China's Foreign Policy," in *Containment and Revolution*, ed. David Horowitz. Boston: Beacon Press, 1967.

Gittings, John. *The Role of the Chinese Army*. London: Oxford University Press, 1967.

Gittings, John. *Sino–Soviet Dispute*. New York: Frederick A. Praeger, 1964.

Gurtov, Melvin. *The First Vietnam Crisis*. New York: Columbia University Press, 1967.

Harrington, Michael. *God, Mammon, and the Japanese*. Madison: University of Wisconsin Press, 1944.

Henderson, Gregory. *Korea: The Politics of the Vortex*. Cambridge: Harvard University Press, 1968.

Hermes, Walter G. *Truce Tent and Fighting Front*. Washington, D.C.: Office of the Chief of Military History, 1966.

Hinton, Harold. *Communist China in World Politics*. Boston: Houghton Mifflin Co., 1966.

Kelman, Herbert C., ed. *International Behavior: A Social–Psychological Analysis*. New York: Holt, Rinehart and Winston, 1965.

Kennan, George. *Memoirs (1925–1950)*. New York: Bantam Books, 1969.

Kierman, Robert. *The Fluke That Saved Formosa*. Cambridge: M.I.T. Press, 1954.

Kim, Ch'ang-sun. *Fifteen Year History of North Korea*. Seoul, 1961. Translated by the Joint Publications Research Service, Washington, D.C. 1965.

Kim, Chum-kon. *The Korean War*. Seoul: Kwangmyong Publishing Co., 1973.

Kim, Eugene, and Han-kyo Kim. *Korea and the Politics of Imperialism, 1876–1910*. Berkeley and Los Angeles, University of California Press, 1967.

Kim, Il Sung. *Selected Works.* Pyongyang: Foreign Languages Publishing House, 1971.

Kim, Sam-gyu. *Konnichi no Chōsen (Korea Today).* Tokyo: Kawade Shobo, 1956.

Klein, Donald W. "The Management of Foreign Affairs in Communist China," in *China: Management of a Revolutionary Society,* ed. John M. H. Lindbeck. Seattle: University of Washington Press, 1971.

Kolko, Gabriel, and Joyce Kolko. *The Limits of Power: The World and United States Foreign Policy, 1945–1954.* New York: Harper and Row, 1972.

Langer, Paul. *The Diplomacy of Imperialism.* 2 vols. New York: Alfred A. Knopf, 1935.

Langer, Paul, and Rodger Swearingen. *Red Flag in Japan.* Cambridge: Harvard University Press, 1957.

Leckie, Robert. *Conflict: The History of the Korean War, 1950–1953.* New York: G. P. Putnam's Sons, 1962.

Lie, Trygvie. *In the Cause of Peace.* New York: Macmillian Co., 1954.

Liska, George. *Nations in Alliance: The Limits of Interdependence.* Baltimore: John Hopkins University Press, 1962.

Malozenoff, Andrew. *Russian Far Eastern Policy, 1881–1904.* Berkeley and Los Angeles: University of California Press, 1958.

McKenzie, F. A. *The Tragedy of Korea.* London: Hadder and Stoughton, 1908.

Mehnert, Klaus. *Peking and Moscow.* New York: Mentor Books, 1964.

Ojha, Ishwer C. *Chinese Foreign Policy in an Age of Transition: The Politics of Cultural Despair.* Boston: Beacon Press, 1971.

Osgood, Robert E. *Alliances in American Foreign Policy.* Baltimore: Johns Hopkins University Press, 1968.

Paige, Glenn D. *The Korean Decision, June 24–30, 1950.* New York: The Free Press, 1963.

Paige, Glenn D. *The Korean People's Democratic Republic.* Stanford, Ca.: Stanford Univ., Hoover Institution, 1966.

Palmer, Frederick. *With Kuroki in Manchuria.* New York: Charles Scribner's Sons, 1904.

Panikkar, K. M. *In Two Chinas*. London: Allen and Unwin, 1955.

Rees, David. *Korea: The Limited War*. Baltimore: Penguin Books, 1964.

Rice, Edward. *Mao's Way*. Berkeley and Los Angeles: University of California Press, 1972.

Ridgway, Matthew. *The Korean War*. New York: Doubleday and Co., 1967.

Riker, William H. *The Theory of Political Coalitions*. New Haven: Yale University Press, 1962.

Rin, Eiju. *Chōsen Sensoshi (History of the Korean War)*. Tokyo: Koria Hyoronsha, 1967.

Royal Institute of International Affairs. *Survey of International Affairs, 1949–1950*. London: Oxford University Press, 1951.

Rubinstein, Alvin. *The Foreign Policy of the Soviet Union*. New York: Random House, 1960.

Salisbury, Harrison E. *The Coming War between Russia and China*. New York: Bantam Books, 1969.

Sands, William F. *Undiplomatic Memories*. New York: Whittlessey House, 1930.

Sawyer, Robert K. *Military Advisors in Korea: KMAG in Peace and War*. Washington, D.C.: Office of the Chief of Military History, 1962.

Scalapino, Robert A., and Chong-sik Lee. *Communism in Korea*. Berkeley and Los Angeles: University of California Press, 1972.

Schelling, Thomas. *The Strategy of Conflict*. London: Oxford University Press, 1963.

Schram, Stuart. *The Political Thought of Mao Tse-tung*. Baltimore: Penguin Books, 1969.

Schwartz, Harry. *Tsars, Mandarins, and Commissars*. Philadelphia: J. B. Lippincott, 1962.

Sebald, William. *With MacArthur in Japan*. New York: W. W. Norton, 1965.

Selected Works of Mao Tse-tung. London: Lawrence and Wishart, 1956. Vols. 1 –4.

Service, John S. *The Amerasia Papers: Some Problems in the History of U.S.–China Relations*. Berkeley: China Research Monograph, 1971.

Sheng, General Shih-ts'ai, and Allen S. Whiting. *Sinkiang: Pawn or Pivot.* East Lansing: Michigan State University Press, 1958.

Shulman, Marshall. *Stalin's Foreign Policy Reappraised.* Cambridge: Harvard University Press, 1963.

Simmons, Robert R. "The Concept of 'Alliance' in the Study of China's Foreign Policy," in *Advancing and Contending Theories of Chinese Foreign Policy,* ed. Roger Dial. Halifax: Dalhousie University Press, 1974.

Simmons, Robert R. "The Korean Civil War," in *Without Parallel: The American–Korean Relationship since 1945,* ed. Frank Baldwin. New York: Pantheon Books, 1974.

Spanier, John. *The Truman–MacArthur Controversy and the Korean War.* Cambridge: Harvard University Press, 1959.

Spiegel, Steven L. *Dominance and Diversity: The International Hierarchy.* Boston: Little, Brown and Co., 1972.

Stairs, Denis. *The Diplomacy of Constraint: Canada, the Korean War, and the United States.* Toronto: University of Toronto Press, 1974.

Stein, Gunther. *The Challenge of Red China.* New York: McGraw-Hill, 1945.

Suh, Dae-sook. *The Korean Communist Movement, 1918–1948.* Princeton: Princeton University Press, 1967.

Suh, Dae-sook. "North Korea: Emergence of an Elite Group," in *Aspects of Modern Communism,* ed. Richard F. Starr. Columbia: University of South Carolina Press, 1968.

Sumner, William Graham. *Folkways.* Boston: Ginn and Co., 1906.

Talbott, Strobe, ed. *Khrushchev Remembers.* New York: Little, Brown and Co., 1970.

Taylor, A. J. P. *The Origins of World War Two.* New York: Bantam Books, 1964.

Topping, Seymour. *Journey Between Two Chinas.* New York: Harper and Row, 1972.

Tsou, Tang. *America's Failure in China, 1941–1950.* Chicago: University of Chicago Press, 1966.

Tucker, Robert C. *The Soviet Political Mind, Stalinism and Post-Stalin Change.* New York: W. W. Norton, 1971.

Tung, Pi-wu. *Memorandum on China's Liberated Areas*. San Francisco (privately printed), 1945.

Ulam, Adam B. *Expansion and Coexistence: The History of Soviet Foreign Policy, 1917–1967*. New York: Frederick A. Praeger, 1968.

Van Ness, Peter. *Revolution and China's Foreign Policy: Peking's Support for Wars of National Liberation*. Berkeley and Los Angeles: University of California Press, 1970.

Weems, Benjamin B. *Reform, Rebellion, and the Heavenly Way*. Tucson: University of Arizona Press, 1964.

Wei, Henry. *China and Soviet Russia*. New York: D. Van Nostrand, 1956.

White, Ralph K. *Nobody Wanted War*. New York: Anchor Books, 1970.

Whiting, Allen S. *China Crosses the Yalu: The Decision to Enter the Korean War*. New York: Macmillan Co., 1960.

Wills, Morris R. *Turncoat*. New York: Prentice-Hall, 1966.

Wint, Guy. *What Happened in Korea: A Study in Collective Security*. London: Batchworth Press, 1954.

Periodicals

Chinese Press Survey. Shanghai, 1949–52.

Foreign Broadcast Information Service, Far East, Washington, D.C.: U.S. Central Intelligence Agency, 1944–1953.

Hsin-hua Yueh-pao [New China Monthly], Peking, 1949–53.

Jen-min Jih-pao [People's Daily].

Shih-chieh Chih-shih [World Culture], Peking, 1949–53.

Summary of World Broadcasts, Far East. London: British Broadcasting Corporations, 1944–53.

Public Documents

Handbook on the Chinese Communist Army. Washington, D.C.: U.S. Department of the Army, pamphlet no. 30–51, September, 1952.

Hearings on the Military Situation in the Far East (MacArthur

Hearings). 82d Congress. Washington, D.C., U.S. Government Printing Office, 1951.

History of the Just Fatherland Liberation War of the Korean People. Pyongyang: Foreign Languages Publishing House, 1961.

History of the North Korean Army. Headquarters, U.S. Far East Command, Military Intelligence Section, July, 1952.

Korea: Origins of the Dividing Line at the 38th Parallel. Washington, D.C.: Library of Congress Legislative Service, June 29, 1950.

North Korea: A Case Study in the Techniques of Takeover. Washington, D.C.: U.S. Government Printing Office, 1961.

Preliminary Study of the Impact of Communism upon Korea, A. Maxwell Air Force Base: U.S. Air Force, May, 1951.

United States Air Force Operations in the Korean Conflict, 1 July 1952–27 July 1953. Washington, D.C.: Department of the Air Force, historical study no. 71, 1956.

United States Relations with China. U.S. Department of State, Far Eastern Series 30, Pub. 3573, Washington, D.C., U.S. Government Printing Office, 1949.

Unpublished Documents

Kim, Roy U. T. "Korea and the Sino–Soviet Dispute." Unpublished Ph.D. dissertation, University of Pennsylvania, 1969.

Min, Benjamin. "North Korea's Foreign Policy in the Post-War Decade, 1953–1963." Unpublished Ph.D. dissertation, University of Massachusetts, 1967.

Tsuan, Tai-hsun. "An Explanation of the Change in U.S. Policy Toward China in 1950." Unpublished Ph.D. dissertation, University of Pennsylvania, 1969.

Yang, Key P. "The North Korean Regime, 1945–1955." Unpublished Master's Thesis, American University, School of International Service, 1958.

Yio, Myung Kun. "Sino–Soviet Rivalry in North Korea since 1954." Unpublished Ph.D. dissertation, University of Maryland, 1969.

Index

INDEX

A

Acheson, Dean, 60, 85, 88, 89, 111, 122, 142, 169n, 205n
Al-Ahram, 182
Alignment, 253
Alliance, 82, 83, 247–48
    definition, 253–62
    model, 246–61, 266–67
    previous definitions, 249–52
    size, 262–66
Aoji, 217
Appleman, Roy, 133n
Aron, Raymond, 251–52
Arthur, Robert Alan, 169n

B

Bacchus, Wilfred A., 205n
Baldwin, Hanson, 133n, 163
Beer, Francis, 251
Beloff, Max, 13n, 134n, 135n
Bridgham, Philip, 243n, 244n
Brodie, Bernard, 197, 244n
Burchett, Wilfred, 246n

C

Chang Chung, 191, 202
Ch'en Yun, 199
Chen, King, C., 101n
Chiang K'ai-shek, 50–51, 65–67, 147–48
China (People's Republic of China)
reaction to the Korean Civil War, 149–51
reaction to latter stages of war, 224
recognition of Ho Chi Minh, 95–97
seizure of consular properties, 93–94
and the Soviet Union, 48–49, 51, 55, 65–66 70, 72–73, 149–52
and the United Nations, 53–54, 89–92, 97–98, 126
and the United States, 50–52

China Digest, 67
Chinese People's Liberation Army (PLA), 23, 182–85, 197, 211
Cho Man-sik, 24
Ch'oe, Ch'ang-ik, 186
Ch'oe Yong-gŏn, 202, 211, 215
Choi, Woonsang, 18n
Chou En-lai, 50, 53, 73, 90, 97, 164, 189, 217, 230, 233
Chu Teh, 199–200
Clews, John, 244n
Clubb, O. Edmund, 78n, 100n
Cohen, Warren, 77n
Conally, Tom, 111
Conroy, Hilary, 20n
Cook, Harold F., 18n
Cumings, Bruce G., 37n

D

Dallin, Alexander, 98n
Dallin, David J., 77n, 130n
Democratic Front for the Liberation of the Fatherland, 104–6
Democratic People's Republic of Korea (DPRK), 201; *see also* North Korean aid from the Soviet Union
Derevyanko, Kuzma, 191

Dulles, Foster Rhea, 170*n*
Dulles, John Foster, 126,
170*n*

E

Emerson, Rupert, 99*n*
Explanation for the war's initiation, 128–30, 159–62
founding, 104
reaction to the 1951
peace proposal, 200

F

Floyd, David, 81*n*
Friedman, Edward, 17*n*, 79*n*,
173*n*
Friedman, Julien, 269

G

Gittings, John, 76*n*, 78*n*, 79*n*,
130*n*, 131*n*, 243*n*
Goodrich, Leland M. J., 204*n*
Gupta, Karunakur, 172*n*
Gurtov, Melvin, 101*n*

H

Haeju, 106
Halperin, Morton, 172*n*
Hammond, Paul, 169*n*
Henderson, Gregory, 18*n*,
35*n*

Henthorn, William, 18*n*
Hermes, Walter G., 246*n*
Hinton, Harold C., 78*n*,
131*n*, 173*n*, 245*n*
Hitchcock, Wilbur, 131*n*
Ho Chi Minh, 96
Hŏ Ka-i, 23, 209
Huang Hua, 69, 160
Hurley, Patrick, 53, 55

I

Inch'ŏn, 16, 157, 178, 216
India, 189

J

Japan, 193, 201, 209
Jeruis, Robert, 116

K

Kaesŏng, 106, 202
Kang Dong Political Institute, 104
Kao Kang, 57–59, 74, 153
Kelman, Herbert C., 17*n*
Kennan, George, 169*n*
Kierman, Robert, 171*n*
Kim, Eugene and Han-Kyo,
18*n*
Kim, Ilpyong J., 37*n*
Kim, Joungwon Alexander,
131*n*